Stories of True Crime in T
Stuart England

Stories of True Crime in Tudor and Stuart England is an original collection of thirty stories of true crime during the period 1580–1700. Published in short books known as chapbooks, these stories proliferated in early modern popular literature. The chapbooks included in this collection describe serious, horrifying and often deeply personal stories of murder and attempted murder, infanticide, suicide, rape, arson, highway robbery, petty treason and witchcraft.

These criminal cases reveal the fascinating complexities of early modern English society. The vivid depictions of these stories were used by the English church and state to describe the proper boundaries of behaviour, and the dangers that could result from the sins of avarice, apathy, vice or violence. Readers will learn about the public interest and involvement in crime and punishment and the way the criminal justice system was used to correct and deter criminal activity and restore social boundaries such as rank, gender, family, religion, and physical boundaries of person and property.

Perfect for the student reader, this collection provides guided access to these exciting sources. Each transcription is modernized and annotated and is preceded by a brief discussion of key historical context and themes. Including an introductory essay on the topic of the English criminal justice system in the early modern period, as well as a glossary of key terms in English criminal law, this is an ideal introduction for students of crime and criminal justice in England.

Ken MacMillan is Professor of History at the University of Calgary, Canada, where he researches and teaches about crime, law, and society in early modern England and the English Atlantic. His previous books include *Sovereignty and Possession in the English New World: The Legal Foundations of Empire* (2006) and *The Atlantic Imperial Constitution: Center and Periphery in the English Atlantic World* (2011).

Stories of True Crime in Tudor and Stuart England

Edited by Ken MacMillan

Routledge
Taylor & Francis Group

LONDON AND NEW YORK

First published 2015
by Routledge
2 Park Square, Milton Park, Abingdon, Oxon OX14 4RN

and by Routledge
711 Third Avenue, New York, NY 10017

Routledge is an imprint of the Taylor & Francis Group, an informa business

British Library Cataloguing in Publication Data
A catalogue record for this book is available from the British Library

Library of Congress Cataloging-in-Publication Data
MacMillan, Ken.
Stories of true crime in Tudor and Stuart England/Ken MacMillan.
pages cm
Includes bibliographical references.
1. Crime—England—History—16th century.
2. Crime—England—History—17th century. I. Title.
HV6949.E5M23 2015
364.10942'09031—dc23
2014037281

ISBN: 978-1-138-85400-0 (hbk)
ISBN: 978-1-138-85401-7 (pbk)
ISBN: 978-1-315-71980-1 (ebk)

Typeset in Garamond
by Swales & Willis Ltd, Exeter, Devon, UK

MIX
Paper from
responsible sources
FSC
www.fsc.org FSC® C013604

Printed and bound by CPI Group (UK) Ltd, Croydon, CR0 4YY

Contents

Illustrations

Acknowledgements

This book has emerged from an assignment I have used for more than a decade in my *History of Crime and Criminal Justice in England* course. The students are asked to examine crime chapbooks written during the seventeenth century and use them to reflect on key themes that are discussed in the course. My first thanks, therefore, are to my past students. Through their written work and the many conversations I have had with them, they have guided me toward certain texts, interpretations, and themes, and have shown me some of the challenges they experience while working with these historical documents. The transcriptions were completed with the assistance of Melissa Glass and Holly Peterson, who transcribed many more chapbooks than ultimately appear in this volume. As members of the target audience of this book, Melissa and Holly also provided helpful guidance with regard to common themes, annotations, and the discussions before each text. Helpful feedback was given by several readers from Routledge, including valuable comments from Andrea McKenzie. Lou Knafla read the entire manuscript and offered many excellent suggestions. A number of original chapbooks were examined at the Huntington Library in San Marino, California, and at the British Library in London. As usual, the staff at both institutions were professional and helpful. At Routledge, Laura Pilsworth and Catherine Aitken have offered expert guidance in getting this book through the press.

The publishers would like to thank The British Library, The Bodleian Library and Lambeth Palace Library for their permission to reproduce copyright material.

Introduction

The texts that appear in this collection have all appeared previously in print, although many have not been read or reproduced for several hundred years. They represent a particular genre of popular literature on the subject of crime that was produced as chapbooks for the semi-literate reading public in early modern England. Crime chapbook literature preceded the better-known *Ordinary's Account* and *Proceedings of the Old Bailey*, which began being published in 1676, and the various versions of the *Newgate Calendar*, which began to appear in the mid-eighteenth century. It also preceded William Cobbett's well-known *Complete Collection of State Trials*, and various newspaper accounts, novels, and biographies about crime and criminals, all of which became common in the eighteenth century (particularly the work of Daniel Defoe and Henry Fielding), and which slowly brought an end to the crime chapbook genre. Reading and listening to the type of tales that are collected in this volume were, therefore, the principal means by which people of sixteenth- and seventeenth-century England gained knowledge of national criminal activity.

These tales clearly satiated a huge appetite for stories of true crime in Tudor and Stuart England. To do so, they had to be simultaneously shocking and entertaining. Even as we read troubling tales of children being murdered and mutilated, women killing and dismembering their abusive husbands, and accused witches being violently tested for signs of their devilish craft, it is difficult not to smile when poor John Foster is tried and acquitted for felony theft for stealing a magpie worth two pence, or when a victim of confidence man Griffin Flood smashes his head with a pewter mug. In addition to being shocking and entertaining, these texts also served as cautionary, religious, and morality tales that reflected on serious crime as one of the signs that English society had become ignorant, irreligious, and immoral. These tales of common, "everyman" criminals – even if their authors often stray from the truth and are sometimes clearly biased against the offender – could be used to remind a wide readership of the wages of sin, thus seeking to deter other would-be criminals from committing similar crimes, particularly those that could cost them their lives.

Crime chapbooks also served to remind husbands, wives, children, servants, apprentices, neighbours, and to a lesser extent wealthy men and women of their legal and social responsibilities toward one another, the church, and the state; of their place in the rigid social hierarchy of early modern

England; and of the dangers that could accrue when these relationships, and society itself, become unbalanced as the result of avarice, jealousy, vice, or violence. This was a society that placed significant constraints on sexual, personal, and religious freedoms, and exhorted obedience, deference, hard work, sexual restraint, and abstinence from all forms of vice. The crime chapbook genre thus served as a metaphor for the social, political, and religious issues of the day. In a society that still had no formal policing beyond the voluntary and untrained constabulary, and had few mechanisms for social assistance beyond the almsmen who provided charity to parishioners at times of desperate need, it was chapbooks such as the ones in this collection that helped to maintain and restore order. Paradoxically, crime chapbooks also served as something of a social safety-valve, in that they became vehicles for vicarious wish fulfillment by harmlessly allowing the reader to become party to the transgressions committed by criminals, without having to face the same fatal consequences.

For a modern audience, this popular literature is an exceedingly valuable tool to learn about the range of serious crime in the early modern period, the relationship between crime and the society in which it was committed, and the inner workings of the criminal justice system. Modern readers who are used to thinking of English people as polite, orderly, and orthodox (though, of course, many were none of these) are often surprised to encounter stories of wives murdering their husbands, children slaughtering their parents, women killing their babies, mistresses roasting their apprentices on spits, and children being assaulted for the clothes on their backs. These stories alter our perception of what constituted "normal" behaviour in this period, while also allowing us to develop empathy for the perpetrators and victims of crime, find the grey area between the "black and white" binary of right and wrong, gain deeper understanding of various social boundaries of behavior (gender, rank, age, family, and religion, for example) that existed in early modern England, and reflect on the efforts undertaken by local and national officials, the church, and the anonymous authors of this literature, to maintain those boundaries against disturbance that threatened to upset the entire society.

***

Chapbooks were initially handwritten in manuscript form and were usually sold by the authors to printers or booksellers, who assumed the costs and risks associated with printing the books and getting them out to a wider audience. The printed books were produced by inserting raised metal letters and symbols into several rows to complete each page, or forme. The forme was then locked into a larger frame known as a chase using wooden or metal furniture and quoins (fixed and expandable spacers) to prevent the forme from shifting in the chase during printing. Ink was applied with a roller or pad, and the chase was pressed onto damp, folio-sized sheets of paper. Folios varied in size but were roughly the size of a regular newspaper page today. Once the forme had been pressed onto numerous sheets, which would depend on the size of the print run, a new forme would be prepared, locked into the chase, inked, and pressed onto the folio.

This process would then continue until each page of the book had been printed. The speed of the printing process depended on the printer's skill, the number of workers in his shop, whether or not multiple formes (on large chases) could be pressed at once, and the extent to which the process of inking and pressing was automated using printing press machines, which sped up the process and improved the quality and consistency of the final product. The double-sided folios were then folded and cut to produce four (quarto), eight (octavo), twelve (duodecimo), or more, two-sided leaves, with the first and last page serving as the cover. Chapbooks typically ranged between eight and thirty-two pages in length, though they rarely exceeded sixteen (octavo printed on both sides). The finished product would usually be hand sewn, either by the printer or seller, using two or three stitches along the spine to keep the pages together in the correct order.

All printers in England, including those who produced chapbooks, had to be registered with the Stationers' Company, the printers' guild that was chartered by Queen Mary in 1557. An unregistered printer was subject to inspection and imprisonment and the confiscation of his equipment and stock. Furthermore, all printed material was subject to censorship, which, depending on their subject matter, was handled by officials such as the archbishop of Canterbury, the bishop of London, and the lord chancellor. For this reason, various publications indicated that the text was "licensed to be printed" or was published "with authority," or used the common Latin phrase "*Cum privilegio*" (with privilege). This protected the printer's investment by advertising to officials that the book had been allowed and by prohibiting others from printing the same or a substantially similar book, an early form of copyright. Unlicensed publications could be confiscated and destroyed, and their printers – whether registered with the Company or not – subjected to fines or other punishments. Thus, with few exceptions, chapbooks were examined before they were allowed to be published, which meant that the censors found the content suitable for a wide readership, or at least not seditious against the church or state. These strict rules regarding printing were relaxed when the Licensing Act was discontinued in 1695. These relaxed rules help to explain the massive increase of newspapers and periodicals about crime after this period, which quickly led to the decline of the crime chapbook genre.

Unlike literature produced for elite and educated audiences, chapbooks were written quickly and printed on poor-quality paper, using substandard ink, and were subject to rapid deterioration, rather like modern newspapers. They commonly contained typesetting errors associated with both the swiftness of production and the limited literacy of their authors and printers. Their covers and occasionally internal pages often contained low-quality woodcut illustrations, which were sometimes reused (along with certain common prefatory information) on several different chapbooks and did not necessarily reflect the actual content of the book. These illustrations usually depicted murder, the Devil, or punishment by hanging or burning. Like modern book covers, the illustrations were intended to entice the public into purchasing the book. Chapbooks were sold throughout the English countryside, frequently on market days, by travelling pedlars, hawkers, and chapmen (which is how the chapbook got its name, "chap" meaning trade), and in urban bookshops, the back rooms of which also often served as the place of printing and publication. In addition to being sold in market squares and bookshops, it was not uncommon for chapbooks to be sold at the place and time of execution – sometimes giving the last words of the condemned before he or she had actually spoken them!

The cost of chapbooks ranged from a halfpenny to six pence, and averaged two to three pence, at a time when the average commoner earned about 12 pence per day. The poor quality and low prices of crime chapbooks often defined the primary audience for this literature: semi-literate common men, and occasionally women. It has been estimated that about 30 per cent of common men, and a smaller, unknown percentage of common women, were literate in the seventeenth century. These readers, whose literacy skills were usually limited to the English language, also read these stories aloud to illiterate audiences, in pubs during an evening of drinking, or among gatherings in country cottages and village markets. This oral consumption thus ensured a wider audience than merely literate readers.

Although commoners were the main audience for chapbooks, it has been demonstrated that elite audiences also consumed this literature, particularly that which took a political, legal, or religious position. In fact, certain chapbooks were clearly targeted toward audiences of a higher social quality, as demonstrated by the use of Latin phrases and classical and scientific references beyond the knowledge of most commoners.

Chapbooks often had a very short existence after they were purchased. Unlike elite literature, which was intended to be held permanently, and consulted regularly, in the libraries of the wealthy, chapbooks were repurposed typically within a week of being consumed by their audience. Their pages were used for lighting pipes, lining pie plates, and as "bum paper" in the "houses of office" throughout the English countryside. This is why, despite hundreds of thousands and possibly millions being printed between 1580 and 1700, chapbooks are considered to be quite rare today and are found only in specialized repositories. These repositories include the Huntington Library (California), the Folger Shakespeare Library (Washington, DC), the British Library (London), and the libraries of Cambridge and Oxford universities, in addition to several other specialized collections in North America and the United Kingdom. This rareness limits modern audiences' access to early modern English chapbooks, which is one of the reasons this volume has been produced.

***

During the period 1580–1700, the English criminal justice system was served by a series of hierarchical courts and court officers. Lesser criminal offences were commonly handled by justices of the peace (JPs). JPs, also commonly known as magistrates, were formally named in the annual Commission of the Peace and held their positions during good behaviour, often for many years. Their ranks comprised a large number of wealthy gentleman, most of whom had no formal legal training but who had experience with the administration of public affairs and, perhaps most importantly, knowledge of the norms of the community in which they presided. A small number of JPs did have professional legal training and were part of the quorum, a select body of magistrates in each county who possessed more powers than their lay counterparts, and generally took a greater role in the criminal justice system. JPs were guided in their actions by experience and common sense, a series of statutes (such as that which established the important Marian Pre-Trial Procedure in 1555), and instructional manuals produced since the 1560s, especially those of William Lambarde, Michael Dalton, and Matthew Hale. These manuals also described the process that needed to be taken against a person accused of a crime, and the court that should take jurisdiction over the case.

Most allegations of criminal offences were first brought to the attention of a JP by a constable, or headboro. The constable was a man of modest standing in the community, who was elected by the village elders (aldermen) and undertook his tasks voluntarily for one year. He was often the initial point of contact between victims, witnesses, and the accused, and was responsible for conducting preliminary investigations that would, it was hoped, lead to an arrest. The JP then examined all parties and decided whether there was enough evidence to proceed and whether the case should simply be dismissed or arbitrated between the parties. Although it is impossible for historians to know how many cases proceeded to arbitration, it is thought that this happened frequently and was the preferred route in all but the most serious of crimes. If it was determined that a case needed to proceed to trial, the JP also determined which court should hear the case, which depended on the severity of the alleged crime, and whether an accused defendant should be remanded into custody (gaol) or granted a recognizance, which might be accompanied by bail, bond, or an order to be of good behaviour and keep the peace until trial.

If the accused was to be gaoled, the JP issued an order (known as a *mittimus*) to the local gaoler to hold the defendant until trial. The gaoler was usually a private person who paid the local sheriff for the privilege of operating the gaol. He received a county rate for each prisoner, which was enough to provide inmates with a rudimentary diet of bread and gruel. The gaoler also charged his inmates as much as he could for luxuries such as mattresses, blankets, cheese and meat, and better toileting facilities. These additional costs were to be borne by the inmate's family and friends, by charitable alms, or, if the inmate was destitute and a stranger, he might be given a "ball and chain." With a cuff attached to the prisoner's leg on one end of the chain and a cannon ball affixed to the other end, the inmate was able to beg for money outside the gaol without risk of him running away. Whatever coins he took in were given to the gaoler in exchange for luxuries. Although it was technically illegal for the gaoler to mistreat prisoners, there is no doubt this happened. Inmates in gaol for more than a few weeks might also succumb to gaol fever (dysentery) or plague, largely owing to an inadequate diet, severe cold, overcrowding, and unsanitary conditions.

The court that took jurisdiction over the accused was determined by the severity of the charge. Misdemeanours, or crimes constituting a minor breach of behaviour, and community regulatory offences, such as the failure to perform community service or attend church, were usually adjudicated summarily (that is, tried by one or two JPs without a jury) or in the presence of several JPs and a trial jury. These included offences such as assault, fighting, slander, drunkenness, gambling, defamation, scolding, bastardy, fornication, adultery, prostitution, vagrancy, trespass, and a number of economic crimes, such as fraud and forestalling (the criminal act of withholding goods from market to create a shortage in supply). The more minor of these crimes might be handled swiftly and summarily in what came to be known as Petty Sessions, conducted as needed by a JP sitting alone. Occasionally, though less frequently as time went on, these lesser crimes might also be heard in borough, manorial, or church leets (courts) adjudicated, respectively, by town officials, manor lords, or church officers. More serious misdemeanour offences were handled by JPs, often members of the quorum, sitting in groups of two or three at Quarter Sessions. As their name suggests, Quarter Sessions were held four times per year, and took place in the presence of a trial jury of twelve men drawn from the community in which the crime occurred. Once capital punishment was formally removed from JPs in 1592 (though in fact it had not been routinely used by JPs since the 1550s), their range of punishment included fines, banishment from the community, imprisonment, and corporal punishment, such as whipping, ear cropping (the removal of the outer ear), and a stint in the local pillory, stocks, or ducking stool (which involved repeatedly ducking women convicted of adultery or scolding their husbands into a body of water).

The most serious crimes in England – and all of the ones that appear in this collection – were known as felonies. With one exception (petty larceny, or minor theft), theoretically all felonies could be punished with death. Felonies included all crimes against property (larceny, burglary, robbery, cutpursing [pickpocketing], counterfeiting, coin-clipping), serious breaches of the peace or crimes against the king (arson, riot, treason), major sexual offences (rape, sodomy, buggery, pederasty [pedophilia]), all forms of homicide (murder, felonious killing [manslaughter], infanticide), and witchcraft. By definition, felonies violated both Biblical injunctions and state law, and their prosecution, therefore, belonged to the monarch, as head of both church and state.

All felonies had elements, or criteria that needed to be proven, in order for the charge to succeed. These included proof that an actual crime occurred (known as *actus reus*, or "guilty act"), and that certain facts about the act could be ascertained from physical evidence and victim and witness testimony. For instance, in the early modern period, the crime of rape included among its elements proof of resistance (by fighting or screaming out) and penetration.

The failure to prove these elements, and especially that of penetration (which was not easy if the woman was married or known to be sexually active), could result in a lesser charge whose elements could be more easily demonstrated, such as "assault with intent to rape." In the eyes of the law, these were important distinctions: whereas a rape conviction would nearly always result in execution, an assault conviction was a misdemeanor offence and the punishment would have been much less serious. Ultimately, it was the task of the judge to identify the elements necessary to prove a crime and of the jury to determine whether or not the victim or prosecutor, and his witnesses, met that burden of proof.

Moreover, certain felonies were deemed to be more serious and subject to greater punishment than others. These were crimes committed *vi et armis* (by force and arms) and in the presence of *mens rea* (a guilty mind). *Vi et armis* did not necessarily mean that either physical force or weapons had to be involved (although their presence during a crime would usually aggravate the offence), but instead implied that the criminal act was somehow clearly injurious to the body of the king's subject, usually by "putting the fear" into the victim. Thus, robbery was more serious than larceny (theft) because the former involved stealing something from a person's body, which placed the victim in greater physical jeopardy and possibly in fear of his life, whereas the latter simply meant stealing something lying about. *Mens rea* meant that, at the time in which the crime occurred, the offender had knowledge that his actions were wrong and acted anyway. This factor distinguished, for example, murder (which was committed with malice aforethought) from manslaughter (or felonious killing, which might occur through accident or misadventure). Felonies committed in the absence of *vi et armis* and *mens rea* might result in dismissal, acquittal, a pardon, or a reduced charge or punishment. Those committed in the presence of these two factors would much more likely result in conviction and execution.

Capital felonies, those subject to the death penalty if the accused was convicted, were heard by crown justices during twice-annual Assizes. In the unique case of Middlesex County, there was a fixed Assizes jurisdiction, the Old Bailey, which sat regularly to hear the many cases committed in London and Westminster, and their environs. The remainder of the Assizes took place throughout the countryside, where the experienced judges from the three Westminster common law courts of Common Pleas, Exchequer, and King's Bench (or Queen's Bench when the monarch was a woman), together with senior barristers known as Sergeants-at-Law, divided into six groups of two and traveled about England between the standard law terms to provide justice at the local level. Their arrival in a community was accompanied by much fanfare, an Assizes Sermon in the parish church, and a formal charge to the jurors and other participants that reminded them of their duty to God, the king, and his royal justices. Over the course of two or three days, one of the judges heard criminal cases – sometimes known as "Gaol Delivery" because one role of the judges was to clear the gaols of all accused criminals – while the other handled civil matters. Usually, the junior judge or sergeant heard the criminal cases, in part because this was considered to be easier law to adjudge, and in part because of concerns for the spread of gaol fever among the senior judiciary.

On the criminal side of the Assizes, the judge first presided over a grand jury as something akin to what today is known as a preliminary trial. These bodies also met for Quarter Sessions under the auspices of the JP or, in the case of homicide, were presided over by the coroner at an inquest. The coroner was a crown appointee who usually had no medical training but was responsible to look into all suspicious deaths and present evidence supporting a murder or manslaughter indictment to the inquest if he believed the death was anything but natural. The coroner's investigation involved seeking and confiscating the weapon used to commit the crime (known as the *deodand*, which was given a monetary value in the indictment and became the property of the crown upon conviction) and interviewing witnesses and suspects. One peculiar method that was commonly used during coroners' homicide investigations, and that will be seen frequently in this collection, involved bringing the suspect into the presence of the dead body to see if, in the presence of the accused, the corpse would bleed afresh, open its eyes and stare at its murderer, or perform any other supernatural act that suggested the guilt of the accused. All of this evidence, together with a physical "viewing of the body" to determine signs of trauma, would then be presented to the inquest.

Grand juries and coroners' inquests were comprised of gentlemen (who commonly served as foremen) and commoners known as "yeoman" or "forty shilling freeholders," who, unlike lesser commoners, were citizens by virtue of their right to vote in elections. As ranking members of society, these men were also expected to take part in local governance, which their service on the grand juries and inquests helped to fulfill. These men would hear testimony from the prosecutor (either the victim or a family member acting on his or her behalf) and victims (through depositions or in person) and determine that the bill of indictment, or presentment, which was prepared by the JP or coroner, was "true" (*billa vera*) and could proceed to trial, or that there was insufficient evidence (*billa ignoramus*), in which case the charge was dismissed and the indictment "rent to pieces" in the presence of the accused. These bodies were expected to indict on the reasonable suspicion that the accused committed the crime for which he or she was being indicted. It has been estimated that approximately 60–80 per cent of indictments were found true, an indication that although most accused were sent on to trial, the process was no mere formality. Grand juries expected to be presented with enough proof to suggest the accused's guilt, which reduced the likelihood that courts were being used maliciously or that trials would ensue in the complete absence of evidence.

In the case of true bills, trials would then commence. Especially when compared to modern criminal trials, the trials conducted in the early modern period were both speedy and inelegant, although they were often accompanied by a certain degree of formality. This included the court clerk calling an "O yez" ("Hear ye") to command the attention of the participants and a formal reading of the indictment. After the recital of the charge, the accused, now known as a "culprit" (a Law French term roughly meaning "we are ready to prove you guilty"), was required to plead guilty or not guilty. The refusal of the culprit to plead could result in an interesting ritual known as *peine forte et dure* ("strong and hard punishment"). The accused was stripped of his clothes and laid on his back on a bare floor, his arms and legs were drawn apart by cords, and weights were applied to his body until he elected to plead or until he died. This rare and excruciating death was sometimes preferred by those who expected they would have been sentenced to execution anyway, but wished, even in death, to demonstrate courage, challenge the jurisdiction of the court, or protect their reputation and families from a felony conviction.

If the culprit pled guilty, which frequently occurred, he was taken away for the time being and his punishment was pronounced at the end of the Assizes session. If he pled not guilty, he was commonly asked "How wilt thou be tried?", to which the common answer was "By God and my country," meaning a trial by a jury of peers from the "country" (community) in which the crime was committed. The trial jury was comprised of "twelve men good and true," whose qualifications to become jurors included being men aged 15 to 70, of sound mind and good character, who had not previously been convicted of a felony offence. They were called to court by the sheriff according to a rotating roster, although many failed to appear when called, and thus constables, who were expected to attend court during their terms of service, commonly supplemented their ranks. The accused was allowed a number of challenges to ensure that the jury panel would be fair and balanced, rather than being composed of individuals with whom the accused had had past indifferences, or who for one reason or another were deemed insufficient to serve. However, challenges were comparatively rare, and because it was common for juries to be empanelled to hear half a dozen or more cases at a time before rendering their verdict on each, juries were rarely hand-picked for each criminal defendant.

Trials usually took fewer than thirty minutes – and very often took as little as four or five minutes – although some took hours. Prosecution witnesses were sworn by the court clerk, but at this time defence witnesses and the accused did not swear an oath because it was believed that there was too much temptation to lie before God, which could sacrifice their eternal afterlife. Historians have suggested that this one-sided oath-taking often made trials more prosecution-minded (because jurors were more likely to believe oath-takers), which in turn sometimes made sympathetic judges more defence-minded (often serving as a legal advisor) in order to balance the scales of justice. Once the prosecution witness were sworn in, evidence would be presented, beginning with the victim's accusation and ending with the accused's defence. Particularly when trials were held outdoors or in town halls that were not formally designed as courtrooms, witnesses usually stood and spoke from wherever they were in the room, rather than take a more formal position in a witness box. This made the proceedings much less formal than the austerity of modern criminal courtrooms.

Although lawyers were occasionally allowed to "open" a felony indictment, or lay out the case for the private prosecutor (the victim or a family member), they did not become common in criminal courts until the eighteenth century, and were not formally allowed to participate in felony trials until 1836. Unlike in civil trials, where lawyers had predominated since the thirteenth century, there were concerns that the presence of lawyers in criminal trials, and the silence of the prosecutor and defendant, would obfuscate rather than reveal the true facts of the case. For this reason, the victim and accused were expected to represent themselves (with the judge offering some counsel and acting, alongside the jury, as a fact finder), and to do so publicly and verbally (the Latin term was *ore tenus*, "to speak openly"), so that the character and demeanour of both parties could aid the jury in its decision. This form of trial has been referred to as the "accused speaks" trial, as opposed to the "accused is silenced" trial that occurred when criminal lawyers became more common and spoke for their clients.

After the completion of the trial, the judge provided some summation and guidance to the jury, informed the panel about the legal elements that had to be met, and often directly advised the members what their verdict should be, although in theory he could not command their verdict. Sometimes, he intoned a simple and preemptory formula: "You have heard the evidence, you are to find the matter of fact as it is laid before you, whereof you are the proper judges, and I pray God direct you." The jury then retired, without food or drink, until it arrived at a decision, which usually took a matter of minutes and, as mentioned, typically involved deciding on several cases at once. Depending on various factors, juries could acquit the accused by finding him not guilty, convict by finding him guilty, or arrive at a "partial verdict," which might involve conviction of a lesser charge or reducing the value of stolen goods to lessen the severity of the sentence, a practice also known as "pious perjury." It has been estimated that approximately 60–70 per cent of those accused of felonies were convicted, another sign that juries took their responsibilities seriously and were neither too lenient nor too harsh. There is evidence, however, that judges occasionally gaoled entire juries that came to conclusions different than those advocated by the judge, which placed limits on the amount of authority that could be exercised by early modern trial juries.

If the accused was convicted by the trial jury, or had pled guilty earlier in the process, he or she was given a brief period of time (an hour or so) to prepare an *allocutus*, essentially a plea for leniency. Unless the crime was particularly heinous – treason, murder, infanticide, robbery, rape, and arson being among the most egregious crimes in this society – leniency was usually granted, either in the form of a judicial reprieve from the judge, which was a stay of execution pending an appeal to the king for a pardon, or a plea for benefit of clergy. The latter, sometimes known as "pleading the book," enabled men to recite a Biblical psalm known as the "neck verse," because its purpose was to save the convict's neck from the noose, and be branded on the hand or thumb ("T" for "Thief" or "M" for "Manslayer") in lieu of death. In theory, benefit of clergy could only be claimed once by a felon, a branded hand being evidence of a malefactor's previous escape from the gallows. Women, who in this period could not claim benefit of clergy, could claim benefit of belly. Following an examination by a "jury of matrons" to ensure the claimant was indeed pregnant, she would be reprieved, at least until the child was born, and usually thereafter because otherwise the child would become a burden on the state. Just as benefit of clergy was a legal fiction that supported the notion that all men were part of the brotherhood of the cloth, so too was benefit of belly often used as a legal fiction to provide women – many of whom were not pregnant when they were granted their benefit – reprieve from the severity of the law. Other mitigations from death that were used in the seventeenth century included transportation to the Americas, enlistment in the military during active wartime, and exile, although these were rarely used.

Those defendants who failed in their plea for leniency, about 25 per cent of those convicted of a felony, would be executed. To a modern eye, this probably seems like a high percentage. The English state and people often analogized society to a human body, in which offending – to extend the analogy, gangrenous – parts needed to be removed in order to allow the remainder to heal and restore balance. Although this society did not generally think of people as having an innate tendency toward criminality (this notion would become common later in British criminal jurisprudence), nor did it believe that certain kinds of malefactors, and particularly those whose crimes threatened the body or property of other English citizens and subjects, could be rehabilitated or reformed once they had begun their decline into vice, sinfulness, and criminality. More practically, early modern English society did not have the centralized mechanisms – financially or bureaucratically – required to place a dangerous criminal into long-term imprisonment, which meant that at this time death was seen as the only means by which a murderer, rapist, or robber – whose crimes were considered morally reprehensible – could be removed from civil society. Later, a massive increase in criminal transportation in the eighteenth century, and the rise of the penitentiary in the early-nineteenth century, would serve this purpose.

A sentence of death was pronounced by the judge after he placed a black cloth (or "cap") on his head, which symbolically recognized the austerity of the occasion and the legitimacy of the court, as a representative of the king, to take a human life. (Oppositely, those sessions in which nobody was sentenced to death were referred to as "maiden sessions," in which the judge donned white gloves before pronouncing mitigated sentences.) Following the pronouncement of death, the condemned was then returned to gaol – in London, this was usually Newgate – and allowed to spend his last few days on Earth consulting with a minister, confessing his sins, and seeking repentance, so that he would be prepared, after death, for his ultimate judgment before God. Common men and women sentenced to execution would usually be hanged. This would occur at a temporary or permanent gallows erected in the town square for that purpose. In London, where hangings were more frequent because of the large population, executions took place at Tyburn Tree. This place of execution was also known as "Triple Tree" because the gallows included three arms to facilitate multiple hangings. It was located at the southeast corner of Hyde Park, where Marble Arch stands today.

Execution at Tyburn, and to a lesser extent at gallows throughout England, was a highly ceremonial act. As least after 1605, the ceremony began the night before, when the Bellman of the Holy Sepulchre walked through the condemned hold at Newgate Prison intoning the following:

> All you that are in the condemned hold do lie,
> Prepare you for tomorrow you shall die;
> Watch all and pray the hour is drawing near,
> That you before the Almighty must appear;
> Examine well yourself, in time repent,
> That you may not to eternal flames be sent;
> And when St. Sepulchre's bell tomorrow tolls,
> The Lord have mercy on your souls.

The next morning, the condemned would line up for the "Newgate Procession," with their nooses around their neck, and would be carted or dragged on a hurdle from Newgate to the gallows, a journey of several miles. As the crowd grew, and jeered or sympathized with the condemned depending on the nature of his crimes, the procession would eventually end up at Tyburn, where speakers would take advantage of the large audience by orating about contemporary events (this is still Hyde Park's "Speakers' Corner" today). After being permitted to make final speeches, which it was hoped would involve confession, repentance, and a warning to others about the consequences of criminal behaviour, the condemned were hanged, as the crowd cheered or recoiled. Hanging was performed by the sheriff or executioner (who was entitled to the condemned's clothing after the hanging) by removing a ladder, box, or cart from under the convict's feet. This allowed the rope to become taut and the noose to tighten and slowly strangulate the condemned to death. This slow and painful process was sometimes hastened by loved ones, who added their weight to the legs of the condemned and brought about a swifter death. After the condemned was dead, the body was usually released to the family for burial or, in the case of a stranger, was buried in a pauper's grave. This method of public hanging continued in England until 1783, when hangings were moved to the courtyard of Newgate Prison and the method changed to the "drop," in which the body plummeted several feet, snapping the neck and ensuring that death occurred almost immediately.

Men and woman of "gentle" status (nobles) were accorded greater legal privilege and were, therefore, beheaded, usually at Tower Hill, if possible with one drop of the axe. This swifter and less gruesome death bestowed the appropriate degree of dignity on the execution of high-profile convicts, as was true of Charles I when he was executed at Banqueting Hall, Whitehall, by his subjects on January 30, 1649. Those found guilty of treason either against the king (high treason) or a social superior (petty treason) received still greater punishment. They were drawn to the place of execution on a hurdle (a wooden trap dragged behind a horse), hanged until nearly dead, and cut down. Men would then be emasculated (a symbolic gesture showing that their children were disinherited) and eviscerated. While his genitals and intestines burned to ash in a fire, the condemned would be beheaded, his body quartered, and the quarters displayed as directed by the king. In London, this was usually on London Bridge or a similarly well-trod route, whereas in other cities, which were commonly walled at this time, the quarters were placed at each of four entry gates. Treasonous women, whose anatomy was not deemed suitable for public viewing, would be burned at the stake, sometimes after being strangulated by hanging. In both cases, this was considered to be the ultimate form of punishment because of the common belief that the body had to be buried whole in order to receive salvation in the afterlife. Quartering and burning made this impossible, and created immense fear in the Christian population that believed life on Earth was a hardship to be endured in anticipation of eternal bliss in Heaven.

Finally, as a further deterrent and punishment, all felons – even those who were granted benefit of clergy or a pardon, or who had elected *peine forte et dure* in lieu of a trial and public execution – could be subjected to "felony forfeiture." This involved the sheriff or another royal official (such as coroners and escheators) seizing all goods and chattels (moveable property) of the felon, itemizing them, and remitting them to the king. The king, in turn, could keep the profits or, as commonly happened, bestow them to a member of his household, to the royal almoner (who distributed the money as charity), to the feudal lord or bishop on whose land or parish the crime took place, or to a private individual who held a patent entitling him to the profits of forfeiture. One of the reasons why suicide, or self-murder, was a felony in this period was because the suicide's property would revert to the king. Although it is still unclear precisely how often felony forfeiture occurred in early modern England, or how many felons received relief from forfeiture, when it did occur this would result in the impoverishment not only of the felon, should he manage to escape the death penalty, but also of his wife and children. Thus, even in death, a felon's crimes continued to be felt by his family and his community.

***

Despite the seemingly rigid system of English criminal justice in this period, historians have identified several key characteristics that mitigated a "black and white" approach to crime and punishment. First, the system was highly *participatory*. A typical case began with the participation of the victim, accused, witnesses, constable, and JP. Many ranking and common men of the community would also participate. They might serve as investigators, members of a "hue and cry" that sought to apprehend the criminal, and grand and petty jurors. Likewise, women might serve on a jury of matrons, who inspected other women for pregnancy and signs of sexual activity and physical abuse. A town gaoler and executioner, and the local sheriff or undersheriff and his bailiffs, who administered the system, also participated in paid capacities. There were also active roles played by some rather unexpected participants: the critical role of, for example, birds, dogs, and very young children in bringing criminals to justice will be seen frequently throughout this collection. Thus, at some point in their lives, nearly everybody living in Tudor and Stuart England would come into contact with the English criminal justice system, either as victims, defendants, witnesses, jurors, or village and court officials. This degree of participation allowed participants to view the criminal law as local and benevolent (serving the interest of the people and the community) rather than central and malevolent (serving only the interests of the state or nobility), which has been seen as a safety-valve regulating centre and periphery relations in this period.

Second, this system was highly *discretionary* and flexible. Although in theory a national "rule of law" applied throughout England, in practice the exercise of law was based on a series of factors. These included the desire of the various participants to prosecute, give evidence, and convict; the unique norms of a local community, which were sometimes at odds with the expectations of the central government; the existence of extenuating circumstances, such as the degree of violence, that mitigated or exacerbated a criminal act; the neighbourliness (or strangerliness) and demeanour of an accused; the extent to which the various boundaries of behavior in society – gender, rank, religious, social, and economic – were upset or restored by a criminal act; and the degree of correction needed to rebalance society after a crime was committed. One historian, for example, has shown how local communities showed discretion based on their perception of whether a crime was committed by a *criminal* – a hardened, violent, unrepentant malefactor who planned his crimes and significantly upset the community – or an *offender* – a repentant, sinful recidivist whose crimes were not particularly heinous and who could be returned to the normal boundaries of behaviour. Typically, participants were much harsher toward criminals than offenders, employing discretion rather than the strict letter of the law to restore order. Still, despite this accepted degree of local discretion, the state occasionally found the need to step in when the local community was too casual or too zealous in its handling of certain criminal cases. This reinforced the fact that, ultimately, the king was the fount of all justice.

Third, the vast majority of crime was *opportunistic* and amateur rather than planned and executed by professionals. That is, most crime was based on dire need or immediate impulse when presented with easy opportunity, and could be committed by just about anybody under the right set of circumstances. Few crimes involved a profit-driven enterprise undertaken by professionals with innate tendencies toward criminal behaviour. Although a few types of crimes – especially highway robbery, smuggling, poaching, and confidence schemes – were "semi-organized," we do not find much organized gang activity, crime waves, or the existence of a criminal sub-class operating among otherwise law-abiding people. This notion of an innate class of professional criminals practicing among an otherwise law-abiding population would not be common features in the criminal justice system until the mid-eighteenth to mid-nineteenth centuries. In fact, criminal opportunism and amateurism are among the chief reasons why the perpetrators of so many crimes were discovered relatively easily. They simply lacked the professional experience of planning and executing crimes and made the amateur mistakes common to first time criminals that soon led to their arrest.

Fourth, crime and criminal justice in England were highly *personal*, rather than the modern notion of a system that is anonymous, impartial, and objective. The vast majority of crimes committed in small communities were committed by offenders known to the community. These offenders sat beside their neighbours at church, reveled with them during days of celebration, suffered with them during times of plight, and mourned with them over the loss of friends and family. Their reputation and character, therefore, were known to jurors and other participants, and these were taken into account at all stages of the process. Indeed, at this time it was seen as beneficial that jurors personally knew the accused, so that they might arrive at a fair decision based on their knowledge of his character. In addition, most serious crimes were also deeply personal. Most criminals knew and were often related – as spouses, parents, masters, or mistresses – to their victims, which resulted in many crimes being committed out of passion or direct, familial conflict. Likewise, many crimes were committed by desperate people seeking to avoid the trauma of social stigma that could easily occur in a society in which everybody knew everybody else. Cases of infanticide and murder, for example, were often committed with the intent to protect a person's reputation in society, even though the result was usually precisely the opposite. In larger centres such as London, anonymity was more common and criminals often had no personal relationship with their victims, which caused participants either to take a stricter view of the criminal act, or to be more forgiving because emotions were less heightened. Oppositely, in small communities, crimes committed by strangers were seen as particularly heinous because a member of the community, with whom the community had a relationship, was a victim to an outsider.

These four principal characteristics – a system of crime and criminal justice that was *participatory*, *discretionary*, *opportunistic*, and *personal* – are amply demonstrated in the texts selected for inclusion in this collection. My goal was to represent a wide range of crime that extended beyond metropolitan London and into the English countryside, where, historians have recognized, the nature of crime and justice were not always the same as they were in the more populated centres. I have deliberately chosen not to include chapbooks describing some of the better-known trials of the period. In part, this is because many of the most important trials during this time – such as the conviction of the Earl of Castlehaven for rape and sodomy, and the treason trials of Sir Walter Raleigh, Francis Bacon, King Charles I, and the participants of the Monmouth Rebellion – have long been reprinted in Cobbett's *Collection of State Trials*, and are readily accessible. My choice to include lesser-known cases is also because some of the more salient aspects of crime in this period can be shown better through everyday crimes committed by everyday people under everyday circumstances. The crimes described in this book were, for the most part, committed by common, "everyman" English men and women, who for reasons ranging from greed and lust, to fear and revenge, stole, raped, killed, and bewitched.

***

Despite their range of crimes and geography over the course of more than a century, the stories in this collection, and those in the crime chapbook genre in general, share a number of common features in addition to those discussed earlier. Although many chapbooks did have named authors, it was usual for those in the crime genre to be written anonymously. The authors often made it clear that they were somehow personally involved in the cases as observers or interested parties, so we can in some cases guess who the author was or why he had personal knowledge of the case. But the intention at the time the texts were written was that the authors remain unknown to the reader. To some extent, this anonymity shielded the author from persecution if the subject of the chapbook was not deemed fit for public consumption because it challenged the politics or morality of the day, or if the crime being described was, in whole or in part, fabricated. Anonymity thus limited an author's liability should there be concerns about a book's content, and helped to ensure that the reader would not interrogate the author's credibility. There was also a certain advantage to the author, like his disorderly subject, being an unknown "everyman." Because of the moral and religious commentary in these texts, the reader could more easily identify with the everyman than with a known person, whose own imperfect life, or whose reputation as a frequent author of sensational literature, might corrupt the moral purposes of the chapbook.

Another common feature of these texts is that the vast majority of them deal with serious and violent crime, in part because minor crimes rarely left enough records for the authors to access, and in part because the authors of these chapbooks preferred, for financial and other reasons, to represent the more salacious and heinous crimes of the time. Retelling tales of murder, infanticide, rape, sodomy, robbery, arson, and witchcraft, for example – which encompass nearly all of these texts – ensured a wide popular audience for this literature and provided the best opportunities for the authors, printers, and booksellers to earn profit and offer religious and moral commentary, which were the two principal purposes of this literature. By comparison, petty crimes such as assaults, breaking the peace, and various minor sexual infractions (bastardy, fornication, and adultery, for example) occurred much more frequently and would not engender the same interest level from popular audiences. These misdemeanours did not significantly upset the balance of society, nor usually scandalize or involve the entire community to the degree that the more serious crimes described in this book caused. Thus, although punishment by death comprised only about 25 per cent of those convicted for felony in early modern England, and a much smaller percentage of those convicted of all forms of crime, it was the punishment for nearly all of the criminals described in this collection.

One very intriguing characteristic of many of these texts is the involvement of animals, often discussed analogously to creatures of the Bible (such as the great sea creature, Leviathan) and as God's servants on Earth. Birds – ravens, crows, roosters, and turtledoves – appear in several of the tales as portents that reveal past or future crimes or events. Dogs often discover dead bodies or critical clues leading to the arrest of the criminals, or are used as examples of creatures that, like backsliders prone to criminality, need to be tamed and disciplined to maintain their domesticity. Cats, cows, geese, moles, beetles, and other common animals appear as "familiars," the imps that were the Devil's physical form when he consorted with witches and took revenge in their names. Many of the criminals in this collection are also accorded the status of animals, or "creatures of the Earth." Criminals are variously referred to as vipers, snakes, caterpillars, wolves, bears, and tigers and are often referred to not only as less than human, but as beneath the status of the more noble birds and beasts of the world. In a society that believed strongly in the *scala naturae* – the hierarchical ladder of nature, or great chain of being – in which man was situated between God and the angels above, and animals and plants below, frequent references to criminals as inferior animals and creatures clearly emphasized their social position in comparison to the law-abiding subjects and citizens of Tudor and Stuart England. In the eyes of the authors, it was this inferiority that, in part, justified these criminals' removal from civil society through execution.

Yet another common feature in these texts is the strong religious language expressed especially in the opening and closing passages of many of the chapbooks. Most serious crime was seen as an affront to God, particularly that which was explicitly forbidden in the Bible (rape, murder, and sodomy, for example). The authors turned to the usual religious explanations, heretics, and scapegoats – the Devil, Catholics, witches, and man's inherent propensity to be sinful without strong religious conviction – to explain why men and women were so susceptible to evil and temptation, and why they turned on their family and their neighbours. The greatest enemy and tempter of mankind, the Devil, in his various physical and spiritual forms, was seen as the driving force behind most criminality. The Devil appears in nearly all of these texts, disguised as Catholics, animals that served as witches' familiars, and as an unseen but eminently real and providential force that infused itself into the minds of malefactors as they formulated and carried out their criminal designs. On the other hand, God is often described variously as the benevolent agent who providentially stopped a criminal before he completed his deed, thus thwarting the Devil's evil designs; the reason why a criminal was discovered and brought to justice; or – because God's will was unknown and mysterious – why a criminal continued to elude the best efforts of the authorities to bring him to justice.

Because of this society's belief in the active providence of God and the Devil, although many of the events in these stories are explained through analogy to classical figures and Greek and Roman mythology, by far the greatest number of references are to the Bible. This was a text with which many readers would have been familiar and which was used on days of worship to provide parables and analogies that taught lessons about morality, character, conduct, and Christian society. References to Biblical psalms, Daniel in the lion's den, and Peter's denial of Christ, for example, would be well known even to the semi-literate readers of early modern England. At their core, despite the often brutal and bloody subjects of their narratives, these texts served the same fundamental purpose as sermons delivered in church: to instill fundamental lessons about the foibles and follies of fallen men and women, and to remind law-abiding Christians how easily they could backslide into sin once they turned away from virtue and started down the path of vice. Like sermons, most of these texts served as cautionary and morality tales, warning readers about the dangers of living too loose a life, which invariably led to fatal consequences.

It is also for similar reasons that many of the chapbooks in this collection focus not only on the crimes committed by the accused, but also on the repentance (or lack thereof) shown by the convicted criminal as he or she awaited execution. If the central purposes of this literature, and of the criminal justice system in general, were to restore order, deter crime, and affirm the role of the church and state in society and punishment, it was important for the authors of chapbooks to demonstrate that the criminals accepted the seriousness of their crimes and the authority of the state, and were penitent and contrite in the face of death. This was usually shown in the chapbooks through a description of the criminal's behaviour, and the religious instruction provided by the Newgate ordinary or other ministers, during the prisoner's final few days on Earth. Remorse and a plea for God's mercy was also shown in the "last dying speech" that the condemned was allowed to make immediately before suffering capital punishment. In this speech, which was eagerly awaited by the often very large audience that turned out to witness the execution, the condemned was expected to confess his crimes and sins (both those for which he was about to die and others committed by him), recant any subversive views he held regarding the church and state, and offer himself into God's hands for ultimate punishment. Onlookers often became hostile when the condemned chose to remain silent, refused to confess, or uttered hateful speech at the gallows. Oppositely, deeply expressed sentiments of repentance could have dramatic affects on audiences (both of the executions and of this literature), who often came to empathize with the perpetrators of these heinous and bloody crimes.

***

The common characteristics discussed above united the texts that appear in this collection into a distinct genre of popular, true crime literature. Although several of the texts that are transcribed in this collection have been printed in modern collections, the majority have not appeared in print for several hundred years. The texts are all listed in the English Short Title Catalogue and are available on the Pollard and Redgrave and Wing microfilm collections of early English books. These collections are reproductions of the original texts that will be found today in various rare book repositories in the United States and the United Kingdom. These texts will also be found in the Early English Books Online database, which contains a selection of the Pollard and Redgrave and Wing collections. Because the microfilmed and digital texts are sometimes incomplete or illegible, I have consulted a number of the originals at the Huntington Library in San Marino, California, and the British Library in St. Pancras, London.

The texts are presented in the chronological order in which they were originally published, although at times they refer to events that happened some years before. I prefer a chronological organization to a thematic one for several reasons. First, this structure gives the reader a better sense of the variety of crimes committed and the changes that occurred in this literature over time. For example, it is easier to discern that, throughout the course of the seventeenth century, the crime chapbooks became shorter because they generally contained little or no moralizing prefatory material and began to take on the characteristics of non-digressive newspaper reporting that would become more common in the eighteenth century. Second, several of the chapbooks discuss more than one type of crime – often ranging from murder and infanticide to robbery and sexual assault in a single text – which would make dividing the texts into certain categories of crimes or criminals impossible. Third, there are a number of themes in this book, such as the important roles of God, the Devil, religion, women, children, and animals that would be obscured through an organization that merely categorized the chapbooks by types of crimes and criminals.

At the beginning of each text I have offered a brief introduction and discussion of the chapbook that follows. These discussions provide some historical context that will facilitate greater understanding of the selection, and reflect on some of the more important or unusual aspects of the story, and on the relationship between the chapbook and the broader subject of crime and criminal justice in Tudor and Stuart England. While these discussions may be considered to be starting points to engage critically with the texts, they are not comprehensive, and many additional elements worthy of discussion and further examination will be found in each transcription. I have also included the complete title and publication information as described on the cover of the original. These "long titles," as opposed to the "short titles" by which these works are usually referenced, are descriptive of the material that follows. These titles help to explain what the author or printer deemed to be particularly important about the text, and provides the "blurb" that might have been used by sellers and read by potential customers in order to transact a sale. The place of publication is always London, the heart of England's bookmaking and bookselling trade. The publisher is typically a named bookshop, bookseller, or printer, most of which operated shops located north of the Thames between St. Paul's and Tower Bridge. The original date of publication ranges between 1581, when this literature began to be commonly printed, until 1693, by which time this genre was quickly being replaced by newspapers and other official accounts.

The editorial conventions used in the transcriptions are straightforward. To aid the modern reader who is not familiar with early modern typography and syntax, spelling (including place and personal names) and capitalization have been modernized, punctuation changed to conform to modern usage, very large sentences and paragraphs divided up, abbreviations silently expanded, and other archaic devices (such as the use of the long s) revised to reflect modern usage. Some dated diction and syntax – such as thee, thou, sheweth, etcetera – have been retained, as have various idiosyncrasies of the authors. These archaic devices, though usually not impacting the reader's ability to understand the texts, serve as reminders that these are, after all, three-hundred-year-old stories, even though some of them appear as if they were ripped from today's newspapers. Cases of dittography (in which the same word or letter is erroneously spelled out twice) and other typesetting errors (such as letters being upside down or backwards, as frequently happened) have also been silently corrected.

On the rare occasions where Latin was used – rare, because this was not a language commoners knew – this has been translated in brackets immediately after the phrase, unless the original text also provides the translation. Marginal notations, which are commonly citations to religious and classical references in the text, have been incorporated into the main text in parentheses. Even with this all of this modernized transcription, readers will undoubtedly experience some difficulties with the language, as many of the authors were themselves semi-literate and were not always clear in their meaning. For this reason, terms that are less familiar today, or that were used differently in the early modern period, have either been defined briefly in square brackets after the term, or have been described more fully in notes. Notes have also been used to provide citations for religious and classical references, unless these are clearly indicated within the text. These editorial intrusions have been kept as minimal as possible to reduce disruptions for the reader, and, in questionable cases, to allow for the widest possible interpretation to be made.

1 The blood-thirsty papist

Unlike most of the chapbooks in this collection, which contain few overt political messages and even fewer signs of advanced learning on the part of the author, this selection is a politically charged and religiously informed text. What makes this chapbook particularly interesting is the manner in which the anonymous author relates the crime of murder to the Catholicism practiced by those involved, without offering any evidence that the two were related. Queen Elizabeth, since she ascended the English throne in 1558, had constructed the Anglican Church of England and experienced a number of Catholic threats. These included the Northern Rebellion in 1569, Elizabeth's excommunication by the pope in 1570, the Ridolfi Plot in 1572, the arrival of the Jesuits into England throughout the 1570s, and various conspiracies engineered by Mary, Queen of Scots. These various threats brought on the passage of several penal laws against Catholics between 1563 and 1593. Praemunire, treason, and recusancy laws collectively made it illegal to defend the supremacy of the pope or recognize a foreign religious authority, call the monarch heretical or schismatic, or practice recusancy (the refusal to accept Anglican communion). The penalty for breaching these various laws ranged from fines to death, but on the whole the state remained relatively tolerant of Catholics, provided they did not challenge the queen's right to rule. Using this unexceptional and financially motivated murder as an example, the author of this tract describes the blood-thirsty nature of Catholics, and encourages his readers, and the English state, to take even stronger action against Catholics. Indeed, beginning in 1581 (the year this chapbook was written) the state increased the number and severity of penal laws against Catholics, particularly those who sought to convert Protestants or officiate Catholic mass. Thus, although this chapbook narrates a fairly standard case of murder, its political message vastly overshadows the crime it describes.

***

A true report of the late horrible murder, committed by William Sherwood, prisoner in the Queen's Bench, for the profession of popery, the 18th of June 1581. *London: Printed by John Charlewood and Edward White, 1581*

I am the more loath at this time to lay open unto the view of the whole world that late foul murder committed by Sherwood, because I would not speak much of them which be gone and be thought to bite them by the back which are dead. And so be like unto those papists which being hot in cruelty, did not only curse the dead continually, but did take up and burn the bones of diverse [many] good men into ashes to signify unto the world that no drink could cool their thirst but blood, no sacrifice could content them but the warm heart-blood of martyrs and the death of the saints of God.[1] But my intent is this, for as much as their scabs now break out and that their cruelty seeketh no corners, but setteth itself upon a stage to be beheld of all men, to give all good Christians warning that as they shall hear of their naughtiness, and see it so, they will learn to spew them out of their stomachs forever. It was wont to be said often and to be true: "envy braggeth but draweth no blood."[2] But now it may be as truly said: the malice of a papist, it braggeth little, but it is hardly satisfied but with abundance of much blood.

Their desired time of revenge is not past, and their malice hath not yet vomited his gall [bile]. We may see this, that because opportunity offereth not itself, to let them delight their eyes with beholding our channels, running and reeking, with the warm blood of Protestants. Rather than they will want this delight, they will wash their hands in the blood of their own brethren, in their own chambers. This is the portion of their cups, which if they might, we should be made to drink to the dregs.

These are the boars which destroy the vineyard,[3] who, because they are not baited with dogs and their ears torn off, they will play like mad dogs themselves, biting all that come in their way. They give out in their libels, which they scatter, friendly advertisements, as Judas offered a friendly kill. They cast themselves wholly like good subjects, at the feet of our gracious sovereign, but their long ears[4] do betray their conditions. Their throats are open sepulchers,[5] they flatter with their tongues: and so it is their kind, for it is as natural for a dog to bark, as to wag his tail. If the commonwealth be not purged of this infection, the plague will be so great that upon every good Protestant's body, Lord have mercy upon us, may shortly be written.

But I will briefly deliver out this fearful tragedy, in which I will set out nothing that is false, nor willingly keep anything back that is true. In the Queen's Bench there were two detained for popery. The one called Richard Hobson, born in the Isle of Wight, of good parentage, young in years, but (as time offereth) many young and green heads are seasoned papists. The other named William Sherwood, a gentleman born to some lands in Yorkshire, at Walkington, by Beverley. A man condemned in a praemunire,[6] for extolling the supremacy, a derider of God's ministers, a disturber of preachers, a contemner [despiser] of the service confirmed by Her Majesty, calling it devilish. One well liked of many papists but best liked of himself. Because he was so disobedient, they accounted him stout [brave]; because he prated much, they accounted him learned; but because he hath shamed them much, they would now accompt [account] him mad. It fortuned before the death of Hobson, about six weeks, that Sherwood for want of payment was removed from his lodging, well shackled, to the common gaol,[7] whose misery being pitied by this young man [Hobson] was also relieved by his means (as at sundry other times he was).

The quarrel, as I am credibly informed, was this: Hobson gave his word for the money that Sherwood owed. A friend of Sherwood's shortly after had sent five pounds for the payment of his charges, which Hobson receiving, disbursed it for himself, and within few days after, satisfied the residue.[8] Because this money was not paid to Sherwood first, at dinner time, with open words he protested that he could not abide Hobson. This young man moved him oftentimes earnestly to be reconciled, showing his grief unto him, in that he took offence at him. But nothing might move his mind that thirsted, or stay his hands that itched to commit murder. It is a speech commonly used, that love waxeth and waneth oftentimes with the moon, but it may be as commonly seen that the hatred of a papist never waxeth and waneth, but still waxeth, still increaseth. He that hath been planted in popery, his grapes are grapes of gall; his clusters are always bitter. If the pope hath once given them a sop [bread soaked in wine], they are never sober after: if he has once poured his liquor into them, their vessels can hardly be made clean.

But to be brief, the day grew on, which was the 28th of June about 8 o'clock in the morning, at which time he had determined to murder his fellow papist. And that the matter might more easily be brought to pass, he caused the night before the keeper to remove all Hobson's weapons, so that the next morning, as Hobson was coming down through Sherwood's chamber from his prayers, Sherwood shutting his chamber door, assailed him with a knife and a stool trestle, astonishing him, afterwards gave him a large wound, keeping him down and struggling till he bled to death, Hobson often crying "help Father Throckmorton, he killeth me with his knife!" Master Throckmorton and others, hearing this noise, came upon Sherwood and by force broke up his doors, found the young man all to be soused in his own blood and gasping for breath: who after a few faint words, yielded his soul into the hands of God. Sherwood, perceiving a great many busy about Hobson, began to practice to escape, but by heed-taking of one Master Smith's man, he was brought to the marshal's hands, and imbrued [stained] in his fellow's blood. Who being examined, he denied the manifest murder, which by witness was proved, and he being brought to the slain body, the blood which was settled, issued out afresh.[9] Thus he slew this young man, in deed and cause, miserably in form and fashion, cruelly and beastly.

Let us advisedly now weigh and consider, what manner of razor this is, that cutteth so sharp. If they be thus unable to master their passions and thus like bloodsuckers, do open them against their own fellow prisoners, what shall we look for at their hands? *Quibus sepibus tam immanes bestuas continebimus*: What hedges can be made strong enough to keep in these beasts? Tully, writing against Antony, Philip 7, sayeth thus: *Qui familiarem jugularit, quid hic occasione data faciet inimico? Et qui illud animi cause fecerit, hunc praedae causa quid facturum putatis?*: He that will kill his familiar friend, what will he do, if occasion be offered, to his enemies? And he that will do this of stomach, what will he offer to do for spoil?[10]

Surely, so they will do as they have done: they will devour poor Protestants as beasts eat grass. We shall (if time served) not only be choked with the smoke of popery, but we shall be burnt up with the fire. Their imprisonments have so enriched them that they abound in all manner of wealth, especially no men better furnished for war, for rebellion, than they. In this great time of mercy they do nothing but gather heaps of stones to throw at us. They are making of the halters [nooses] to hang us. They are whetting [sharpening] of their knives to cut our throats. These tied dogs, when they shall be let loose, they will bite us, nay, they will bite us to death.

It is time to cut off the Hydra's heads,[11] and to strangle him within his cave, for howsoever it commeth to pass, they lift up their heads on high. Papistry began to wax dead and to be cold in the mouth: it beginneth now to warm again and to kneel. We poor Protestants are afraid, but that God and our gracious prince [queen] is with us and hath broke still the arm of the wicked. Our hearts would melt like war in the midst of our bowels: the Lord hath delivered Her Majesty hitherto from them, as a doe from the hand of the hunter, and as a bird from the hand of the fowler, and God grant they be never taken for good subjects, till they become subject to God and his gospel. This subjection of theirs and false protestation of faith to Her Majesty is a false colour. We wink hard or else we be marvelously blinded if we perceive it not. It is piety that these black ravens should go for birds with the rest. I hope God will so bless us, especially all magistrates, that they will look to it at the last that they shall not be in account with them as to be the finger next the thumb.

But now to return to his end, *Qualis vita, finis ita*, as he lived so he died. Being arraigned at Croydon, he continued still obstinately denying the fact, hoping for some help by pardon, but a just judge prevented an ungracious hope. The 12th of July he was returned home manacled with another, who was condemned for a rape. His behaviour the night before he suffered was according to his accustomed usage, resolute in opinion, though false and dissolute in behaviour, driving off his Christian brethren that exhorted him, with dry scoffs. And no marvel, for scoffing, mocking and moaning, licking of chalices and all manner of toying, is the life of their religion.

The next day was the 13th of July, the appointed time for the execution. In the morning certain devout Christians had access unto him, whom at the first entrance he cut off, or hearing a small time, despised. The time of the execution drew nigh, which was performed over against the Queen's Bench, where the murder was committed, by the undersheriff of Surrey and the bailiff of Southwark. From the White Lion[12] to the place where he should suffer, after many vain words of conceived reprieve had by the way, he was caused to climb the ladder, on which being placed, he entered this kind of discourse: "I beseech all Romish Catholics to help me in this my extremity, with their virtuous and godly prayers for other which are of a contrary profession, as I abhor their religion, so I will [have] none of their prayers. But if there shall be here present any one of the true Catholic Romish faith, I beseech them of their prayers of my behalf."

The people hearing these his obstinate speeches, with sundry exclamations, cried out, "Hang him, hang him, there be none here of his profession!" Nevertheless he continued his wicked speeches, proclaiming the pope of Rome the supreme head of the universal church, Christ's vicar here upon Earth. Yet notwithstanding, though by evident reasons he was confuted, yet the God of this world had so blinded him that no reason could prevail with him.

And farther, whereas the preacher persuaded him to lay his hope on Christ, whose mercy was infinite, he vehemently cried out, "Away with the wolf, he perverteth the truth and troubleth me, away with the wolf!" Being farther inquired of the murder, he persisted in his unjust denial, laying contrary to all evidence and probability the death of the young man Hobson to his own charge.[13]

When no hope of confession or recantation was to be conceived, the sheriff caused him to be removed higher, to the end that execution might be performed, wishing him by earnest and devout prayers to call for mercy and repentance, to crave grace. But he by these tokens perceiving death at hand, contrary to a meek lamb, as he termed himself, fled down the ladder to fly from the butcher, thereby showing the unstableness of his faith. So that the hangman was forced to undo the halter which he had fastened to the gibbet, and to put it about his neck below, and so by little and little to draw him up. Where resting, after many persuasions by the sheriff and the preacher, and no profit in the midst of his Latin pater noster,[14] was turned off to the mercy of God.

I am persuaded if all the rest were thus handled, no one faithful subject should draw less breath, and then I am sure (through God's great goodness) the happy peace of this land should be made perfect. You see how boldly he embraced foreign jurisdiction, all they which be papists, heartily do the like. I pray God that if they be not haltered, yet that they may be bridled with shorter reins, that they be not so headstrong, as this man was.

If a sheep worrier[15] be well cudgeled [beaten] at the first, he forsaketh his trade. So if papists were thoroughly dealt withal, they would forget to make the pope supreme head of the Church of England. I beseech those that be in authority to look to it, and thus committing the poor (yet quiet) estate of the Church of England to the old and wonted care of our gracious prince, and the rest that bear any office, I end, not willing to spend many words upon so vile a generation. But as Peter Act 2[16] exhorted his scholars in many words, saying, "save yourselves from this forward generation," so I with few words exhort all estates to look to themselves, and to take heed of this viperous and pestilent generation from ancient cruelty, of the which the Lord deliver this whole land of England both now and forever. Amen.

Notes

1 This is a reference to the Roman Catholic inquisition, initiated by Pope Paul III in 1542 and still ongoing at the time of this chapbook. Its purpose was to persecute Protestants, usually by having them burned at the stake, thus making them martyrs. In England, the inquisition was carried out by Mary I ("Bloody Mary") from 1553–58, which became a central subject in John Foxe's famous *Book of Martyrs* (1563).

2 From John Lyly, *Euphues: The Anatomy of Wit* (1578).

3 Psalm 80:8–13, an allegorical reference to an enemy trying to destroy true religion.

4 To Christians, the goat, distinguished by its long ears, reflects fraud and sin. Matthew 25:31–46 analogizes Christ's return to separate the believers who will go to Heaven from the sinners who are damned as a shepherd separating the sheep from the goats.

5 A place, such as an altar or mausoleum, where sacred objects (relics and the dead), are stored. Generally, a reference to Catholic idol worship.

6 A law that forbade clergy from recognizing papal supremacy in religious or secular matters.

7 It was common at this time for those who owed money to be placed into "debtors' prison," which was usually the local gaol in smaller communities. The debtor was often allowed to transact normal business in order to raise funds, but remained imprisoned or under a keeper's watch until his debt was satisfied.

8 That is, Hobson intercepted the money and used it to pay Sherwood's creditors, paying the remainder from his own purse. Sherwood was angry because Hobson did not give the money directly to him.

9 A common method of determining a murderer was to bring the suspect into the presence of the corpse to see if the latter gave signs of the suspect's guilt. This usually involved the corpse opening its eyes and looking upon the suspect, or the wounds bleeding afresh in the suspect's presence.

10 Marcus Tullius Cicero, *Orations Against Marc Anthony*, Philippic 7, section 18.

11 In Greek mythology, the Hydra was a many-headed water serpent whose heads grew back when they were cut off. It was defeated by Heracles (Hercules), who with the help of his nephew systematically cut off each head and cauterized the stump so that a new head could not grow. Heracles cut off the last head with a golden sword, killing the Hydra.

12 A prison in Southwark, London.

13 Sherwood claimed Hobson committed suicide.

14 The Latin (and thus Catholic) version of the Lord's Prayer.

15 A wild dog known to roam among sheep and cause them distress.

16 Acts 2:40.

2 The jealous mercer and the smitten lover

The violent and bloody murders that are described in this chapbook cover most of the seven deadly sins. Thomas Smith suffered from wrath, greed, hubris, and envy, while Mrs Beast and Christopher Tomson both suffered from greed, lust, and perhaps a measure of sloth, too. Both homicides involved a significant degree of malice aforethought, a vital element to prove murder in court. In order to avoid any suggestion that the victims deserved their fate, the author also emphasizes how honest, hardworking, and friendly the victims were in their community. Given the bloody and premeditated nature of their crimes against good, law-abiding subjects, execution was the only punishment that could rebalance society after the upset and scandal caused by the murders. As a common murderer, Smith was hanged by the neck until dead. But as petty treasoners – because they had killed a social superior, in this case a husband and master – Beast and Tomson suffered a greater punishment. She was burned at the stake, a common punishment for women who were treasonous or heretical. Although he would normally have been hanged, drawn, and quartered, his punishment was commuted to being hanged to death. Then, to send a strong message of deterrence, Tomson's body was hanged in chains at the place of his crime. This process could result in the body being placed on public display for months or years, until somebody petitioned the king for its removal. By that time, the body would have decomposed and been ravaged by birds, rats, and insects, leaving little to bury.

***

A brief discourse of two most cruel and bloody murders,
committed both in Worcestershire, and both happening
unhappily in the year 1583. The first declaring how one
unnaturally murdered his neighbour, and afterward buried
him in his cellar. The other sheweth how a woman unlawfully
following the devilish lusts of the flesh with her servant, caused
him very cruelly to kill her own husband. *London: Printed by
Roger Warde, dwelling near Holburn Conduit at the Sign of the
Talbot, 1583*

That the days of danger and iniquity are as now, not only our own frail nature
may sufficiently certify us: but also the irksome examples and unwonted prodigious spectacles every day and hour (almost) apparent in our eyes, may drive
from us any doubt to the contrary. For if we enter into examination with ourselves, as well of our negligence of duty to our God, as also our lack of love to
our neighbour, we shall find that we are not, neither do as the holy evangelist
wisheth us, when he saith (1 John 4:7): "Beloved, let us love one another, for
love commeth of God, and every one that loveth is born of God and knoweth
God: but he that loveth not, knoweth not God, for God is love." And I find in
Ecclesiasticus these words (Ecclesiasticus 25:1[1]): "Three things rejoice me and
by them am I beautified before God and men: the unity of brethren, the love
of neighbours, and a man and wife that agree together."

How then can we otherwise judge but that we are in that iron and crooked
age,[2] wherein iniquity should vaunt [boast] and shew herself, being made
acquainted every day with the lack of that heavenly ornament, love, the memory thereof almost defaced and pulled up by the root in so grievous and vehe-
ment manner that it may be hardly said to have any abiding among us at
all? And that I may not wade into abundance of matter without due proof to
affirm anything alleged: I pray you look into these tragical accidents following, which albeit they carry terror sufficient to forewarn the unnatural children of this world, yet daily do fresh enormities spring up, able (had nature
so agreed) to urge the very bowels of the Earth to yield forth fearful acclama-
tions against us. Shall I withhold to say, that the father hath not procured the
death of his own natural child, and the child risen in like occasion against his
father? Shall I not say, the husband hath abridged the life of his espoused wife
and mate, and she likewise committed the like unnatural act on her husband?
Hath not one brother murdered the other, one neighbour killed the other, one
friend been false to the other, yea and very nature turned against itself?

These unlooked for examples are daily before us, so that we cannot shun
the sight and hearing of them, and yet shall we pass them over with a slender
or light regard? Oh my friends, do we not see the heavens frown? And why?
Because the sins of the Earth hath fumed up into the nostrils of the Almighty
with a savour [smell] so irksome and insufferable that he cannot in justice, but
strike stiff necked Pharaoh with the rod of his fury,[3] yea, and bereave the Earth
of those benevolent blessings, which he hath suffered it so quietly to enjoy

and so great abuse rendered unto him for them. Can we reprove the father for disinheriting his son, when he seeth his dealings such as deserveth nothing? Can we blame that master, who thrusteth his servant forth of his doors, when he beholdeth his behaviour unworthy of house-room? Even so, can we otherwise say, that our heavenly Father doth unworthily cast us out of his favour, when instead of love, we render him hatred, for duty, negligence, and for all his good gifts, ungracious thanks? Oh no, let us not enter into such questioning with ourselves, for if we look into our iniquity, and then into his mercy, our daily falling from one sin into another and his so long fatherly forbearance. We will then quickly return from the fleshpots of Egypt,[4] and from our own filthy and odious vomit, and every one of us say heartily with the psalmist (Psalm 51:3): "I do know mine own wickedness, and my sin is ever against me." And likewise confess with Daniel the prophet (Daniel 9:9–10): "To thee (oh Lord God) belongeth mercy and forgiveness, for we have gone away from thee and have not harkened to thy voice, whereby we might walk in thy laws which thou hast appointed for us."

It is high time that we should thus consider with ourselves, if we but look into the present occasions offered unto us, and mark how busy the Devil is to work mass utter overthrow: The rather by two grievous and horrible mischances which hath lately happened, wherein may be seen, how needful it is for us to call for the grace of our heavenly Father, to strengthen us with such assured confidence, that we fall not likewise into such evil, but may show such hearty repentance of our former offences, as the very wicked, by our good example, may be drawn to glorify the eternal God.

A most cruel and bloody murder, committed on New Year's Eve last past, being the last day of December, 1582 in the town of Esam in Worcestershire, by one Thomas Smith a town dweller, upon his neighbour Robert Greenoll, who when he had cruelly murdered him, made a grave in his cellar and there buried him

In Esam,[5] a handsome market town in Worcestershire well known, dwelled two young men, who by their usual trade were mercers,[6] as in the country they call them so that sell all kinds of wares. The one of them they called Robert Greenoll, a bachelor, and of such an honest conversation as he was not only well beloved in the town where he dwelt, but also of those who had every market day access thither for their needful necessaries, so that he was as well customed as any occupier in the town. The other was called Thomas Smith, of indifferent [moderate] wealth likewise, and son to one of the most substantial men in the town, and joined in marriage with a gentlewoman of very good parentage. So that he likewise was well thought on of most and least [more or less].

This Thomas Smith, seeing Greenoll have so good utterance [sales] for his wares and so well esteemed in each company, if not upon this cause alone, though chiefly it be accounted so, he began to envy the prosperous estate of him being his neighbour and friend. And the Devil so far ruled the course of his envious intent, as nothing would suffice the desire thereof but only making away of Greenoll by death, which though he had no reason for, yet such was the persuasion of the evil spirit with him. Many platforms were laid, a thousand devises [plans] canvassed over by this lewd man, which way he might work the death of his friendly neighbour. At last, as the Devil wanteth no occasions to help man forward to his own destruction, so he presented Smith with a fit opportunity, whereby he might execute the sum of his bloody will. And as the repining at our neighbours' prosperity is not only monstrous, but a devilish nature, so had this man compassed a monstrous and most devilish devise, the very conceit whereof is able to astonish the heart of a Jew or Mahometan [Muslim] recreant,[7] and thus it was as followeth.

On New Year's Eve last past, this Thomas Smith, longing and desiring the end of his unnatural will, bearing the image of a friendly countenance in the face but the very perfect shape of Judas's treachery in his heart, invited his neighbour Greenoll to his house, where he promised to bestow a quart of wine and an apple upon him. Saying further, they would pass away the evening pleasantly in friendly talk and drinking together. Greenoll, being one desirous of each man's friendship, and much the rather of his being his neighbour, and one of the same trade himself was, nothing mistrusting the villainous treason hid under so smooth a show of neighbourhood, gave him thanks, promising to come to him at night and not to fail him. This pleased well the blood-thirsting man, so that home he went to determine the instrument to do the deed withal. Then down into his cellar he goes, to dispose [arrange] a place wherein he might convey the body when he had slain him. There he digged a grave about six or seven inches deep, thinking there to bury him that he should never be found.

It drew toward night, when as a play was cried [announced] about the town, whereto both old and young did hastily repair. This Smith, having a boy that served him in his shop, fearing lest the boy should perceive anything, gave him money and bade him go see the play and bring him the whole report of the matter. This he did in the presence of Greenoll, who was come according to his promise to keep him company. The boy, having fetched a quart of wine and apples as his master willed him, ran merrily to see the play, leaving Greenoll and his master by the fire pleasantly talking. They two, thus sitting alone, did drink to each other very familiarly, till at last, Greenoll stooping to turn an apple in the fire, a fit time that Smith espied to accomplish his will. Taking an iron pestle, wherewith he used to beat his spice in the mortar, and which he had laid by him ready for the nonce [occasion], with this pestle (as Greenoll stooped to turn the apple) he gave him two such mighty blows on the head as he fell down backward to the ground yielding forth a very pitiful and lamentable groan.

Smith, hearing him to give such a woeful groan (as himself said to me, when I came to him into the prison), began to enter into some sorrowfulness for the deed, wishing that he might recover again. But when he perceived he had smote him so sore that there was no hope of his recovery, he took the pestle again and gave him three or four more cruel strokes about the head, which made him to lie trembling and shaking in such pitiful manner as would have made a heart of adamant [stone] to melt in grief. For to behold how life and death made strife together, life for the sweetness, to resist death his bitterness with many a gasp for breath, with struggling and often folding his arms together: thus lay this innocent and martyred course. Not sufficed with this, the bloody murderer taketh a knife and therewith cut the throat of Greenoll, but as Smith himself says, he did not cut the weasand [windpipe], but pierced the skin somewhat, and then would have stabbed him to the heart with the knife, but missed and smote him on the shoulder blade, whereupon he struck again, and then indeed pierced him to the heart. What a cruel and monstrous hard heart had he, that could endure this rueful stratagem?

When he had sufficed his bloody mind upon his friend and loving neighbour, he drove him down into his cellar, where his grave was ready prepared for him, and there buried him. Which being done, he smoothed it over so finely with a trowel that plasterers use so that it could be hardly discerned. Because he would work the surer, he took bales of flax which lay in his cellar and so shaked the shellings thereof on the floor in all places, as no one could say (but he that knew it) where the grave was, setting likewise dryfats [baskets] and chests over it so that he judged it should never be found. Afterward he went and took water, wherewith he washed and dried his house so clean in every place that one drop of blood could not be espied. Behold how subtly he went to work. But God, who in no case will have bloody murder hid, prevented all his crafty policies.

Smith, having thus played his tyrannous pageant and having taken Greenoll's keys of his shop from him, went thither and likewise robbed it, bringing a great deal of the goods from there into his own house. But this, by the way, is to be considered, that in the town of Evesham, all the time of Christmas and at no other time, there is watch and ward kept that no misorder or ill rule be committed in the town, which doubtless is a very good and commendable order. To one of the watchmen had Smith given this watch-word, "See and see not," which was only to this end, that he might go by them unseen when he carried the goods out of Greenoll's shop to his own house. On the morrow, when it was known that Greenoll's shop was robbed, question was made through the town who was abroad that night that might be suspected, because of the play that was in the town? Upon which demand, the watchman to whom this message was sent declared how Thomas Smith was abroad somewhat late and sent him this watch-word, "See and see not," but what was meant thereby he could not gather. Upon this, Smith was sent for before the chief of the town and demanded if he knew where Greenoll was, for that it was reported he had been in his house overnight and since that time no man could tell any tidings of him. Moreover, his shop was robbed that night, and that Smith being abroad and sending such a by-word "See and see not" to one of the watchmen, it was a shrewd presumption against him to be somewhat faulty in the matter.

So after his answer that he knew not where Greenoll was become, and by his late walking and words sent to the watchman no harm was meant, they said that they would go to search his house. Whereupon Smith answered that his house they could not as then see because his wife was at Kings Norton, a town not far thence, and she had the keys of his house. "But," quoth he, "if you will search my cellar you may," and so took the keys from his girdle and threw them onto them. Then went to search Smith's cellar, whence they were coming again without finding such matter as they looked for, till by chance one of them happened to espy a little piece of earth, as it were new broken out of the ground, lying under the nethermost stair, which he taking up, said it were good to see where any earth was lately broken there about, for if they chanced to find the place something might come to light worth beholding. Upon this counsel they began all to look earnestly about the cellar, if they could find the place where that earth had been broken up. At last they removed the chests and dryfats, where they felt the ground more soft than all the rest, which caused them (suspecting somewhat) to fall to digging, where presently they found Greenoll buried, not past six or seven inches deep, and looking upon him, beheld how cruelly and unnaturally he had been murdered.

This news brought to the bailiffs of the town, where Smith was kept till they returned, not without great lamentation for this bloody deed of all that knew or heard thereof, he was sent to Worcester gaol, where he remained till such time as the cruelty of his unneighbourlike deed might be determined by justice. When the Assizes came, the apparent truth of his offence laid before the judges, he was condemned to the death which he suffered very lately since. But yet by the earnest entreaty of his friends, who were of great wealth and credit, the severity of the law was not altogether ministered, for whereas he should have been hanged in chains, he had more favour shewed him, he was hanged to death, and afterward buried.

Thus my friends, have you heard the true discourse of this most bloody and monstrous act, according as in great grief, with like sorrow for the deed, himself did utter it, both unto me and diverse others being present, preachers and gentlemen. And truly this much I must say, for the man truly he was both a handsome and well featured a young man as one shall likely see, his father of good wealth and one of the chiefs in the town of Esam. And he had been married not past eight weeks, by credible report, before he did the deed, to a gentlewoman of very good parentage who no doubt remaineth in great grief for this unlooked for mischance, she being abroad with her friends when her husband at home committed this cruel deed. I commit it to the judgement of all virtuous women, what a grief it was to her, when first she heard of this unhappy news.

But here I may not make a final pause, for that another horrible and wicked deed, committed in June last 1582 in the same shire, constraineth me to speak somewhat thereof, and for that I beheld the death of one of the parties. I am the more willing to pass it over in a brief discourse.

Another most cruel and bloody murder, committed in the same shire the same year as the aforesaid

At a place called Cotheridge, about four miles distant from Worcester, dwelt an honest husbandman named Thomas Beast, one very well reputed among his neighbours, as well for his housekeeping as also for his godly and honest behaviour. This aforenamed Thomas Beast kept a handsome young man as his servant, called Christopher Tomson, to whom (by the wicked instigation and provocation of the Devil) the good wife of the house used far better affection than to her own husband. Oftentimes they would carnally acquaint themselves together, till lust had gotten so much power of the woman as she began altogether to loathe and dislike her husband and prefer the fleshly dealings of her new companion so much as she must needs[8] seek and practise the death of her husband.

The neighbours not suspecting, but credibly perceiving, the common and unhonest behaviour of this wicked woman and her lusty yonker [youth], began so much to dislike thereof as it came at last to her husband's ears, who as well to slake [relieve] the rumour of the people, as also the pleasure these two unhonestly enjoyed, gave his servant warning to avoid his house, who packed up his clothes and was departing. But that this filthy desirous woman so much prevailed in the matter with her husband, that her companion departed not, but tarried [lingered] still. At length, so great grew the hatred of this harlot against her husband, as she must needs have Christopher her sweet dallying friend to dispatch the life of him. Whereto a great while he would not consent, persuading her still from it, so much as in him lay. But it grew to such an issue at the last as she must needs have her will, and Christopher must not deny her thereof. For she conjured [implored] him by the love that he bore her, and if any way he would witness his affection unto her to manifest it in the killing her husband. "For," quoth she, "with money and friends I will warrant thee to save thy life, and then thou and I will live merrily together."

Oh most horrible and wicked woman, a woman, nay a devil! Stop your ears, you chaste and grave matrons, whom God's fear, duty, true love to your husbands, and virtue of yourselves hath so beautified as nothing can be more odious unto you than that such a graceless strumpet should be found, so much to dishonour your noble sex.

Well, when neither entreaty nor all the fair means Christopher could use to subvert this devilish desire, solemnly at the eating of a posset[9] the night before he did the deed, he promised her faithfully to accomplish her will. On the morrow when his master was in his field at the plough, he takes a long pikestaff on his neck wherewith he would go do the deed. But his wicked mistress misliking the weapon, saying that it was nothing fit for the purpose, delivered him a forest bill,[10] which she herself had made very sharp for the same intent and said: "Be sure to hit him right, and thou shalt speed him I warrant thee, so that he shall never tell who did hurt him." Christopher taketh this bill on his back and comes into the field to his master, where he began quarrelingly to say unto him after this manner: "Seeing you are willing I shall serve you no longer, give me that which is my duty and so fare-ye-well." With other words of quarrel he used about the sum of the money, but his master granted him so much as he demanded, and turning from him to open his purse to give him the money, Christopher stroke at him with the bill in such cruel manner that there he killed him.

After the deed was done he fled, but not far before he was taken, when presently he exclaimed on his mistress how she was cause that he committed the deed. Whereupon they were both sent to Worcester gaol, where very often she would solicit her sweet Christopher with money, handkerchiefs, nose-gays,[11] and such like amorous and loving tokens, and he besotted [infatuated] in his naughty affection, would shape all his conditions to please her. The more to witness his dissolute [licentious] folly, he made a triumph (as it were) in carrying a lock of her hair about him and would sit kissing and delighting in any token she sent him. One day he desired the gaoler, that if he were a man that regarded the extreme afflictions of those whom the tyranny of love possessed, that he would do so much for him, to rip forth the heart of him, and cleaving the same in sunder, he should there behold the lively image of his sweet mistress, to whom (as the chiefest jewel he had) he desired him to make a present of that precious token.

When time came that justice should determine of these twain [two], being worthily found guilty and condemned: she was adjudged (for an example to all light and lascivious women) that she should be burned, and Christopher, to be carried to the place where he did the deed, there to be first hanged dead, and afterward to be hanged up again in chains. The Assizes being holden at Esam, she was laid upon a hurdle and so drawn to the place of execution, which was without the town, and there being bound to the stake and the fire made to burn about her, her wretched carcass was soon dissolved into ashes. Christopher Tomson, he was carried back again to Worcester where he like-wise (for an example to all lewd livers) was drawn on a hurdle about the city, and so conveyed to Cotheridge, where according to his judgment he hangeth in chains.

Notes

1   The book of Ecclesiasticus (or "The Wisdom of Sirach") is apocrypha (or deuterocanoni-cal). Although they will rarely be found in modern Bibles, the apocrypha were included in many early modern Bibles, including the 1611 King James Bible, from which they were removed in 1885. Thus, these books were well known in the late sixteenth century, although they are rarely referenced today.

2   The Iron Age, in which humans were still living in the early modern period, is one of the five ages identified by the Greek poet Hesiod in *Work and Days* (circa 700 BCE). This is an age in which humans live in misery, children dishonor their parents, men lie to get ahead, and humans no longer feel shame. In a later work, the Roman poet Ovid's *Metamorphoses* (circa 8 CE), the Iron Age is likewise associated with men being jingoistic, greedy, immod-est, and disloyal.

3   A reference to Moses, in the book of Exodus, using his staff (or rod) to initiate the plagues of Egypt, eventually causing the stubborn Pharaoh to allow Moses to lead the enslaved Israelites to out of Egypt and into the Promised Land.

4   A fleshpot was a large pot used to cook flesh, or meat. As Moses led the Israelites, they only had manna to eat, which was nourishing but light, and some wished for the more

substantial food they had in Egypt. More generally, this is a reference to failing to appreciate a life of simplicity, honesty, and integrity.

5 Evesham, commonly pronounced "Asum."

6 A dealer in textile fabrics, such as silk, and other exotic items.

7 This statement betrays a common early modern prejudice toward non-Christians. In this context, even a non-believer in Christ would find Smith's actions reprehensible.

8 "Must needs" is an archaic term that means "found it necessary to."

9 A hot drink of spiced milk and wine, sometimes used to settle the nerves.

10 A pikestaff was a stick of up to 16 feet in length, upon which a pike (or spike) was placed during military combat. A bill was a curved blade, often attached to a pikestaff, and used to clear brush or for military combat. Thus, a bill was a much more effective murder weapon than a pikestaff.

11 A small bouquet of fresh or dried flowers that is held up to the nose to reduce the offending smells that were believed to cause illness.

3 The strange discovery of sundry murders

This long chapbook describes many senseless and unconnected murders, most of which are revealed by the providence of God and portents that stretch the modern imagination. Two suspected murders were brought before three dead children, who, though they had been dead for more than a week, regained their former colour and "blushed on the murderers," resulting in the men confessing their crimes. A shoemaker was brought before his victim, causing the corpse to bleed afresh, open his eye, and stare at his murderer. A murderous mother's crime was revealed when the body of her baby was discovered by a dog. These discoveries are attributed by the author to "the will and wonderful work of Almighty God." On the other hand, the murderers of Master Padge were not revealed by God, but were brought to justice by a responsible body of private individuals who based their accusation on old-fashioned observation and detection, which led to the arrest of the suspects. Even in the murder of Padge, there were various portents that revealed the criminals: a bear with eyes like fire bearing a kerchief, the weapon used to murder Padge, and a raven that hanged itself on the mast of a ship that mysteriously turned itself around, stem to stern. To this author, as to many others in this collection, these were signs that, even if His providence was not immediately obvious in this case, "by one means or other" God always reveals himself as the bringer of justice.

***

Sundry strange and inhumane murders, lately committed. The first of a father that hired a man to kill three of his children near to Ashford in Kent. The second of Master Padge of Plymouth, murdered by the consent of his own wife. With the strange discovery of sundry other murders, wherein is described the odiousness of murder, with the vengeance which God inflicteth on murderers. *London: Printed by Thomas Scarlet, 1591*

The heavy sentence that Almighty God pronounced upon the parricide[1] Cain when he said, "thou are cursed from the Earth that hath opened her mouth to receive thy brother's blood from thy hand" (Genesis 4), showeth how odious murder is in his sight. It therefore behoveth everyone to have a special care what actions we commit, not seeking to murder those that have in some sort offended us, but to leave, as we ought, the revenge of all wrongs unto the Lord. For we may be assured we cannot deal colourably [deceptively] with God, as Pilate thought to have done when he pronounced sentence against his own conscience. For he having, at the importunate [persistent] suit of the Jews, pronounced death upon our saviour Christ, thought to have washed away the fact with the washing of his hands and his protestation in saying "I am innocent of the blood of this just person," whereby indeed he could not clear himself. But according to the saying of [Desiderius] Erasmus, "in murder the consenter is as evil as the deed doer," so Pilate's conscience made him guilty of Christ's death, for which the wrath of God still followed him. For after that time Pilate, in executing his office, did nothing but that which was injustice. And being thereof accused in Rome, he was by the Emperor Caligula banished and went to Lyons, the place (as some say) of his birth, through grief of which disgrace, by the sufferance of God, he desperately slew himself, that he might die by the hand of the most wickedest person that lived.[2]

God said unto Cain, "the voice of thy brother's blood cryeth unto me out of the ground."[3] And Plutarch doth describe many strange discoveries of murders, among which he sayeth, that a monstrous son slew his own father, the act being so much against nature as no man suspected his graceless child for the same.[4] Yet in his own conscience he saw millions of accusers standing before him and ready (as he thought) to attach [arrest] him for the same. Insomuch as upon a day sitting in a tavern with a companion of his, he suddenly thrust his sword up into the chimney and cried out, saying, "Ah you villain swallows," quoth he, "leave your babbling and exclaiming that I slew my father, or I will do by you as I did by him." His companion, hearing this his voluntary accusation, secretly bewrayed [divulged] the matter to the magistrate, whereby the ungracious son was soon apprehended and executed according to his demerits.

Horror and fear always accompanieth the murderer. His own conscience is to him a thousand witnesses. He standeth in dread of every bush, beast, and bird. He imagineth that every thing discovereth his evil and many times it falleth out that the silly [innocent] creatures of the Earth detecteth him. Oh, what a strange and unlooked for discovery was this, yet nothing strange considering the horror of the filthy fact. God seldom or never leaveth murder unpunished, nor will the mark of murder go forth of the murderer's weapon, neither can murder be kept so close, but that by one means or other the Lord will compel the murderer to discover and lay open the truth unto the world, as by this lamentable accident following manifestly appeareth.

A declaration of the monstrous cruelty of a father, that hired one to murder three of his own children

In the town or parish of Warborne within four miles of Ashford market, being within the county of Kent, dwelled one Lincoln, the unnatural father

Sundrye ſtrange and inhumaine Murthers, lately committed.

The firſt of a Father that hired a man to kill three of his children neere to Aſhford in Kent:

The ſecond of maſter Page of Plymoth, murthered by the conſent of his owne wife : with the ſtrange diſcouerie of ſundrie other murthers.

Wherein is deſcribed the odiouſneſſe of murther, with the vengeance which God inflicteth on murtherers.

Printed at London by Thomas Scarlet. 1 5 9 1.

Figure 3.1 Title page from *Sundry strange and inhumaine murthers, lately committed*, 1591. The woodcut image depicts a father murdering his three children while the Devil guides his hand, and a dog that uncovers a child who was murdered and buried by its mother.

Source: By kind permission of the Trustees of Lambeth Palace Library.

of four unfortunate children. This man being about fifty years of age was a widower and therefore became a suitor to a widow not far from thence, who, being of some reasonable wealth, refused to marry with him in respect of his great charge of children. Whereat, as it seemeth, the Devil entered so far into his mind that he cast many ways in his thought how to make them away. Returning home, [he] sat down in great heaviness by the fireside. Whereupon, he having a married man that wrought [worked] with him in his house, demanded of him why he was so pensive, who requiring him also to sit down by the fire, told him that he could not be merry.

"Why," said he, "how comes it that you marry not some honest woman to comfort you, considering you have wherewithal to keep her?"

"Oh," said he (fetching a great sigh), "there is none will have me, in respect of my great charge of children. But," said he, "if I could make them away by any means, I could marry with a rich widow."

And thereupon (as it was since confessed) none being present but themselves, the said Lincoln persuaded this labouring man to perform his request and to take this matter in hand so should he have forty shillings in money and a good cow for his pains. But the poor man notwithstanding he seemed at the first unwilling, yet as he was poor so he was covetous and the hope of the money and the cow so wrought in his thought that forgetting God and all godliness, in the end without any great delay he consented to the fact. And the rather he was induced thereunto, for that this unnatural father promised that when the murder was committed not to pursue or make after him for the same and that if he were compelled thereunto, yet would he deal in such sort, that he would let fall suit[5] rather than to take his oath to say he was the murderer.

Thus concluding between themselves, the day came wherein the wicked act was performed, which was upon a Saturday in November last, on which morning the father and all his children with the murderer broke their fast at home together. That done, old Lincoln prepared himself to go to Ashford market, which he did. Taking his eldest son with him and the murderer, they departed towards Ashford but on the way the murderer returned home again to the three innocent children, whom he speedily murdered, knocking them on the heads with a hatchet and cutting all their throats. The father, the better to colour [disguise] his unnatural consenting to the death of his own children, bought three pair of new shoes for them, whom he knew should be murdered before he came home, and sent his eldest son home before, being about fifteen years old. He could not get in at the doors, which was barred on the inner side, and seeing he heard none of the children stirring, stayed there until his father came. Who seeing no light nor hearing of the children, contrary to his usual custom (yet might have gone in on the back side) came to his next neighbour's house and prayed that some body would go home with him to see what had happened. In conclusion, he came home with company, who were eyewitnesses of this tragical spectacle. For having entered the house they found murdered two pretty boys and a girl, which grievous and unexpected sight made the beholders to stand amazed. Nevertheless the hard-hearted father made no sign of sorrow for them, neither would he seek means to pursue the murderer, which by the report of his neighbours seemed to be his man, who only was seen about the house after his departure and none else. But this wretched man commended him to be a very honest fellow and therefore supposed his eldest son to be the author of this murder and upon him would willingly have imposed the same.

The next day following, the father would seek no means to bury the children, nor that the coroner should view them, but suffered them most unnaturally to lie above the ground for the space of three days, until a gentlewoman named Mistress West came and reproved him of his unnatural dealings towards them. Which done, he digged a hole in the house about two foot deep and laid them in it, but by reason of springs in the ground, the water issued into the pit and thereby soaked the children's wounds and body and made them very clear and white.

Within five days after the coroner came thether, being procured thereunto, and found the children covered with a little earth and a board over them, whom he caused to be taken up. This was the eighth day after the murder was committed, in which time the murderer was apprehended and accused thereof, but he utterly denied the fact. But being brought before the dead bodies of the children, the father being there also, the wounds began to bleed afresh, which when the coroner saw he commanded the party apprehended to look upon the children, which he did, and called them by their names. Whereupon, behold the wonderful works of God, for the fact being still denied, the bodies of the children, which seemed white like unto soaked flesh laid in water, suddenly received their former colour of blood and had such a lively countenance flushing in their faces as if they had been living creatures lying asleep, which indeed blushed on the murderers, when they wanted grace to blush and be ashamed of their own wickedness. Which wonderful miracle caused the murderer there present not only to confess and acknowledge himself guilty of that damnable deed, but also to accuse the father of the children as principal procurer of their untimely deaths. Whereupon they were both sent prisoners to Canterbury, where they remained until the last Assizes holden at Sevenoaks in Kent, eighteen miles from London, where they were arraigned and condemned to die for the same. So that upon the seven and twentieth day of February last past they were both executed near to Ashford, where the father of the children confessed himself guilty of the murder, having before denied it even till the hour of death. Whereby appeareth that his own conscience was overcharged with this foul and odious offence and therefore would not suffer it to be concealed.

Thus may you see how murderers are overtaken and their actions opened by themselves. Yea, if there were nobody to accuse the murderer, the murdered corpse would give evidence against him. It hath been a mean [method] appointed by the Lord to discern the murderer, that when he approached the dead carcass would at some issue [opening] or other bleed. Many have by this miraculous work of the Lord been discovered when the proof hath been only bare suspicion. This example ensuing is much to that purpose.

There was not long since at Uppingham in Rutlandshire a shoemaker that had murdered a young man, who was buried and the murderer little suspected for the same. Nevertheless upon bare suspicion he was apprehended and the dead corpse digged up again, before whom this shoemaker was brought, upon whose approach the murdered corpse not only bled, but with one of his eyes standing wide open he stared upon the shoemaker that murdered him. The standers by, wonderfully amazed thereat, removed the shoemaker and presently the eye closed up, and being brought again, the corpse with his eye wide open stared upon him as before, as who would say, "This is the murderer, stay him, my blood asketh for vengeance." I have here published this matter upon such due proof as cannot be reproved, it is not yet long since the murderer was executed at Oakham in the foresaid county, an example of great terror to such as delight in blood. But what may examples prevail where grace and the fear of God is wanting, as appeareth by this sequel:

Of late there was dwelling in Salisbury a young damsel named Alice Shepheard, who, being with child and yet never married, would swear when she was charged therewith that it was most untrue. But the time coming on when she should be delivered, she was constrained to reveal the truth to her mother and grandmother, who presently fetched a midwife, making none other acquainted therewith. Neither did she after her coming stay very long before this maid was delivered of a manchild, whose neck they presently broke and secretly buried it in the churchyard, thinking thereby to escape worldly punishment: not fearing the wrath of God for their willful murder, nor considering that He saw the secrets of their hearts, nor that He would not suffer innocent bloodshed to go unpunished. But now see the will and wonderful work of Almighty God to reveal this most wicked act.

It happened a dog came over the place where the child lay buried, and having found the scent of the flesh he never rested until he had with his feet scraped it up out of the ground, leaving it bare above the earth, whereby it seemeth that they buried it but very shallow and was fearful to be espied, lest the fact should thereby be discovered. Now when the dog had laid it open to the eye of each passenger, it happened that one Hugh Mawdes of Salisbury coming by, chanced to spy the same and was greatly amazed to see so grievous a sight, who presently went and told the masters of the parish what he had seen. Whereupon they came to behold this grievous sight, which they perceived was but newborn, and therefore concluded that it was the child of some strumpet and that she had murdered it and then buried it in that shallow place.

Which done it was conveyed into Our Lady Church in Salisbury, where all the chief of the town came in and gave their censures [opinions] for finding out the unnatural mother and murderer thereof. Among whom Mistress Shepheard's daughter was nominated and greatly suspected for the same. Notwithstanding, upon this bare suspicion the suspected person with her mother, grandmother, and midwife was sent for, who being examined before a justice confessed that the said child was stillborn, and that therefore they privily [privately] buried it in that sort. Whereupon the justice caused them to be sworn upon a book that they had said nothing but the truth, which they severally did. But here God showed a miracle before them all, for they having taken their oaths before the justice they were discharged and sent away, not meaning to deal any further therein.

But the midwife, being touched in conscience with her oath which she had then now taken, going forth of the justice's doors suddenly fetched a great sigh and said, "Oh what a wicked woman am I to swear that the child was stillborn, when in truth it was born alive." Which words being overheard by one of the justice's servants, they were all called in again, where they were charged with the murdering of the said child, which after a faint denial, they generally confessed. Then were they committed to prison until the last Assizes, where they received the doom of judgment by death, which of duty they had deserved for so wicked a deed. Thus we see that although God suffer the murderer to escape for a time, yet doth he follow them with so sharp revenge as either they desperately slay themselves or reap such shame as the world may be satisfied, that God hath dealt justly with them.

A true discourse of a cruel and inhumane murder, committed upon M.
Padge of Plymouth, the 11th day of February last, 1591, by the consent of
his own wife, and sundry other[s]

In the town of Tavistock 10 miles or thereabouts from Plymouth, there dwelled one Master Glanfeeld, a man of as good wealth and account as any occupier in that country. This Master Glanfeeld favoured a young man named George Strangwidge, who was of such great credit with him that he turned over all his wares, shop, and dealings into his hands, and took so good liking of him being a proper young man, that it was supposed he should have had his daughter in marriage. And the rather for that he had learned the full perfection and knowledge of his trade in London, in the service of a worshipful citizen called Master Powell in Bread Street, and grew so painful [diligent] and seemed so good a husband[6] as the said Master Glanfeeld's daughter did wholly resolve that the said Strangwidge should be her husband and no other, whereto in truth her parents never did condescend. But Satan, who is the author of evil, crept so far into the dealings of these persons that he procured the parents to mislike of Strangwidge and to persuade their daughter to refrain his company, showing her that they had found out a more meeter [appropriate] match for her and motioned unto her that it was their pleasures she should marry one Master Padge of Plymouth, who was a widower and one of the chiefest inhabitants of that town. And by reason that the said Master Glanfeeld did mean to abide at Plymouth, he thought it a more sufficient match to marry her in Plymouth where she might be hard [close] by him, than to marry her to Strangwidge who dwelt far from him.

In the end such was the success that although she had settled her affection altogether upon Strangwidge, yet through the persuasion of her friends, though sore against her will, she was married to Master Padge of Plymouth. Notwithstanding that she had protested never to love the man with her heart, nor never to remove her affection settled upon the said Strangwidge, which she performed as the sequel maketh manifest. For this Mistress Padge had access to Strangwidge and he to her at his coming to Plymouth, whereby the Devil so wrought in the hearts of them both that they practiced day and night how to bring her husband to his end. And thereupon the said Mistress Padge, as appeareth since by her own confession, did within the space of one year and less attempt sundry times to poison her husband, for it was not full a year but that she had procured him to be murdered, as you shall hear immediately.

But God, who preserveth many persons from such perils and dangers, defended still the said Master Padge from the secret snares and practices of present death, which his wife had laid for him. Yet not without great hurt unto his body, for still the poison wanted [lacked] force to kill him, so wonderfully did Almighty God work for him, yet he was compelled to vomit blood and much corruption, which doubtless in the end would have killed him, and that shortly. But to prosecute, and that with great speed to perform this wicked and inhuman act, the said Mistress Padge and Strangwidge omitted no opportunity. They wanted no means nor friends to perform it for their money, whereof they had good store and more than they knew how to employ, except it had been to better uses. For she, on the one side, practiced [plotted] with one of her servants named Robert Priddis, whom as she thought nothing would more sooner make him pretend [carry out] the murdering of his master than silver and gold. Wherewith she so corrupted him with promise of sevenscore [140] pounds more, that he solemnly undertook and vowed to perform the task to her contentment. On the other side, Strangwidge hired one Tom Stone to be an actor in this tragical action, and promised him a great sum of money for performing the same, who by a solemn vow had granted the effecting thereof, though to the hazard of his own life.

These two instruments wickedly prepared themselves to effect this desperate and villainous deed upon the 11th of February, being Wednesday, on which night following the act was committed. But it is to be remembered that this Mistress Padge lay not then with her husband by reason of the untimely birth of a child whereof she was newly delivered, the same being dead born. Upon which cause, she then kept her chamber, having before sworn that she would never bear child of his getting that should prosper, which argued a most ungodly mind in the woman, for in that sort she had been the death of two of her own children.

About ten o'clock at night, Master Padge being in his bed slumbering, could not happen upon a sound sleep and lying musing to himself, Tom Stone came softly and knocked at the door, whereupon Priddis his companion did let him in, who was made privy to this deed. And by reason that Mistress Padge gave them straight charge [command] to dispatch it that night whatsoever came of it, they drew towards the bed, intending immediately to go about it. Master Padge being not asleep as is aforesaid, asked who came in, whereat Priddis leapt upon his master being in his bed, who roused himself and got out upon his feet and had been hard [strong] enough for this man, but that Stone flew upon him, being naked, and suddenly tripped him so that he fell to the ground. Whereupon both of them fell upon him and took the kerchief from his head and knitting the same about his neck, they immediately stifled him.

And as it appeareth even in the anguish of death, the said Master Padge greatly laboured to pull the kerchief from about his neck, by reason of the marks and scratches which he had made with his nails upon his throat. But therewith he could not prevail, for they would not let slip their hold until he was full dead. This done, they laid him overthwart [across] the bed and against the bedside broke his neck, and when they saw he was surely dead, they stretched him and laid him in his bed again, spreading the clothes in ordinary sort as though no such act had been attempted, but that he had died on God's hand.

Whereupon Priddis immediately went to Mistress Padge's chamber and told her that all was dispatched. About one hour after he came again to his mistress' chamber door and called aloud: "Mistress," quoth he, "let somebody look into my master's chamber, me thinks I hear him groan." With that she called her maid, who was not privy to anything, and bade her light a candle, whereupon she slipped on her petticoat and went thether likewise, sending her maid first into the chamber where she herself stood at the door, as one whose conscience would not permit her to come and behold the detestable deed which she had procured. The maid simply felt on her master's face and found him cold and stiff and so told her mistress, whereat she had the maid to warm a cloth and wrap it about his feet, which she did, and when she felt his legs they were as cold as clay, whereat she cried out saying her master was dead.

Whereupon her mistress got her to bed and caused her man Priddis to go call her father Master Glanfeeld, then dwelling at Plymouth, and sent for one of her husband's sisters likewise, willing her to make haste if ever she would see her brother alive, for he was taken with the disease called the Pull as they term it in that country. These persons being sent for, they came immediately, whereat Mistress Padge arose and in counterfeit manner sounded, whereby there was no suspicion a long time concerning any murder performed upon him, until Mistress Harris his sister spied blood about his bosom, which he had with his nails procured by scratching for the kerchief when it was about his throat. Then they moved his head and found his neck broken and on both his knees the skin was beaten off, by striving with them to save his life.

Mistress Harris, hereupon perceiving how he was made away, went to the mayor and the worshipful [aldermen] of the town, desiring them of justice and entreated them to come and behold this lamentable spectacle, which they immediately performed and by searching him found that he was murdered the same night. Upon this the mayor committed Priddis to prison, who being examined did impeach Tom Stone, showing that he was a chief actor in the same. This Thomas Stone was married upon the next day after the murder was committed and being in the midst of his jollity suddenly he was attacked and committed to prison, to bear his fellow company. Thus did the Lord unfold this wretched deed, whereby immediately the said mistress was attached upon the murder and examined before Sir Francis Drake,[7] knight, with the mayor and other magistrates of Plymouth, who denied not the same, but said she had rather die with Strangwidge than to live with Padge.

At the same time also the said George Strangwidge was newly come to Plymouth, being very heavy and doubtful by reason he had given consent to the said murder. Who, being then in company with some of London, was apprehended and called before the justices for the same. Whereupon at his coming before them he confessed the truth of all, and offered to prove that he had written a letter to Plymouth before his coming thether, that at any hand they should not perform the act. Nevertheless, Master Padge was murdered before the coming of this letter, and therefore he was sent to prison with the rest unto Exeter. And at the Assizes holden this last Lent, the said George Strangwidge, Mistress Padge, Priddis, and Tom Stone, were condemned and adjudged to die for the said fact, and were all executed accordingly upon Saturday being the twentieth day of February last, 1591.

Other strange things seen at that time

Upon the same night and three nights after, there was seen an ugly thing formed like a bear, whose eyes were as it had been fire, bearing about him a linen cloth representing the instrument wherewith the said Master Padge was murdered.

Also in Plymouth the same week in the presence of sundry honest persons was visibly seen a raven, which did alight upon the head of a ship's mast sunk at the end of the town. This raven standing upon the top of the main mast did with her talons pluck up certain rope yarns that hung down from the head of the mast and fastened them about her neck and often turned them about her neck with all her force. Which done, she plunged herself right down, clapping her wings close to her body and never left until she had hanged herself.

Now the ship was all this while aground, lying with her stern to the shore, and suddenly the said ship turned herself round and brought her stem where erst [before] her stern did lie. All which are strange, yet is the same so true as it cannot be disproved, being justified by those that saw the same.

The Lord bless us and give all other grace to be warned by these examples and inhumane action before recited. That we may avoid the danger of shedding of innocent blood, and fear the judgment of God which continually followeth willful murderers. Eternal God preserve this little island, bless the Queen's Majesty and her honourable [Privy] Council, turn thy wrath away from us O Lord, and pour down thy blessings upon Her Highness, that she our Moses, may long live to hold up the Tables of the Law in her gracious hands,[8] and that we may seek continually to please her in such due sort, as she may have no just cause to throw them down, which God grant for his mercy sake. Amen.

Notes

1 The text reads "parricide," which is the killing of one's father, though really the author should have written "fratricide," the killing of one's brother.
2 The Roman historian Eusebius (AD 260–340) recorded that following his condemnation of Jesus, Pontius Pilate was recalled to Rome to answer for another incident, this one involving mass murder. He was sentenced to banishment in Vienne, Gaul (France), about 30km south of Lyon, where he later committed suicide.
3 Genesis 4:10.
4 The following tale is taken from Plutarch's *Moralia* (circa AD 100), specifically the essay "On the Delays of Divine Justice."
5 That is, he would decline to prosecute, without which the case would not be heard.
6 He was good at his affairs and seemed an excellent prospect as a husband.
7 This is the same Francis Drake who had circumnavigated the earth from 1577–80. As a substantial gentleman who resided in Plymouth (many places in the region are named after Drake today), it is not surprising that Drake would have taken on some responsibilities of the magistracy, as befitted his rank and position.
8 As the founder of the Anglican Church of England, Elizabeth is being compared to Moses, who led the Israelites out of slavery and brought them God's commandments on Tables, or tablets.

4   The boy without any fear

This brief chapbook exemplifies the participatory, personal, and opportunistic nature of crime in this period. Many people were involved in bringing Ralph Deaphon, his wife's murderer, to justice. These included his neighbours, the accused's co-workers, a constable and coroner, the judges of the Assizes, and, most importantly, a fearless five-year-old boy who twice testifed against his father and helped to secure his conviction. As was common at this time, the victim and perpetrator knew each other and the crime was, by all appearances, one of opportunity, committed in the heat of passion. For all of its unremarkableness, therefore, this case reflects many of the key themes that characterized crime and criminal justice in early modern England. Perhaps the most interesting part of this story is the preface that opens this chapbook. It has strong religious and moral overtones, but has little to do with the story of murder that follows. The author is pessimistic about the nature of his fellow man, suggesting that greed, jealousy, fear, vanity, and the Devil constantly tempted husbands to turn against wives, sons against fathers, friends against friends, neighbours against neighbours, and so on. This preface also introduces a key theme in the punishment model of the early modern period: deterrence and reformation. Tales of murder, such as this one, "hath been published for our example to the world, thereby to put us in mind of our duties to God, and withhold us from like trespasses, by viewing their shameful ends." Thus deterred by their knowledge of crime and its consequences, readers are exhorted to seek reformation, by performing charity and good deeds and always living as if they might, at any moment, be called to God's judgment. Unmentioned by the author, but perhaps more to the point, is the harsh reality that a young boy has lost his parents and will live out his childhood as an orphan.

***

A most horrible and detestable murder, committed by a bloody-
minded man upon his own wife, and most strangely revealed
by his child that was under five years of age, at Mayfield in the
County of [East] Sussex, for which he was executed the 27th of
February now last past, at Grinstead in the same county. *London:
Printed by John Danter and are to be sold by William Barley at
his shop in Gracious {Gracechurch} Street over against Leadenhall,
1595*

To the Christian reader, peace in Christ

What Christian endued [endowed] with any motion of pity, my loving countrymen, that seeth and noteth with advice the many mischances and cruel
murders in these times committed, and with a heart charged with grief and
eyes gushing floods of tears, unfeignedly desires not to see the coming of that
dreadful judge which will and must come? That this tempter with allur-
ing baits entice no more those children of his to such horrible sins, as he
daily doth. How many most execrable [unpleasant] murders have there been
done of late times, which hath been published for our example to the world,
thereby to put us in mind of our duties to God and withhold us from like
trespasses by viewing their shameful ends, whom deservedly the law cuts off
for such offences?

But so rageth the enemy of mankind, day and night, restlessly with his
temptations, that he ceaseth not to urge us to all mischief. The son desiring
his father's living and to be great before his time, murdereth him. The friend
his dearest friend, the wife the husband and the husband the wife: brother
against sister and sister the brother. Whereby the world is grown to such a
pass that no friend dare commit any secret to his most nearest and dearest
friend without some jealousy of his truth and faithfulness. If he have money,
he feareth to reveal it to his wife, his servants, his children, his friend, or any,
doubting lest the knowledge thereof shall abridge his days. If he have a wife
which as himself he loveth, although he sees with his own eyes her chastity
given over to the lecher and another enjoy that only proper to himself, yet
with heart's grief he is fain [willing] to smother so vile and most odious [feel-
ings], doubting the revealing thereof should work his shame in the world, and
his life thereby dangered. If his children neglect their duties, he is forced to
bear with their enormities lest it happen to them as to many fathers who have
lost their lives in seeking to correct such head-strong youth. Is there not the
like in servants, whose credit with their masters hath been admirable, that in
the end have enriched themselves and beggared their masters?

Ah, would every estate would but look into himself and every one in himself seek a reformation. Then should the vainer's flock decrease, when charity
doth abound. The covetous grazier[1] and farmer should take such reasonable
prices for their corn and cattle that their poor brethren handcraftsmen [arti-
sans] might live by them without oppression. Lawyers should not then be so

followed, neither of poor or rich, which every term from their own habitations follow them many miles to their great damage, in neglecting their business at home, and large expenses abroad, running like a bondman (bound by duty) after lawyers, capless, to beseech them to take their monies, fed with a belief of good success in their suits, when oftentimes it proves to their undoing, with their wives and families. And when it is too late, then they repent their follies, and cry out on that headstrong vain that would not suffer them to yield to reason. And then what have they, but a flout [disregard] of him that had their money, etc., they themselves become a scorn to their neighbours, a grief to their friends, and to their children common rebuke.[2]

These be the fruits of our days, which the Lord for his mercy give us grace to foresee and seeing to avoid them. Forgetting the world and to mind the joys of the glorious Kingdom of Christ, whom we with grief of mind sorrow to offend, which hath so highly esteemed of us, to give his precious blood for our redemption. A notable and most worthy mirror to all his, to frame our lives thereafter, if we had grace to look into it, which God grant. And that the falls of others may make us to leave those sins so deeply ingrafted [held] in our hearts, that in the last day we may reap the reward of our charity and other good deeds to our needy brethren extended. Taking such firm hold on that anchor of faith, Christ Jesus, that neither Pope or Devil may have power to harm us. And we all freed from that heavy vengeance, which is likely without speedy amendment to fall upon us, which though it be deferred for a season, will come when we think least thereon. Let us therefore (like the five wise virgins[3]) be ready furnished against that day, that we may be ready with the bridegroom to enter.

And now to the matter which we have to entreat, the truth whereof here particularly set down, may move all pitiful hearts to lament, which thus followeth.

A most horrible and detestable murder, committed by a bloody-minded man, upon his own wife

In the town of Mayfield in the County of [East] Sussex, there dwelled one Ralph Deaphon, whose trade was to dig in the iron mines and to make coals. This Ralph being at his work in the wood making coals, as he usually did [went home] about five o'clock on the 8th of October now last past, in the evening being dark (as some in their examinations and confessions on their oaths before the Coroner Master Magnus Fowle saith), returning unto them about nine o'clock that night. Coming home, his wife with her son of five years of age, or scarce so much, being abed, he knocked and was let in, where he fell to railing and chiding with her. In the end, whether it were a matter pretended, or otherwise, but led thereunto by the Devil, the ancient enemy of our salvation, which doubtless provoked him thereunto, he drew out his knife and cut her throat.

And so leaving her weltering [lying] in her own gore, [he] went again to his work without making any semblance of sorrow for this most odious murder, leaving some candle or fire in such place of danger, that the house therewith was fired, which the neighbour adjoining and the whole town came to quench, marveling where the good man and his wife were that they heard none of them, thinking them to be from home. Amongst them that durst venture most, an honest woman named Joan Baylie, espying first the fire, cried out for help, who with her neighbours did what she could to save the child which was like to perish with the fire. Who when she had recovered [the boy], they sought to save the goods, but little they could do unto it, but there was the dead body found. The constable, a very honest man, having viewed the same, could not tell what course to take to find the murderer. Sending for the coroner, they examined this Joan Baylie to find what they could of the death of the woman, who could say nothing. Then was the child, whose name was Ralph (called after the name of his father), brought before them and required to tell when his father came home. The boy, without any blushing fear (as commonly is seen in children), told them that his father came home when his mother was abed, and first used some churlish [mean-spirited] speech unto her, then he drew out his knife, cut her throat, and so left her. Describing in good order the bigness of the knife and the colour of the haft [handle], but wherefore [why] his father did this wicked deed he could not say anything.

This confession of the boy being ended, they presently sent for his father from work and strictly examined him of the same, who stoutly [obstinately] and most audaciously denied the fact. Then being demanded where he was when his house was on fire, he answered he was all day hard at his work, and so continued his tale. Then the coroner required to have a sight of his knife, which he pulled out of his pocket, and was in all points for bigness, colour of haft, and all other marks, even as the child had before at large repeated unto the said coroner. Then being demanded if that were his own knife, he said no, he borrowed the same. But the child affirmed it was his own.

His fellow workmen were hereupon likewise examined, who said that about five o'clock the night before he left them and returned not unto them again until it was nine. Upon which evident proof, and the deed being so apparently open by the boy, he was for that night committed to the stocks in the town. The next day, being more thoroughly again examined in the cause and the evidence being found too apparent, yet he still denied it. The coroner committed him to the queen's gaol at Lewes. From whence, with other notorious malefactors not unlike himself, he was brought to Grinstead on the 24th day of February last past, where before the right worshipful Baron[4] Clarke and Serjeant Drew, judges of the Assizes, he was for the fact arraigned, and on the evidence of his son, which was present before the judges with a voice laudable, which was in the child admired, he delivered the evidence as before. On which he was found guilty and had judgment and on the 27th of February, 1595, he was executed at Grinstead, in the County of Sussex.

Thus God revealeth the wicked practices of men, who though the act be kept never so secret, to their great rebuke he discovereth. Especial notes in scriptures and grave examples we have, how the fowls of the air and the stones in the wall shall declare such horrible sins, that the punishment due for the same may be worthily rewarded, as we see by this and many others. Which I pray God may move us to repentance, and give us grace to eschew the like. Amen.

Notes

1 A person who grazes animals, also known as a husbandman.
2 The author is criticizing the frequency with which men, who are oppressed by greedy farmers, bring legal suits in order to enrich and improve themselves, which has precisely the opposite effect, by making them impoverished at the hands of lawyers and enemies of their neighbours.
3 A reference to the Parable of the Ten Virgins (Matthew 25:1–13), in which five wise virgins were prepared to meet their grooms by ensuring their lamps were always full of oil, while five foolish virgins, in failing to bring oil for their lamps, arrived too late for their wedding banquet and were shut out. The parable has clear analogies to the Day of Judgment, when those who were prepared – by giving help to those in need and keeping Christ in their hearts – will be accepted into Heaven, while the remainder are damned to Hell.
4 Judges of the Court of Exchequer, which supplied judges to the Assizes, were known as Barons.

5 The minister's mutilation and murder

The description of the mutilation and murder of the victim in this story is, perhaps, the most horrific in this collection. The story begins with a dispute over the use of common land. Historically, common fields had been used by freeholding tenants (owners) to graze their livestock and access water to irrigate their fields, and by copyholding tenants (renters) to grow crops for personal use in small plots. By the early seventeenth century, these common rights were under attack as landlords increasingly sought to enclose common fields with fences and deny tenants access to them. The enclosed land would then be repurposed for farming or husbandry using the benefits of the ongoing agricultural revolution. This slow but steady effort to deny rights to commoners naturally caused controversy between aristocrats and their tenants. In this case, Reverend Storre, the town minister, was asked to adjudicate the matter, and also to give his own opinion on the issue. As heir to a wealthy lord, Francis Cartwright had a vested interest in changing common rights toward the landlords' favour, whereas Storre, using sound legal arguments, sided with the commoners and with tradition, thus making an enemy of Cartwright, and giving rise to the minister's gruesome murder.

There is evidence that social rank heavily informed the outcome of this case. Cartwright, as the heir to an aristocrat, was of a higher social status than Storre, who, though a master of arts, was but a mere minister. Evidently, Cartwright felt wronged when his social inferior decided against his interests and then chastised him publicly in church. Cartwright's ability to secure bail from a "corrupt" magistrate was also likely because of his social rank, though the Privy Council did not support this decision, an example of how local and central officials did not always agree. Cartwright's social status also permitted him the ability to flee England while his friends succeeded in securing a pardon from the king, thus perverting the course of justice. Finally, despite testimony provided by the victim's parishioners, fellow ministers, the town's gentry population, and the fellows of Oxford University, Cartwright's rank helped to ensure that, ultimately, the pardon was not overturned, which meant that Storre's widow failed to get justice for the murder of her husband. Had Cartwright been a commoner, the situation would likely have been quite different. He could not have hidden behind social status, nor his right to correct social inferiors, and probably would not have secured bail, let alone a royal pardon before the case even went to trial. This is an example in which the privileges of social rank, and the boundaries of behaviour permitted to the wealthy and powerful, impacted the efficiency and fairness of the criminal justice system.

***

The manner of the cruel, outrageous murder of William Storre, master of arts, minister and preacher at Market Rasen in the county of Lincoln, committed by Francis Cartwright, one of his parishioners, the 30th day of August Anno 1602. *Oxford: Printed by Joseph Barnes, 1603*

About Lammas[1] last, viz. August 1602, there happened some controversy between the Lords and the rest of the inhabitants of Market Rasen in the County of Lincoln, concerning their commons and liberty in the town fields.[2] The matter being moved by one of them in the Church immediately after evening prayer, on a Sabbath Day, diverse hot intemperate speeches passed among them. Whereupon their minister, whose name was Master Storre, much disliking so indiscreet a course, willed them to have respect both to the time and place where they were. And further advised, seeing the cause in hand concerned a multitude amongst whom some of the least government [discretion] would always be the readiest to speak, that they would therefore make choice of two or three of the fittest and most substantial men to answer and undertake for all the rest.

This motion seemed to please them well and thereupon they entreated him that he would, as a man indifferent,[3] speak first what he thought concerning the cause. But he not willing to intermeddle in that matter, twice or thrice denied their request. And the rather, for that there was present one Francis Cartwright, a young man of an unbridled humour, the only son and heir to one of the same lords of the town, betwixt whom and himself there was grown no small unkindness. Yet in the end, being pressed thereunto by their importunity [persistence], with the consent of both the parties he delivered his opinion, using therein such discretion and reasons to confirm the same that they could not directly except against him. Notwithstanding, seeing him incline more to the right of the freeholders and the rest of the commons than to favour their intended purpose, they seemed to dislike his speeches and to cavil [object] at the same.

Young Cartwright standing by, not able any longer to contain himself, took occasion hereupon to break forth abruptly into these words: "The priest deserveth a good fee, he speaketh so like a lawyer." Master Storre, having often aforetime had experience of his hot stomach and hastiness as well towards others as himself, thought it best to reply little against him for that present. But the other, respecting neither the time, nor place, nor yet the dutiful regard

he should have had to his father's presence, uttered many more such base and
odious terms, that for modesty's sake, I forbear to rehearse them. The next
morning, as Master Storre and some others of his neighbours were talking
with the elder Cartwright about these his son's abuses, he came unto them
where they were, interrupting their conference, and fell into the like outrageous railing as he used the night afore. The minister, seeing this second
incursion more violent than the former, replied to some of his words, returning them back again, as more properly to be applied to himself.

This reply he took in such high disgrace, that had not his father hindered
it, he had there presently with his dagger effected some part of that mischief
which afterward he put in practice. But being not suffered to do what he would,
he departed from them into the open marketplace, and there proclaimed: "That
Storre was a scurvy, lousy, paltry priest: that whosoever said he was his friend,
or spake in his cause, was a rogue and a rascal: that he would (but for the law)
cut his throat, tear out his heart, and hang his quarters on the maypole."[4]

These speeches, and many more of the same quality being daily given out,
occasioned Master Storre to think it now high time to provide for his own
safety, and therefore he went to some justices near adjoining, acquainted them
with these proceedings, and desired the good behaviour[5] against the said Cartwright. But they, doubting whether they might grant the same in this case or
not, offered him for his present safeguard the peace,[6] and the other at the next
Quarter Sessions, if occasion so required.

He not resolved what were best to be done, whether to accept of this
offer or to complain himself before the high commissioners,[7] came home
and the next Sabbath took his text out of Isaiah chapter 1 verse 9 in these
words: "Except the Lord of Hosts had reserved unto us, even a small rem-
nant, we had been as Sodom, and like unto Gomorrah." The which words,
by the general report even of his enemies that heard him, he handled very
learnedly and delivered out of the same many points of necessary doctrine;
using ever among sundry loving exhortations, now and then also, as occasion
served, inserting some sharp and nipping reprehensions. Young Cartwright
seemed to note it diligently with his pen, but as the stomach, filled with
raw humours,[8] corrupteth all good nourishment that cometh therein, so this
man's mind, fraught with rancor and malice, wrested all things he heard into
the worse sense, as purposely spoken against him, and after that, more and
more thirsted for revenge.

About a week after, he espied Master Storre walking about eight o'clock
in the morning alone by the south side of the town in his cloak, went to a
cutler's[9] shop, and took out of the same a short sword which he had, formerly provided and made very sharp, and presently overtook him. The other,
hearing one at his heels, looked back and saw him drawing his sword as he
came, noting also, by the paleness of his visage, how mightily he was incensed
to mischief, and seeing no means either to escape or to defend himself, was
greatly aghast and purposed to use some speeches (if it were possible) somewhat to assuage his passions.

Figure 5.1 Woodcut image from *Three bloodie murders*, 1613. This image depicts the gruesome murder of minister William Storre by Francis Cartwright.

Source: Reproduced by permission of the Bodleian Library, Oxford University.

But he being double armed both with force and fury, would abide no parley, but presently at the first blow cut his left leg almost off. And then making at his head, the other [Storre] casting up his arms to defend it (for other weapon had he none), he gave him two mortal wounds on the forepart thereof through the brain-pan [skull], cut off three of his fingers, and gave him two other grievous wounds on the outside of either arm between the elbow and the hand: the one to the middest of the arm, and the other more than half in sunder, dividing the main bone above two inches one part from another. Thus massacred, he fell backward into a puddle of water, and striving to recover himself, the splinter-bone of his leg half cut through afore, snapped in two, and his heel doubled back to the calf of his leg. Cartwright, not yet satisfied with the blood which he had already gotten, continued his rage still more fiercely upon him, and gave him another gash on the outside of the right thigh to the very bone. And again on the left knee, his leg being bended as he lay, he cut him the fashion and compass of a horseshoe, battering in pieces the whirlbone [femur] and the nether part of the thigh bone that it was most grievous even to behold. Some smaller wounds he had, and sundry other blows which came not to his skin, as appeared by the mangling of his apparel.

A maid, coming that way by occasion of business, cried out, whereupon he fled. Many of the neighbours came presently to the place, and beholding this woeful spectacle, their minister thus wallowed in the mire and his blood so extremely gushing out, ran some of them into the town with such a confused noise and outcry of murder that others hearing it supposed on a sudden there had been fire and went with all speed to toll the bells. Thus was all suddenly in an uproar, yet few or none could tell what the matter was. The rest of more discretion took up the wounded man, carried him to the next house where one of the constables dwelt, and made very good and speedy means to bind up his wounds and to staunch his blood.

Against the next day was provided a bone-setter and three or four of the best surgeons thereabout, who, when they came to dress him, were of opinion that if he died not at the opening of his wounds and forcing together of his bones, he would at the least be very subject to often sounding [fainting]. Yet he, beyond all their expectation, endured all extremities which necessity in that case imposed on him to abide, for three hours space at the least, and never fainted or changed colour. The which thing induced them to alter their mind and to hope (as it were) past all hope, that he would escape it. But the deadly blows had so perished his brains, and let out so great a quantity of his blood in other parts of his body, that it was not possible he should recover. So that after he had languished in very great pain from Monday morning till the next Sunday after midnight (which was at the change of the moon), he ended his life.

The time that he thus continued, he spent much to the profit of himself, and to no less comfort of those that came to visit him. For besides many divine meditations he daily uttered, and thanks to God for his so merciful a visitation in giving him both time and memory to prepare himself, he also heartily forgave and continually prayed for his greatest and deadliest enemy, whom he esteemed now in worse state and more miserable than himself.

Now to leave the dead man (as no doubt he is) with the Lord. It is not amiss briefly to declare by what means the offender escaped.

Presently after he had committed this cruelty, he posted [hastened] home to his father's house, on the backside, and the truth of his fact being now known, many that were already assembled and knew not at the first about what matter, came to apprehend the felon. But his father, fearing lest in that desperate heat he should do some more mischief, did what he could to pacify the tumult until the constables came and then delivered him. They sending for three or four of such as they thought best, which had some of them seen the wounds as well as one of the constables himself had done, carried him to a justice. Where, either for lack of their due information of the truth or by the corrupt and favourable affection of the magistrate, or both, there was a very slender bail taken, and the malefactor by this sleight sent away.[10]

Presently after his escape, the manner of this murder being so barbarous, and coming to the ears of the late[11] Lord Archbishop of Canterbury and of some other of the Privy Council, a pursuivant [attendant] or messenger was by them directed forth for the justice that thus had bailed him. Who not willing to make his appearance before their honours, obtained by great and special means, and the rather, because of his age and impotency (being not able to travel) to have the hearing of the cause referred to the judges of that circuit, at their next Assizes. In the meantime (as still he remaineth), he was put out of commission,[12] and the constable also, in whose house Master Storre died, was bound over to answer for his contempt.

When the Assizes should have been kept, upon some occasion, [it was put off half a year and before which time Cartwright's friends (he believed remaining in France and another winter in the Low Countries [Netherlands]) laboured by corrupt dealing about His Majesty to purchase his pardon, and in the end, notwithstanding the foulness of the deed],[13] obtained the same, and sent for him over again into England. The course of justice (contrary to all expectation) thus being recessed, the poor widow, though both herself and her five small children depended only on such charitable relief as it pleased God to move others to bestow upon them, was driven with all speed, in the most dangerous time of sickness, to travel to London, and there in her own person (for none other might do it) to sue forth her appeal.

Hereupon he durst never shew himself openly but lurked in secret among his friends, hoping that either the widow might be compounded[14] withal, or else to find some error in her proceedings to overthrow her appeal. But when he could no way prevail, either with the large offers daily made to her for agreement, nor his counsel find any erroneous proceeding that might hold plea in law to stop her suit, he fled the second time, and (as it is thought) remaineth beyond the seas where he was before.

To the reader[15]

For that some of Cartwright's favourites, wanting colour [deceitful reasons] to excuse altogether the foulness of his fact, do yet endeavour to qualify the same in what measure they can, affirming that he, being a young man, was provoked and stirred up by evil words to commit that in the heat of his blood which otherwise he would never have committed. And some others, being themselves either of a loose conversation or at the least enemies to the ministry of the Gospel, would seem to extenuate the crime by imputing it as a just reward due, not only to the party murdered, but also to the most of his calling for their over-bold checking and (as they term it) domineering over their betters, because indeed, they reprove the general corruptions that so abound in every corner. And lest also it might happily be surmised by some indifferently affected, that many things in this relation might partially proceed in favour of the dead man from some of his friends, it is therefore thought fit, for the better satisfying of the latter sort, to assure them that there is nothing set down but that which is to be justified by very sufficient proof. And for the better answering of the former scandals and such like, here be annexed the testimony (as it were) of four substantial juries, which speak of their credit what they knew concerning the man. The first doth consist of the better sort of his parishioners where he remained; the second of the chief of such ministers among whom he conversed; the third of the worshipful in the country to whom he was best known; and the fourth of the learned men in the university where he was brought up.

The testimony of his parishioners

For as much as some uncharitable people, not satisfied with the guiltless blood of Master Storre, our late minister, give out slanderous speeches against him now dead, as proceeding from us his parishioners, we therefore willing to clear ourselves from such untruths, do give to understand to whom these presents shall come,[16] that as (no doubt) the fact was heinous before God, so is it a thing most grievous unto us. As well in regard of his wife and five small children, whose staff of bread[17] (as himself said) by this means is broken. As also chiefly that such a man should thus perish among us, whose learning, diligence, and dexterity in teaching the word of God was equal (as we are persuaded) to the better sort of his fellow ministers, his conversation so answerable to his doctrine, and his carriage such in all his affairs that (in our judgment) it might have been a precedent to direct a civil and Christian life. Thus having witnessed the truth in the premises, we cease, from Market Rasen this 17th of April, 1603.

Edmund Wright	Mich. Jesoppe	Tho. Harwicke
Hum. Chapman	Rich. Wright	William Dannotte
John Dannotte	Chris. Gyfford	John Cater
John Rutter	Will. Wright	William Hansley
Rich. Pockley	Christ. Wright	Leonard Hill
Alexan. Lamming	Mich. Hanson	John Tayler
Robert Lillie	Hen. Parker	James Robinson
Tho. Brakes	Pet. Parker	Edw. Fawsitte

The testimony of preachers, half of them doctors & bachelors of divinity, and the rest masters of arts

Whereas upon the late murder of William Storre, Master of Arts and preacher of Market Rasen in the county of Lincoln, there have been set abroach [in action] certain reports tending to his disgrace in favour (as it is thought) of the offender. We therefore, the Ministers to whom he was best known, either by nearness of dwelling or by conversing with him, do signify to all those to whom this our testimony shall come, that we always held and reputed the said William Storre, not only for his learning and sufficiency in his calling, a man far passing many others. But also of such honest and commendable bearing of himself in his life and conversation, that his greatest adversaries could never, while he lived (as we are verily persuaded), justly take exception against him. In witness whereof, we have subscribed our names this present April 1603.

Law. Stanton	Roger Parker	Mich. Reniger
Greg Garth	Rich. Turswell	George Eland
Alex. Southwicke	Theo. Tanzey	Hen. Nelson
John Chadwicke	Tho. Burton	William Mason
John Downes	David Hatcliffe	Samuell Allen
Amos Bedford	Will. Symonds	Paul Balgaie
Cuth. Dale	William Lownd	Richard Bateman
John White	Hugh Browne	Nic. Clarke

The testimony of knights and esquires

Being requested for some special causes to deliver under our hands what we knew concerning Master Storre, late vicar of Market Rasen, we whose names are subscribed, neighbours somewhat near adjoining, thought it our Christian duty to yield testimony therein accordingly. And therefore do signify that as we accompt [account] the manner of his death a part of most barbarous cruelty, so we much lament that it happened to a man so well approved generally for a good scholar, a painful [careful] preacher, and for many other commendable parts, which (if by untimely death he had not been cut off) might otherwise have been greatly beneficial both to the Church and Commonwealth. Given at Lincoln the 29th of April 1603.

George S'poll	Phillip Tyrwhitt
Edward Ayscoghe	Thomas Grantham
Edward Tyrwhitt	Thomas Dalison
Char. Metham	Vincent Fulnetby
Ric. Rossetter	Richard Gedney
Fran. Bullingham	Edward Saltmarsh

The testimony of doctors and bachelors of divinity in the university

For as much as we are entreated by certain ministers of the county of Lincoln to signify what opinion we held of William Storre, Master of Arts and late fellow of Corpus Christi College, we whose names are underwritten, do by these presents give him this testimony: that for the time of his abode in our University he shewed himself very sober and honest in his conversation. He was of quiet carriage in his place, studious, learned, and religious, of great and special hope to prove a worthy member in the Church of Christ. Oxon.,[18] June 29, 1603.

John Howson, Vicechancellor, Oxon.

Edmond Lillie	John Rainolds	Thomas Holland
Richard Kilby	John Peron	George Abbott
Raph Kessell	John Williams	Henry Airey
John Aeglionbye	Leon. Hutton	William Thorne
Nicholas Higges	Thomas Luddington	Rich. Crakenthorpe
Edward Hyrst	Chris. Membry	Sebastian Benfeld
Thomas Burton	Chris. Chalfount	Peter Hooker
Henry Hindle	Robert Burhill	John Barcham
	Richard Alleyne	

Notes

1 Lammas Day is August 1, the day in which the wheat harvest was celebrated.

2 That is, the open fields on which husbandmen grazed their cattle, farmers used to access water to irrigate fields, and small copyholders used to grow crops for personal use.

3 As a minister, Storre had no stake in the outcome of the dispute.

4 The maypole was a fixed pole usually located in a town square traditionally used to celebrate May Day (the beginning of spring).

5 A recognizance issued by a JP that required an individual to be of good behaviour, typically until a case came for hearing. Normally it was issued to a person who was suspected of committing a crime and was thus denied as Cartwright had not yet done so.

6 A recognizance ordering a named individual to keep the peace against the person who made the complaint until further action was taken.

7 The Court of High Commission was an ecclesiastical court in England between circa 1540 and 1640. It had wide powers in civil as well as church matters.

8 This is based on the notion of the Galenic humoral theory, in which it was believed that four humours (blood, phlegm, yellow bile, and black bile) needed to be in balance for the body to be healthy. In this case, a "raw humour" was developing, and unbalancing Cartwright's mind.

9 A dealer in cutlery and knives. In this case, Cartwright had brought in one of his own knives for sharpening.

10 The next three paragraphs do not appear in the 1603 chapbook, but instead in *Three Bloody Murders* (London: John Trundle, 1613), the first part of which recounts Cartwright's murder of Storre almost verbatim, and adds these paragraphs to complete the story. It is possible that this information was not known when the 1603 edition was published.

11 John Whitgift (in office August 1583 to his death in February 1604); by the time these paragraphs were written in 1613, Whitgift was the "late" archbishop.

12 Removed from the Commission of the Peace, and therefore no longer a JP.

13 The chapbook is damaged, although the part between brackets is a very close approximation of the original text.

14 That the dispute could be brought to resolution, usually through a monetary settlement.

15 This section, which appeared in the 1603 version, was presumably written to ensure Storre's name was not besmirched by Cartwright's wealthy friends. The testimonies might have been written in support of his widow's attempts to have the pardon removed so that Cartwright would stand trial.

16 Variants of the phrase "to whom these presents shall come" were formulaic ones commonly used for English charters, patents, and depositions. The phrase was meant to indicate the document was "open," or intended for public viewing.

17 A reference to Leviticus 26:26, in this case, the killing of Storre cut off his family's livelihood.

18 An abbreviation for Oxoniensis, the Latin name for Oxford University.

6 The cock-a-doodle-doo miracle

Several salient features of the early modern English criminal justice system are revealed in this story of the murder of young Anthony James and the mutilation of his older sister, Elizabeth. Based on the quality of clothing found on his body, the murdered boy was obviously wealthy, which prompted the community to offer a 40 shilling reward – more than a month's salary for the average commoner – for information leading to the murderer's arrest. It is unclear how the case would have been pursued had the child been a vagrant stranger. It is also interesting that the outcome of the case critically depended on the testimony of an eight-year-old girl, who recounted four-year-old facts. This is a somewhat surprising in a society where women had less legal agency than men, and children were not usually seen as reliable witnesses in criminal courts. Perhaps anticipating the reader's suspicions about the veracity of the girl's testimony, the author takes pains to note that she answered the questions posed to her "with more reason and sense, than is common to one her age." Probably the most notable aspect of this chapbook is the role the author attributed to God. God's benevolence in keeping the girl alive in a tree (like "Daniel in the lion's den"), ensuring she would be found by a stranger ("surely the providence and appointment of God"), helping her to find her way back to Hertford ("to give these wicked wretches some part of their reward"), sending a cock as "his first messenger of this mighty miracle" (the same messenger who reminded the apostle Peter of his denials of Christ and forced his "remembrance"), and God's choice to conceal that which remained unknown about the case, would certainly have resonated strongly with an audience of early seventeenth-century Anglican readers.

***

The horrible murder of a young boy, of three years of age, whose sister had her tongue cut out, and how it pleased God to reveal the offenders by giving speech to the tongueless child, which offenders were executed at Hertford the 4th of August, 1606.
London: Printed by Ed. Allde for William Firebrand, and are to be sold at his shop in Pope's Head Alley, over against the tavern door, 1606

In Hatfield in the County of Hertford dwelled an old widow, called Mother Dell, who had abiding with her in the house only her son, named T. Dell. Into the house of this old woman (some four years since) was seen go in two pretty children, a boy and a girl.[1] The boy seemed not three years of age and the girl not much above four. These children were led into the said house by a wandering pedlar and his wife (or punk [harlot]). The going in of these children was noted by diverse [people], but especially by a tailor dwelling in the town called A. C. Which tailor marked them so much the more for that they were handsomely appareled, and their coats made with new wings, skirts, and tags, such as he had not seen the like of before, which made him presently upon the sight of them to make a pattern of those wings and tags. But doubting that he had not taken a true pattern, he watched to have another sight of those children. When for two or three days space he could not see them, he went to the house of Mother Dell and did ask her for those children? She answered him very shortly, saying they were safe enough, for they were gone again with them that brought them.

With this answer the tailor was satisfied because it no further concerned him than the getting of a piece of a new fashion. But within a while after, the boy was found dead in a ditch of water not far from the town, with a great piece of wood tied to his back. The child being taken out, it did plainly appear that he was murdered before he was thrown in. The poor harmless infant being found thus cruelly murdered, and none that looked on him taking knowledge of him, his pretty little coat was taken and hanged up in diverse market towns and proclamation made in every one of those towns to this effect: that if anyone whatsoever could and would tell where the father or mother of the murdered child (which wore that coat) dwelt, he should have forty shillings for his pains and his charges borne to bring him from and to the place where he dwelt. But all this proved to little or no purpose, till at the last this news came to the hearing of the tailor, who coming to the place where the coat was to be seen and taking good notice of it, he presently called to his remembrance that that coat was worn by one of those children which he had seen go into the house of Mother Dell.

The news of this coming to the ears of Sir Henry Butler and one other knight, being both justices and both dwelling near to that place, a warrant was made. By virtue whereof, the said Mother Dell and her son were brought before them both and strictly examined, where they both confessed the two such children as the tailor spake of came into the house with a pedlar and his wife, and that they verily thought the boy at that time had that coat on his back. But all this was nothing to them, for they neither knew the pedlar nor his wife, only they came thether to see if they had need of any of their ware (as it is a common use for traveling pedlars to call at diverse houses). And when they had bestowed some little money with them, both he, his wife, and those children (which they said were theirs) went out on the backside of the house, and what after became of them, they knew not.

Upon this their confession, they were both bound over to appear and answer at the next Assizes, the justices hoping ere that time to find out the actor or actors of that more than monstrous tragedy. But alas their hopes were deceived, for the time was not yet come wherein God had decreed to bring this cruel, barbarous, and bloody massacre to light. Yet notwithstanding, they were still bound over from Assizes to Assizes, almost for four years, in which time, the said Mother Dell bestowed great cost in altering, repairing, and furnishing of her house, which made many of her neighbours much to wonder, for that they knew not from whence she should have wherewith to defray that charge.[2]

But now let us leave both her and her son to the hell and horror of a guilty conscience, which always waits and attends on murderers, and let us now speak of the poor mangled and dismembered girl who was now in far worse case than her dead brother, had not He which provides for the whole world, in His good appointed time, provided for her. For her tongue was first cut out of her head by the roots, then was she led by this said mother of mischief and her son (at a time when they were not seen) to the side of a wood which was seldom frequented, in which place stood an old great hollow tree which was not very high.

Having brought this helpless and hopeless child to this tree (which they meant should be her grave), the son got up to the top and rudely hauled up after him this harmless girl, who having seen her brother murdered before her face, had no reason to hope of life, yet did she not cease with tears and signs to beg for pity of these pitiless wretches, whose hearts being much harder than stone, would not relent. For this merciless villain let her slip into the tree where they left her, in hope never more to see her or hear of her.

But he that preserved Daniel in the lion's den[3] and made the blind to see, the lame to go, and the dumb to speak, did not only preserve the life of this child, but also did give unto her an extraordinary strength and vigor, whereby she was able and did make such a noise that a man coming by that way (not by chance, but surely by the providence and appointment of God), hearing a strange humming and hollow crying, drawing near to that tree, perceived the noise and cry to come from thence, which made him get up to the top of it, where being and looking down into it he beheld that pitiful, ruthful, and bloody spectacle. Which when he had a while looked on with pity and compassion, and having spoke to her and perceiving by her signs that she could not answer him, he made means to draw her out. Which when he had done, he began (as may be easily imagined) to bethink with himself what great trouble he might come into if he were found with the child, he being a stranger as it seems he was.

And this fear of trouble (as was supposed by the grave and wise judge and justices of the bench when the matter came to their hearing) made this man, after he had pulled her out of the tree, to make from her with all the haste he could. But the poor soul pursued him with all the haste she could, crying and calling unto him for succor [aid] and help in the best manner she could, being thereunto urged by pain and hunger, the least of which will force a man of a resolute and resolved spirit to break silence, had he vowed the contrary. Much more than being joined both together must they force a child.

In brief then, when she had lost the sight of him, God knows what became of her, but no one man or woman can tell any certain place of her abode for almost these four years. Many say they have seen such a dumb child wander up and down a-begging, and she herself hath confessed (since the time that God hath lent her use of her speech and utterance, that she may be easily understood by any that shall hear her) that she did beg for her food all that time. And questionless, the Lord who had reserved her, both to bring so monstrous a murder and cruel a massacre to light, and also to make manifest His almighty power to many misbelieving and unbelieving miscreants (Athiests, I mean), He, I say, as may most evidently appear, did both preserve her and provide for her.

And now the time drawing near wherein it pleased God to give these wicked wretches some part of their reward, he so directed the course of this poor wandering child that she came back again to the town of Hatfield, where she received her wrongs, having yet no use of speech nor utterance whereby she might be understood. And wandering up and down the town, little thinking she had been near the place where her innocent brother lost his life and herself the instrument of her speech. But going along the street, gazing here and there, as children will do (yea and old folks too) when they come into a strange place, at last she came by the house where this bloody tragedy had been acted. Which house she no sooner saw but she knew, as did appear by the signs of grief and sorrow which she made at the sight thereof. For what with her crying and the extraordinary noise which she made, she drew people about her who did in some sort seem to grieve at the moan she made. But surely they could not choose but wonder and desire to know what the sorrow and signs meant which the child made. For one while she would gape wide with her mouth, drawing her forefinger to and fro it as though she had been cutting off something, then would she with her finger point into the house. And when this Mother Dell and her son came to the door, then her crying and her signs did seem much to increase, which made the lookers on to suspect much, but alas they knew not what.

But at last amongst other folks came the tailor before spoken of, and he no sooner saw the child, noted her signs, and remembered the other child found in the water and murdered as is aforesaid, but straight he says, that this was the other of those children which was led into that house long since by the pedlar and his wife. Then some of the neighbours, together with the tailor, took the child and led her into the house. She being within, stood staring wildly round about her, at last she spied a pair of stairs, to which she went directly, and coming to them, she looked earnestly on them. Looking about the house again, she first pointed to the stairs, and then to a corner of the house, as though to say, these stairs did stand there. This sign the neighbours understood well because they knew the stairs had been removed, and that made them think some foul matter would be picked out of her other signs.

Hereupon they began to lay hands on the mother and her son, to have them again (now with the child) before the justice, at which the child seemed to rejoice. Being brought before Sir Henry Butler, who was the next justice (and had examined them diverse times before concerning these children) the constable or headborough began to tell unto His Worship the cause of their coming. And having related unto him from point to point what they had seen, the child, marking and understanding them well, fell to her former signs again before the knight. Whereupon he did, with great wisdom and discretion, examine them apart, one from another. But they both remained still obstinate and in their old tale, confessing nothing, nor would any of them acknowledge that they have ever seen the girl before. Notwithstanding, the tailor did still affirm it to their faces that that was the girl which the pedlar and his wife led into their house long since with the boy.

The justice assuring himself now that these were the actors of that bloody tragedy and hoping that God would in time make it yet more plain than it was, he caused a mittimus to be made and sent them to the gaol, there to remain without bail or mainprise until the Assizes. And further he willed the constable to take the child back again with him to the town and to have a great care that she might be well looked unto and to see the house of Mother Dell safely shut up. All this being done according to the knight's command, and the child's lodging and diet being much better than it had been long before, she began to gather both strength and spirit upon her and to take delight to play amongst children.

But now (gentle reader) let me entreat thee as thou readst, not only to admire and wonder, but to praise and magnify the mighty maker and preserver of us all, for His great mercy and might shewed to this poor child, in this next succeeding action, which if we look into but with the eyes of natural reason and human sense, it will be thought incredible and impossible. But with God nothing is impossible, and this ought not to be thought incredible because it was so lately and so near unto us done, and for that the child is yet living in Hatfield to affirm for truth all that is here written of her.

Now you shall understand, that this girl being playing with other children in the backside of some man's house in the town where cocks, hens, and chickens were feeding, it pleased God at that time to make a cock to be (as it were a tutor to the child) his first messenger of this mighty miracle, like as a bird of the same name and nature, using the self same note, put Peter in mind that he had denied his master,[4] from which his remembrance sprung his true and hearty repentance. But to proceed: this child being playing (as I said before), one of the cocks in the yard began to crow and another answered him and thus they continued a pretty while. At last one of the children began (after their manner) to mock the cocks, crying "cock-a-doodle-doo!" In the end, this dumb child, straining herself, cried as the rest had done, "cock-a-doodle-doo!," which made all the children amazed. And one of them that stood next her said: "What, canst thou speak now?" "Aye, that I can," said she, speaking it so plainly that they all understood her.

The hearing of this made the children break up their play and run home with joy to the house where this child was kept to carry [the] news. And when she came home to the house where she was kept, and the folk of the house finding the report of the children to be true, with exceeding joy (after the asking of her some few questions, to which she did answer very directly) they led her again to the knight before named, to whom they told what had happened. Which when he had heard (he being furnished with the fear of God, which is indeed the true fountain and foundation of wisdom), he first of all gave thanks to God, and then he did ask her who cut out her tongue? She said, the old woman and her son that killed her brother and put her into the tree. Then he asked her who took her out of the tree? And she said, a man, that when he had done did run away from her because she could not speak to him. He likewise asked whither she went then? But alas, she could not tell him. Then he did ask her, who brought her to the old woman's house first? And she said, a man and a woman that had killed her father and her mother and taken a great bag of money from them. And she said that the man and woman had given a great deal of that money to the old woman, and that the old woman did at that time lift up her hands three times and did swear three times that she would never tell anybody who they were. These and many other questions the knight did ask her, to all which she did answer with more reason and sense than is common to one of her age.

To conclude, the Assizes being come, an indictment was preferred against the mother and the son, to which indictment they pleaded not guilty and put themselves to the ordinary trial. Whereupon the child was brought before the bench and stood upon the table between the bench and the jury. Where after that the foresaid knight had opened some part of this foul offence, the child was asked diverse of the former questions, to which she answered as before. The tailor likewise was there, who told unto the jury what he had seen. Then the jury was willed to go together, but before they went they did look into the child's mouth, but could not see so much as the stump of a tongue therein. The jury stayed not long before they returned with their verdict, guilty, whereupon they had sentence of death pronounced against them and were both hanged at Hertford the fourth day of August, 1606.

Thus far (gentle reader) have I set down briefly and truly the manner of this monstrous massacre. And how far it hath pleased God to reveal some of the authors and, for some secret purpose best known to himself, to conceal the rest, which questionless shall be made known in his good appointed time when it shall be most for his honour and glory. In the meantime, let me entreat all you which do read or hear this ruthful discourse to meditate (as I do and will) on the many miseries and mischances mankind is subject to, which if you do, questionless you will make less joy at the birth of your children and less sorrow at their death than commonly you do, and rather seek (in some sort) to imitate those heathens which did sing and dance at the death of their children than those Christians which do mourn and sorrow as men past hope.

As for the love which ordinarily men bear unto their children, it may more fitly be called love to themselves than to their children. For notwithstanding we all know, or ought to know, that no one is truly happy till his end, if he die well, yet many (nay most of us) do rather desire to have our children survive us than to see them fairly bestowed before us. Never thinking, respecting, or regarding what may come to them after our death, so our humours be fed in our lives. And if this may not truly be said to be self-love, I know not what is self-love. Therefore let us all and every one of us refer and put our wills to God's will, assuring ourselves that all things shall work together for the best for them that love and fear him.

As for the pedlar and his wife which the child hath confessed to have robbed and killed her father and mother, they are not yet found out, nor is the place and abode of her too unfortunate parents yet known. But yet all in good time, if it be the will of the Almighty, both the one and the other shall come to light. Amen.

Notes

1 Another version of this story appears in *The Most Cruel and Bloody Murder Committed by an Innkeeper's Wife . . . and her son* (London, 1606). In this second version we learn how the children's parents suffered their horrific deaths. We also learn that the Dells are innkeepers named Annis and George (not "T" as in this version), and that both the murdered parents and their children are named Anthony and Elizabeth James.
2 They didn't know where she got the money to make improvements and buy furniture.
3 Daniel 6:12–24.
4 Peter's denials of Christ are described in the New Testament gospels: Matthew 26:73–75; Mark 14:69–70; Luke 22:54–62; John 18:13–27.

7   The life and death of a bawd

Perhaps the most interesting aspect of this chapbook is that there was little evidence proving that Margaret Fernseed murdered her husband, which was the crime for which she was convicted and executed. Although Fernseed confessed to running a bawdy house, corrupting many maids and married women, being a receiver of stolen goods, and adultery, all of which were crimes in their own right, she was adamant right up to the brink of death that she was innocent of her husband's murder, which was "proven" using solely circumstantial evidence. Despite this, Fernseed was convicted based on her poor reputation in the community and her flagrant abuse of the boundaries of behaviour expected of women in this society. Rather than being a good neighbour and a submissive and modest wife, Fernseed breached nearly every gender, sexual, and social boundary that was used to maintain order in early modern England. For these reasons, even if the evidence linking her to Anthony Fernseed's death was sketchy, Margaret Fernseed had to be executed, so that balance could be restored. This tale is an excellent example of how the criminal justice system of early modern England was used to restore boundaries of behaviour in society, even it sometimes meant working within the grey area of the criminal law.

***

The arraignment and burning of Margaret Fernseed, for the murder of her late husband Anthony Fernseed, found dead in Peckham Field near Lambeth, having once before attempted to poison him with broth, being executed in St. George's Field the last of February, 1608. *London: Printed for Henry Gosson, and are to be sold at the Sign of the Sun in Paternoster Row, 1608*

The grossest part of folly and the most repugnant, even unto our own natural reason, is to think that our hidden abominations can be concealed from the eye of the Almighty or that, He seeing our bloody and crying sins, will not either reveal them before His ministers of public justice or, in His best pleased time, power down sharp vengeance for such presumptuous and rebellious offences.

Oh! The miracles in these revelations are such and so infinite that the thought of man or his wisdom is but mere weakness, going about to comprehend such unspeakable judgments.

And of this we have before our eyes a most notable example in this wretched woman, of whom my present discourse entreateth, named Margaret Fernseed, a woman that even from her time of knowledge [puberty] (if the general report of the world, according to the old adage, may be taken for an oracle) was given to all the looseness and lewdness of life, which either unlawful lust or abominable prostitution could violently cast upon her with the greatest infamy, yea, and with such a public and irrespective unchastity that neither being chaste nor caught she regarded not, either into what ear the loathsomeness of her life was sounded or into what bed of lust her lascivious body was transported.

In this more than bestial lasciviousness, having consumed the first part of her youth, finding both the corruption of her blood to check the former heat of her lust and the too general ugliness of her prostitution to breed a loath in her ordinary customers, being then confirmed in some more strength of years, took a house near unto the Irongate of the Tower where she kept a most abominable and vile brothel house, poisoning many young women with that sin wherewith her own body long before was filthily debauched. From this house at the Irongate she was married unto one Anthony Fernseed, a tailor dwelling in Duck Lane but keeping a shop upon Addle Hill near Carter Lane. This Anthony was amongst his neighbours reputed to be both sober and of very good conversation.

Now it happened that some few months ago, in the fields of Peckham near London, there was found a man slain having his throat cut, a knife in his hand, gold rings upon his fingers, and forty shillings in money in his purse. His wounds of so long continuance that it was not only corrupted but there was also maggots, or such like filthy worms, engendered therein, which gave testimony to the beholders that he had not slain himself in that place, as well because the place was free from such a spectacle the day before, as also that such corruption could not proceed from a present slaughter. Again, what the person slain no man knew, both because his physiognomy[1] was altered in his death and because his acquaintance was little or none in those parts about Peckham.

In the end, searching his pockets and other parts of his apparel, amongst other notes and reckonings they found an indenture[2] wherein a certain youth which did serve him was bound unto him. This indenture gave them knowledge both of his name and of the place of his dwelling, whereupon certain discreet persons of Peckham, sent to London to Duck Lane and inquiring for the house of one Anthony Fernseed, delivered to his wife the disaster and mischance which had befallen her husband, which her hardened heart received not as a message of sorrow, neither did the grudging of an afflicted countenance gall her remembrance, but as if it had been the report of some ordinary or vulgar news. She embraced it with an irrespective neglect and carelessness, and demanded instantly (before the message would tell her how he died) whether his throat were cut or that he had cut his own throat, as either knowing or prophesying how he died. Yet to observe a customary fashion or (as the proverb is) to carry a candle before the Devil,[3] she prepares herself and her servant in all haste to go to Peckham to behold her husband.

And in this way, as she went, it was her chance to meet with one of her husband's ancient acquaintances, who, feeling that in charity which she ought to have felt in nature, began to complain her misfortune, telling her she had lost a most honest and good husband. She, whom the Devil now would not suffer to dissemble [pretend] (though his greatest act be in dissimulation), told him her fear was she should not hear so well of him. He, wondering at her ungodly carelessness, let her pass, when presently she met another of her acquaintance, who, with like charity to the former, began to pity her griefs (though grief was never further from her heart) and to wish her those comforts which are fit for affliction. But she as careless as before gave him (by the neglect of her words) true testimony how far sorrow was from her heart, which when he noted, he said, "Why Mistress Fernseed, is the loss of a good husband so slightly to be regarded? For mine own part, had such a mischance fain [come] to my fortune I should ere this have wept out mine eyes with true sorrow."

But she quickly made him answer, "Tut sir, mine eyes are ill already and I must now preserve them to mend my clothes, not to mourn for a husband." After that, in her going, the wind blowing the dust in her face, she takes her scarf and wiped her eyes and said she should scarce know her husband when she saw him. These courtesan-like speeches made her acquaintance leave her and wished her more grace.

So she and her boy came where the body was, where more for awe of the magistrate than any terror she felt she made many sour faces, but the dryness of her brain would suffer no moisture to descend into her eyes. Many questions were asked her, to which she answered with such constancy that no suspicion could be grounded against her. Then was her boy taken and examined, who delivered [revealed] the abomination of her life and that since her marriage with his master, she had lived in all disquietness, rage, and distemperature, often threatening his life and contriving plots for his destruction. That she had, ever since her marriage, in most public and notorious manner, maintained a young man with whom (in his view) she had often committed adultery. That the same young man, since his master's loss, was fled he knew not whither, and that his mistress had even then before the message of his master's death sold all his goods (as he supposed) to fly also after him whom she loved.

All these speeches were not only seconded but almost approved by some of her neighbours, which lived near unto her, insomuch that she was the second time taken into a more strict examination. Wherein, albeit she could not deny any of her general assertions, yet touching the death of her husband, that she forswore [swore falsely] and renounced the fact or practice thereof to be hers with such a shameless constancy that she struck amazement into all that heard her.

In the end, by authority of justice she was committed to the White Lion in Southwark. During the time of which imprisonment till her time of trial, thinking to outface truth with boldness and sin with impudence, she continued out all her examinations taken before several justices in her former denials, and whereas the rod of imprisonment laid upon others is received as a gentle correction whereby to look into themselves, it was to her rather the bellows of indignation than a temperer to patience. Rather a kind of frenzy than a cooler of fury, and rather a provoker to evil than a persuader to goodness. For she was seldom found to be in charity with any of her fellow prisoners nor at any time in quiet with herself, rather a provoker than an appealer of dissensions, given to much swearing, scarce praying but continually scolding, so that she was as hateful to all them that dwelt with her in that her last home, the prison, as she was to people of honest conversation (having deserved the name of a bawd [madam]) while she lived abroad.

In this uncivil order spending her hours, the time of trial coming on (when such offenders were to appear before the earthly Judge to give account of their lives past), amongst many others this Margaret Fernseed was one. At the Assizes last, according to the order of law, she was indicted and arraigned, the purpose of which indictment was to have practiced the murder of her late husband Anthony Fernseed, who as before was found dead in Peckham Field near Lambeth. To the indictment she pleaded not guilty, putting her cause to God and the country, which were a credible jury paneled, and had there made their personal appearance for that purpose. Then were these several witnesses produced against her, namely of the incontinentness of her life past, her attempt to poison her husband before this murder, as also to prepare broth for him and put powder in it, her slight regard of him in his life, and her careless sorrow for him after death. With other circumstances, as the flight of the fellow whom she had lived long in adultery withal, her present sale of her goods upon her husband's murder, as it may be justly thought, with purpose to fly after him. On which lawful evidence she was convicted and after judgment given her to be burned, and from thence she was conveyed back to the White Lion till the time appointed for her execution.

How Margaret Fernseed spent her time in prison, from Saturday, the day of her conviction, till Monday the last of February, when in St. George's Field she was executed

Being come back to the prison, for the first night she disposed herself according to her ancient habit, being as it were so rooted and accustomed to evil that as even death itself had not power to make her forget it and endeavour a better course. But being at the same time in the prison with her, three gentlemen who likewise were condemned and who through the course of their lives had not taught them to live well, yet the care of their souls remembered them to die well. These gentlemen, having heard how ill her life past had been and that her countenance was as resolute, importuned the keeper that they might have her company, partly to instruct her, but especially that she might see them, and by the reformation of their lives she might learn to amend her own and as they did, to prepare herself fit for death. Whose persuasion and whole-some counsels of their own, with comfortable promises of our merciful sav-iour Jesus Christ to them that unfeignedly believe in him and by unfeigned repentance make way to their salvation, as also with threatening her with the terrible judgments of Hell which are prepared for them that perish through lack of grace, they so wrought in her, she was at last drawn to make a confes-sion of her former life past, and to repent her of the same. The form of which was in this manner:

The confession and repentance of Margaret Fernseed, after her condemnation in the White Lion

To prepare the reader for this confession of hers, know that I was credibly sat-isfied that, when the heat of her fury was past (to which she was much subject unto), she was a woman well-spoken, of fair deliverance, and good persuasion. And so to her confession:

"To excuse myself, O Lord, before thee who knows the conspiracies of our thoughts even to the utmost of our actions (how ever so private or publicly committed), were folly or to justify myself were sin, since no flesh can appear pure in thy sight. I here, therefore, with prostrate knees and dejected eyes as unworthy to look up unto thy Divine Majesty, with a contrite heart and peni-tent soul, also here voluntarily confess I am the greatest of sinners which have deserved thy wrath and indignation."

In this good manner she proceeded and withal satisfied all that came and desired to have private conference with her of the whole course of her life. That in her youth, even from the age of aptness [adolescence], she had been a pros-titute, whore, but growing into disabled years, to please the loose desires of such customers she after turned bawd, a course of life more hateful in tempt-ing and seducing youth than the other in committing sin. The one makes but spoil and ruin of herself and the other of a multitude.

"For," quoth she, "I myself have had ten several women retaining to my house for that purpose. Some were men's wives, which repaired thither both by appointment and at convenient hours when their husbands might least sus-pect or have knowledge of their absence. And these women did I first tempt to their fall, some by persuading them they were not beloved of their hus-bands, especially if I could at any time have note of any breach or discontent between them. Others, that their husbands maintained them not sufficiently to express their beauty and according to their own deserts. Of these, them having brought my purpose to effect, and that I knew they had offended, they were as fearful to offend me as their husbands should have knowledge of their offences. And these allowed me a weekly pension for coming to my house, and durst not at all times but find opportunity to come whensoever myself or such loose friends, whom either they had been familiar withal or now desired to be acquainted with them, should send for any of them to supply my house, and make spoil of young maids who were sent out of the country by their friends, here with hope to advance themselves. I went weekly to the Carriers,[4] where if the maid liked me I so wrought with the Carrier that she seldom left me till I had brought her to be as bad as I purposed, which effected, every one of them I compelled to give me ten shillings a week out of their gettings. Having, as I said, seldom less than ten whose bodies and souls I kept in this bondage, besides I confess I was a continual receiver of theft stolen. But in all this, as it was badly got so was it worse consumed, for nothing of it did prosper with me, whereby," quoth she, "I acknowledge I have deserved death and in the highest degree, but for this which I am condemned, Heaven that knoweth best the secrets of our hearts, knows I am innocent."

But who knows not that in evil there is a like impudence to deny as there is a forwardness to act: in which we will leave here whom the law hath found guilty, and having thus truly related her own confession we proceed to the manner of execution. First only touching the evidence of two sailors, given to the jury at her arraignment. Among other circumstances that was availablest to condemn her, this was one and the chiefest. During the time while she kept a bawdy house about the Irongate by Tower-ditch, there happened a couple of bargemen to come to revel at her house with such guests as she kept to entertain loose customers, and having spent the whole day in large riot and much expense, the night being late, for that time they made their lodging there. They being abed, it happened that night (which was seldom) her husband came to make his lodging there also, and being chambered with his wife, but a wall between where these bargemen lay, they could expressly hear them every word that passed between them, the effect of which was the reproving of her for her bad life, his persuading her to amendment, which she not willing to listen unto, fell a-scolding at him and so left both his bed and chamber some time passing.

At last Master Fernseed heard these bargemen cough, and wondering to have strangers lodged in his house (for it was not common to his knowledge) arose out of his bed and demanded of them what they were? Who asked of him also wherefore he questioned them?

"Mary," quoth he, "for if you be honest men and have a care either of your bodies or souls, avoid this house as you would do poison, lest it be the undoing of you all."

They seeing him of a comely personage, and that his words tended to some purpose, demanded of him what he was that gave them such wholesome counsel?

"I am," quoth he, "the master of this house (if I had my right), but I am barred of the possession and command thereof by a devilish woman, who makes a stews [brothel] of it to exercise her sinful practices." So, with some other admonishment, left the room, when these bargemen told Mistress Fernseed what they had heard of her husband.

To which she replied, "Hang him knave and villain! I will before God be revenged of him (nay ere long), by one means or other, so work, that I will be rid of him." Which making good, in the judgment of the Judge, to gather with her life and practices, she as aforesaid was condemned.

On Monday being the last of February, she had notice given her that in the afternoon she must suffer death, and a preacher commended unto her to instruct her for her soul's health, who laboured much with her for the confession of the fact which she still obstinately denied, but made great show of repentance for her life past. So that about two o'clock in the afternoon she was stripped of her ordinary wearing apparel, and upon her own smock put a kirtle of canvas pitched clean through,[5] over which she did wear a white sheet, and so was by the keeper delivered to the sheriff, on each hand a woman leading her and the preacher going before her. Being come to the place of execution, both before and after her fastening to the stake, with godly exhortations he admonished her that now in that minute she would confess that fact for which she was now ready to suffer, which she denying, the reeds were planted about, unto which fire being given, she was presently dead.

Notes

1 The shape of his face had changed.
2 A legal contract binding an apprentice or servant to a master for a period of time.
3 As Catholics typically held candles before saints to venerate them, to do so before the Devil was to tempt evil.
4 Carriers were companies or drivers that contracted to transport goods and people in carriages, carts, and wagons, often between the country and the city. By the seventeenth century, the term had also come to mean individuals who informed criminals about the arrival into the city of potential marks.
5 A kirtle was a loose-fitting one-piece garment worn over a smock (underclothing). In this case, it was soaked in tar (pitched) to facilitate burning and accomplish Fernseed's death at the stake.

8 The cripple's complaint and the strumpet's repentance

The "monsters" in this chapbook both engaged in sexual relations outside of marriage, came to resent these acts, and committed murder in order to remove the shame of their "wickedness." The author makes it clear that the reader is not supposed to be sympathetic to the murderers, even if one was a cripple and the other a hapless woman. Instead, the author frequently refers to the murderers as sub-human creatures. John Arthur is described as an "unperfect wretch," a "decrepit creature" and a "deformed lump of flesh," while Martha Scambler is a "she-wolf, more unnatural than either bird or beast," and a "caterpillar of nature." Even the title of this chapbook, *Deeds against nature, and monsters by kind*, emphasizes the inhumanity and animalistic tendencies of these two criminals, and thus clearly distinguished them from civilized, law-abiding people. The cripple's "complaint" and the strumpet's "repentance" are particularly interesting aspects of this chapbook. Although it was not unusual for chapbooks to show how convicted murderers confessed and repented before their executions, this author evidently elected to reproduce these in poetic form. Even though these poems are written in the first person, it is clear that the same person – likely the anonymous author – wrote them both, and of course it is possible that no such penitence was demonstrated by Arthur or Scambler at all. The semi-literate and common audience that would have read and experienced this chapbook likely found these poems especially satisfying, particularly if they were read out to a wider audience.

***

Deeds against nature, and monsters by kind, tried at the Gaol
Delivery of Newgate, at the Sessions in the Old Bailey, the 18th
and 19th of July last, 1614. The one of a London cripple named
John Arthur, that, to hide his shame and lust, strangled his
betrothed wife. The other of a lascivious young damsel named
Martha Scambler, which made away the fruit of her own womb,
that the world might not see the seed of her own shame. Which
two persons with diverse others were executed at Tyburn the
21st of July following. With two sorrowful ditties of these two
aforesaid persons, made by themselves in Newgate, the night
before their execution. *London: Printed for Edward Wright, 1614*

Is it not a marvel that fire falls not from Heaven to consume an infinite
number of worse than savage-natured people in this land, when vile wretches,
whom God hath marked with his secret brand of secret purpose, so impi-
ously attempt things against nature? As for example (which God grant it
may so prove for our amendment), here remained amongst us in this city a
deformed creature, an unperfect wretch wanting the right shape and limbs of
a man, though in form and visage like unto one of us. This decrepit creature
(as I said), named John Arthur, lived and maintained himself with the charity and devotions of alms-giving people, and by his lame and limbless usage
purchased more kind favours than many others of his bare fraternity. Money
and means being easily gained by a few beggarly observations, as a wretch
graceless and unthankful for God's blessings thus bestowed upon him, [he]
made no good use thereof but spent the same in the service of the Devil, as in
blasphemy, swearing, drunkenness, and such like, all damnable sins and such
as be the nurses and breeders of others.

This aforenamed cripple, being on a time in the middle of his drunkenness,
heated with lust, fell into familiarity with a certain woman of his own condition, who purposing to live as he did, upon charity and good men's alms, and
seeing good benefit to come by his "Amens," unto whom many people grew
willing to give, promised to be his associate and, as his companion and wife,
to beg with him. Many days and months spent they together, continually
abusing the gifts of charity and wasting away the same with drunkenness in
the by-places and suburbs of the city, which is evermore the receipt of such
begging vagabonds and disordered livers, instruments of the Devil prepared
still for deeds of mischief. This cripple, having not one good thought of God's
grace, so lusted after his begging companion that he obtained the daily use of
her body, and continually committed so that sin of lust and shame, making a
practice thereof in the contempt of God's Laws, that the eye of Heaven could
no longer wink at them but with a clear sight see into their base wickedness.
Yea, more than base, in that a deformed lump of flesh and no perfect creature
should thus abuse the seed of generation and now and then in the fields and
highways commit such beastly offences.

But God, we see, hath iron hands and will at last strike heavily, as he did upon these two shameless malefactors. For the cripple, in time surfeiting upon this his shame and growing weary of this hated offence, as all people will do, being not lawfully married, began to cast her off and to loath her company, though he himself might be thought the more loathsome. Which she (abused woman) perceiving, and knowing herself to be but his strumpet, challenged of him the promise of marriage, and so importuned him thereunto by his former vows and promises, and that Heaven would otherwise call his perjured oaths to account, all instigations of the Devil, and subtle policies to draw them both to destruction. Her importunate suits to marriage so troubled his mind, bred such a rage in his heart, that a purpose came into his mind to rid her away by some untimely death: a motion no sooner set on fire, but the Devil was ready to bring more fuel, and never rested till it was all on a flame.

So upon a night, a time fitting for such a dark deed, the cripple enticed her forth into the fields near Islington, where secretly at the brick kilns, the lodging place for rogues and night walkers, he renewed his former familiarity and with a dissembling kindness persuaded her to lodge there with him all night. Which she, mistrustless [trusting] woman, consented to and little misdoubting his devilish intent, laid her down upon a pallet of straw by him to sleep, which as a token of hard misfortune suddenly possessed her. The cripple, perceiving all secure and silent and now thinking to be rid of the shame thus daily following him, took the woman's own girdle and putting the same slyly about her neck. Where though nature had denied him strength and limbs, yet by the help of the Devil, which always adds force to villainy, he made means in her sleep to strangle her and to take away her life, as it were suddenly without repentance. Therefore, all people by this example ought still to be prepared for death, for he comes as a thief in the night and gives no warning. Who would have thought such an outcast of the world, such a lame deformed creature, not able of his own strength to help himself, should have power to take away another's life? But the Devil, we see, is a-cunning and will still make the simple his strongest assisters and those that be the most weakest to be of the vilest thoughts.

But to conclude, the cripple, blinded thus with his own shame, had that ignorant opinion of the discovery hereof, that he thought the world too simple to look into his life and his decrepit carriage would keep away all suspicion, and that no man would think a lame creature could be able to do so wicked a deed. But graceless varlet[1] as he was, too much flattered in his own opinion, the Devil, as he was first beginner of his sin, so was he last end of his shame, for the same morning the woman was found thus murdered and being seen the night before in his company, with slender examinations confessed the fact. Wherefore the same he had his trial at the Sessions by a jury of twelve men and his execution at Tyburn in the sight of many hundreds of men, women, and children, which accounts him to be a monster by kind and the doer of a deed against nature.

The cripple's complaint in the dungeon at Newgate[2]

Methinks I hear a doleful sound,
Within this dungeon underground:
Prepare thyself (poor soul) to die,
For so the bellman's voice doth cry.

And beggars all come ring my knell,
The cripple now bids all farewell:
Both crutches, scrip, and patched gown,
Wherewith I begged from town to town.

Though limbs I want and could not go,
Yet was my mind not pleased so:
But had my faults, as others have,
Which brings me thus unto my grave.

In vain delights I spent my days,
And wronged my fortunes many ways:
The alms that good men gave me still,
I wasted to content my will.

For Heaven had marked me out for shame,
Whereto I did my courses frame:
And as I was misshaped by kind,
Deformed also was my mind.

For by that sweet enticing sin,
My sudden downfall did begin:
Wherein I set my heart's delight,
On wanton women day and night.

At last when I love's pleasures proved,
I hated her whom late I loved:
And sudden loathing, soon begun,
Ashamed sore, of follies done.

And still desired to end the life,
Of her I promised to make wife:
For love so gained can never last,
No sooner done, but love is past.

Then as my shame I hated her,
And would her death no time defer:

But armed with wrath in dead of night,
I trained her from all people's sight.

That never more my follies great,
To my disgrace she should repeat:
Nor say unto the world that I,
Had lived with her most wantonly.

For in the fields we two alone,
With weeping tears and bitter moan:
She craved amends for my amiss,
To make her wife as reason is.

But I refused that honest course,
But did an act of sad remorse:
To end her shame with mine as then,
I did exceed the deeds of men.

The Devil my helper at that hour,
For he as then had strongest power:
Nor by his means I could not faint,
Though I was lame and limbs did want.

My heart with furious rage possessed,
About her neck her girdle cast:
And forced so away her life,
Rather than make her married wife.

Never like deed by cripple wrought,
For pleasures being too dearly bought:
Both old and young, both rich and poor,
Make never maid a common whore.

For doing so my life I lose,
With burdens of repentant woes:
For wanton loves are wicked things,
And with them still much sorrow brings.

Adieu, vain world, the cripple dies,
In this my life much wonder lies:
That born a lame deformed wight,[3]
Should thus take pride in love's delight.

Like unto this viper of our age, we are to place in our discourse another caterpillar of nature, a creature more savage than a she-wolf, more unnatural
than either bird or beast, for every creature hath a tender feeling of love to
their young except some few murderous-minded strumpets. Women I cannot
call them, for a woman esteems the fruit of her own womb, the precious and
dearest jewel of the world, and for the cherishing of the same will (as it were)
spend her life's purest blood. Where contrariwise, the harlot (delighting in
shame and sin) makes no conscience to be the butcher of her own seed, nay,
the image of God created in her own body, and now and then in the concep-
tion makes spoil of the bed of creation before it can receive true form.

Therefore, for an example likewise cast your eyes upon this other monster
of nature which was a lascivious, lewd and close strumpet, a harlot lodging
privately near Bishopsgate in Bedlam[4] at a kinsman's house of her, which
little suspected this her unwomanly carriage. But shame long raked up in
the ashes of secrecy, though close smoking, will at last break forth into open
flame: so this graceless wanton (spending her youth in lascivious pleasures,
as many a-one doth in and about this city) happened to prove with child,
and having no husband to cover this her act of shame and withal fearing the
disgrace of the world, by a devilish practice sought to consume it in her body
before the birth. But not prevailing (as God would have it), she was forced by
nature to deliver it alive to the world and so was made the unhappy mother of
a man-child. Unhappy I may name her, for her own hand made her unhappy.
To our purpose, her lusty body, strong nature, and fear of shame brought an
easiness to her delivery and required in her agony no help of a midwife, which
among women seemeth a thing very strange, for not so much as the least child
in the house where she lodged had knowledge of her labour, nor hardly was
she thought to be with child, so closely demeaned she herself. But the Devil,
we see, adds force unto wickedness and puts a kind of strength to nature in
that kind, otherwise had she been discovered in the childbirth.

Consider this: the child being born with shame, and she by it made a
scandal to her acquaintance, renewed the remembrance of her past sins and
presented present shame unto her grieved thoughts, which troubled cogitations, by the persuasions of the Devil, put her in mind violently to make it
away, and to give it death before the body had well recovered life. Whereupon
taking the poor tender babe as it were new dropped from the mother's womb,
and, not like a mother, but a monster, threw it down into a loathsome privy
house, therein to give it an indecent grave and, as she thought, thereby make
to herself a riddance of a further infamy. But God is just and will reward
shame where it is deserved, and such unnatural deeds, let them be acted in
deserts, in the caverns of the earth where never light of day nor sun shines, yet
will they be discovered and brought to the world's eye. So happened it with
this harlot, when all fear of suspicion was past, she safely delivered, the child
in the privy smothered, and in the world no notice taken thereof.

Yet in the end was it thus most strangely discovered: the tunnel of the
aforesaid vault or privy ascended up into the next neighbour's house, as in

many places they do, where by chance (as God had ordained) dwelled an untoward lad that, in taking delight in knavish pastimes, took a cur dog[5] then using the house and carelessly threw it down the tunnel into the vault where the murdered infant lay, and taking no regard thereof, [he] suffered the dog to remain there starving and crying for food the space of three days and nights. During which time the yelping of the dog much disquieted the neighbours and so troubled the dwellers thereabouts that they could not sleep a-nights for the noise. But especially the good man of the house, who grieved to see a dumb beast so starved and for want of food thus to perish, like a kind natured man caused the privy to be opened and the poor cur taken up. Which proved by God's justice the only discoverer of the aforesaid fact, for in taking up the dog, they were woeful witnesses of the sweet babe lying all besmeared with the filth of that loathsome place. The sight whereof caused no small amazement, especially to the good man of the house, who with a diligent care (as his duty was both to God and his country) and that all such inhumane deeds might be brought to light, made it known to the magistrates. Which likewise, with Christian care, caused a certain number of substantial women to make search of suspected persons and of such who were like to be the murdered infant's mother or murderer, amongst many other loose livers and common harlots of which number those by-places have too many, the more is the pity.

This aforesaid murderess came to the touch,[6] where upon examination she confessed the child to be born with life and herself not worthy of life. And so pleading guilty, she was brought to her trial, and for the same arraigned and condemned by the bench of Assizes in the Old Bailey the 18st and 19th of July last 1614 and hath suffered death at Tyburn the 21st following as an example, that God, either by beasts of the field, fowls of the air, fishes in the seas, worms in the ground, or things bearing neither sense nor life, will by one means or other make deeds of darkness clear as day, that the world may behold his high-working powers, and that no malefactor can escape unpunished though his deeds be as secret as the work of Hell, beyond the thought of human imagination. Convert us from sin, great God of Israel, so shall we never be endangered with the like persuasions which God in his mercy grant. Amen.

Martha Scambler's repentance

Poor I, the poorest now on Earth,
May well accuse my cause of birth:
Not being born I ne'er had known,
This guilt that hath me overthrown.

Wo worth the cause of sin and shame,
Which stains my credit and good name:
Wo worth the trains which still are laid,
Whereby we women are betrayed.

When I was won to folly's will,
And took delight in doing ill:
No thought I had of pleasures past,
But still my youth did vainly waste.

Till at the length my womb did breed,
A substance of unlawful seed:
Which I suppos'd a shame to be,
(God knows) unto my friends and me.

And to prevent the world's disgrace,
I sought to find a secret place:
My shameful burdened womb to ease,
That way which did my God displease.

O, when my hour of labour came,
To bring to light this fruit of shame:
No midwife's help at all I sought,
But soon my own delivery wrought.

The babe being home and in my arms,
I should have kept it from all harms:
But like a bear or wolf in wood,
I wished it smothered up in blood.

Whereat strange motions without fear,
From Hell to me presented were:
And bade me bury it in a vault,
For none alive did know my fault.

And so my credit and good name,
Should take no spot of black defame:
And I as pure and chaste should be,
From such a crime as any she.

My soul then blinded by the Devil,
Bid me consent unto this evil:
Where I full soon thereto agreed,
To act a more than woman's deed.

The loathsome jakes [privy] received my child,
Which all misdoubts and fear exiled:
For being tumbled down therein,
There well might end my shame and sin.

But God, this deed more dark than night,
In wondrous sort did bring to light:
For by a dog the child was found,
As it was thrown therein to drowned.

Three days and nights with yelping cry,
It troubled much the dwellers by:
Which caused them to release him thence,
And so found out this vile offence.

For which I surely now must taste,
Rewards for my offences past:
And die for that accursed crime,
That makes me monster of my time.

Both maids and men, both young and old,
Let not good lives with shame be soiled:
But bear true virtues to your grave,
That honest burials you may have.

Notes

1 A dishonest or unprincipled person.
2 In the original, both ballads appear at the end of the text, rather than the structure shown here.
3 Commonly used to describe a person with a deformity or disability.
4 Bedlam is the derisive name given to Bethlem (or Bethlehem) Royal Hospital, which was then located at Bishopsgate, where Liverpool Street Station is today. It was commonly used to house mental and terminal patients.
5 Although the term "cur" usually refers to a mongrel or mutt in modern day, "cur dog" referred a dog bred for a specific purpose, such as herding cattle or hogs.
6 That is, she came within their grasp.

9 The hog-keeper and her daughter

Accusations of witchcraft were common occurrences in the seventeenth century. English society was in crisis politically, economically, and agriculturally (this was a time of frequent dearth and crop failure) and witchcraft was the safety-valve society used to explain its many misfortunes. The most common targets of witchcraft were poor, widowed, "relict" (post-menopausal) women, particularly those with contentious dispositions who operated outside of the normal gender and social boundaries of behaviour. Witches forsook God and consorted with the Devil, who entered into a covenant written in their own blood and suckled from them. This suckling was typically done by the familiar on a "third nipple," a blemish that was commonly sought on the witch's body as proof of her consortium. Once the covenant had been consummated through suckling, the Devil arranged vengeance on the witch's behalf. This was essential to demonstrating *maleficium*, or using witchcraft for evil deeds, which was an element that needed to be proven in felony trials for witchcraft. Another key means of determining whether a woman was a witch was to subject her to a "trial by water." This involved placing a rope around her waist or feet and thrusting her into the water. If she floated, she was guilty of being a witch because it meant that God had rejected receiving the fallen woman into the water, which was a symbol of baptism and belief in Jesus Christ. If she sank, she was accepted by God and acquitted, in which case the rope was used to haul her out before she drowned.

This richly detailed story of widow Sutton, her daughter Mary, and Mary's son Henry, was, therefore, entirely consistent with the early modern stereotype. Widow Sutton was poor and unpopular, her daughter Mary was a lewd woman with three bastard children, and Henry was a quarrelsome youth who disrespected authority. The women confessed to consorting with suckling familiars, taking on animal forms (a cow and a beetle), and directing their *maleficium* toward Master Enger's cattle, his horses, his servants, and finally his son, in the process bringing about perplexity, lameness, languor, and death. Various tests were conducted on Mary – who was quite violently handled in the process – to confirm their suspicions: drawing blood from her, which helped to revive the servant, and subjecting her to both the trial by water and the searching of the body for the Devil's mark. These tests proved that Mary

Sutton was a witch and she and her mother were subsequently brought to the Assizes, convicted, and executed. Whether or not the Suttons were witches, they certainly breached the boundaries of behaviour that were expected of women and poor people at this time, and the community was brought back to balance by the removal of these women from society.

***

Witches apprehended, examined, and executed, for notable villainies by them committed both by land and water. With a strange and most true trial how to know whether a woman be a witch or not. *London: Printed for Edward Marchant, and are to be sold at his shop over against the cross in Paul's Churchyard, 1613*

The several and damnable practices of Mother Sutton and Mary Sutton, her daughter, of Milton Mills[1] in the county of Bedford, who were lately arraigned, convicted, and executed

Pliny writes of some kind of serpents that dare not approach the wild ash tree,[2] nay, the sight of it is so terrible to them, they fly from it and will not draw near the shadow thereof. But if they be walled round with fire they will rather run through to the confusion of themselves than endure it. If it were so with us which profess ourselves Christians and should be Christ's sons to imitate our Father and Saviour in His life, which He left as a lesson to mankind His children to learn, we should then, having reason (part of the inheritance of angels), be more provident of our proper good than serpents are. Who, to avoid the persecution of their mind, will endure the affliction of their body, and to shun the very shadow of the ash tree will thrust themselves into torment of fire.

So should men, who seeing sin like a wild ash tree grow in the world, and that to lurk under the shadow thereof is a whip to their conscience, when to feed on the sap is damnation to their souls, in this like serpents avoid it for the relief of their minds, though with the painful dissolution of their bodies. But such is the deafness of our ears, that though Heaven itself speak in thunder to remember [remind] us a day shall come when we must give account for our willful transgressions, we do not regard it, and such is the hardness of our hearts that neither treasons, murders, witchcrafts, fires, floods, of all which the impetuous course hath been such in this age, that we have cause to think our day of summons is tomorrow, if not this hour. Yet we are unprepared of our account, and as if it were lawful that evils should grow, many from one, and one from another, are as corn is fruitful from one seed to several ears. So from one sin we multiply to diverse, not dreading vengeance till our iniquities be numberless, as shall appear by this following discourse.

At a place called Milton some three miles from Bedford was lately dwelling one Mother Sutton, who, being a widow and of declining years, had her daughter called Mary Sutton (as it was thought by the neighbours thereabouts) resident with her as a stay and comfort to her age, when [in fact] she kept her but as a furtherer to her devilish practices, nay, indeed to make her to a scholar to the Devil himself. This widow Sutton, having been dwelling a long time in the foresaid town of Milton and not suspected as then to have been a practiser in this devilish exercise of witchcraft, was by the townsmen (being held but poor) for her better relief chosen to be the hogherd or hog-keeper. In which service she continued long, not without commendations for her dutiful care had therein. And though many cattle oftentimes miscarried and were taken with staggerings, frenzies, and other diseases to their confusions and impoverishing of the owners, yet she not till of late suspected to be a cause thereof, though since it hath evidently been proved against her.

Continuing thus almost for the space of twenty or one and twenty years, and in that time had brought her daughter to be as perfect in her devilish charms as herself, there grew some difference between a gentleman of worship called Master Enger dwelling at Milton Mills, and this mother Sutton, on whom she had vowed to take a strange and actual revenge for the discontent she had conceived against him. Which rancour of hers she thus prosecuted: His horses that were left well in his stable overnight, she caused them to be found dead in the morning, some strangled, some having beaten out their brains, others dead, and no cause perceived how. Besides this loss, which for the strangeness bred some amazement in him, for that it happened not once but often, this also did second it: When his swine were in the fields at their troughs eating their meat, some of them would suddenly fall mad and violently fall to tearing out the guts and bowels of their fellows. Others, by ten and twenty in a company as if they had been carried with one desire, would leave their feeding and run headlong into the mill dams and drown themselves. So that not by accidental means but the hellish and most damnable witchcrafts of this Mother Sutton and her daughter, many these harmless cattle and oxen, made as needful reliefs to the necessity of man, were thus perplexed, and an honest and worshipful gentleman, Master Enger, from whom she had oftentimes both food and clothing, damnified [injured] by her means to the value of two hundred pounds in less than two years.

In the time these aforesaid losses happened to Master Enger, one Henry Sutton, the bastard son of Mary Sutton (for it is to be noted that although she was never married, yet she had three bastards), coming to play himself about the mill dam, fell to throwing in of stones, dirt, and filth with other such unhappiness incident to children. Of which having been often forewarned by an ancient servant of Master Enger's, who was then about the mills, and finding the boy notwithstanding his admonishment rather to persevere than to desist from his knavery, he came to him and giving him a little blow or two on the ear. The boy went home crying and the ancient fellow went back to his labour. This Henry Sutton, coming home, began to tell his mother how a man of Master Enger's (naming him) had beaten him, whose venomous nature being soon enkindled, though he had received no hurt, she vowed to take revenge, and thus it followed:

This ancient servant with another of his master's men were on the morrow, being market day at Bedford, appointed by their master to carry a cartload of corn for the furnishing of the market. Being on their way at Milton town's end, they espied a goodly fair black sow grazing, who, as they drove their team, still kept pace with them till they came within a mile of Bedford. Where on a sudden they perceived her to turn twice or thrice about, as readily as a windmill sail at work, and as suddenly their horses fell to starting and drawing, some one way, some another. At last the strongest prevailing, they drew away the cart and corn and left the wheels and axletree behind them. The horses, they ran away with their load as if they had been mad and the two fellows after the horses. The horses, being affrighted half out of their strength, and the fellows as much mad to see them, down went one sack on this side the cart and another on that. The horses, they ran as if they would have swelted [exhausted] themselves, and the fellows after them breathless and sweating to make the wild jades stay. All which till the Devil and the witch had played their parts would not serve turn.

At last this tragic comedy drawing to an end, they made a stand, when the servants bringing them back and finding their axletree, pins, and all things unbroken, took up their corn, made fit their cart again, and the horses drew as formally as could be. And they went forthwards towards Bedford, mistrusting nothing though they saw the sow following and grazing as they did before.

Being come to Bedford and having unloaden the cart and made sale of the corn, the one fell to driving the team home again, leaving his ancienter fellow behind him at Bedford, who happening into company fell a-carousing with boon [pleasant] companions like himself, and in the height of their cups, they as desirous to hear as he to tell, he related unto them the manner and form how his cart and wheels were divorced as he was coming to town. Some wondered, all laughed. The company broke up, and this ancient servant took his horse with purpose to overtake his fellow who was gone before with the cart.

Who no sooner was out of Bedford town's end but he might behold the same sow (as near as he could judge) grazing again, as if the Devil and the witch had made her his footman to wait upon him. But the fellow, not mistrusting anything, made his nag take a speedy amble and so to overtake the cart, while the sow side by side ran along by him. When he overtaking his fellow, and had scarce spoken to him but the horses (as before) fell to their old contention running one from another. Only the horses were better furnished than before, for where at first they left both wheels and axletree behind them, they now had the axletree to take their part, leaving the wheels in the highway for the servants to bring after. The horse, in this manner coming home, drove all the beholders into amazement, and the servants beginning to have mistrust of the black sow, they watched whither she went, whom they found to go into Mother Sutton's house. Of which they told their master, and of all the accidents aforesaid, who made slight of it to them, whatsoever he conceived of it himself, and saying he supposed they were drunk, they departed.

The same old servant of Master Enger's, within few days after going to plough, fell into talk of Mother Sutton and of Mary Sutton her daughter, of what pranks he had heard they had played thereabouts in the country, as also what accidents had befallen him and his fellow as they had passed to and from Bedford. In discoursing of which a beetle came and struck the same fellow on the breast, and he presently fell into a trance as he was guiding the plough, the extremity whereof was such as his senses altogether distracted and his body and mind utterly distempered. The beholders deemed him clean hopeless of recovery, yea, his other fellow, upon this sudden sight, was stricken into such amazement as he stood like a lifeless trunk divided from his vital spirits, as far unable to help him as the other was needful to be helped by him. Till at length being somewhat recovered and awaked from that astonishment, he made haste homeward and carried his master word of what had happened.

Upon delivery of this news (for he was a man highly esteemed by him for his honest and long service) there was much moan made for him in the house, and Master Enger himself had not the least part of grief for his extremity, but with all possible speed hastened into the field and used help to have him brought home. After which he neglected no means nor spared any cost that might ease his servant or redeem him from the misery he was in. But all was in vain, for his ecstasies were nothing lessened but continued a long time in as grievous perplexity as at first. Yet though they suspected much, they had no certain proof or knowledge of the cause, their means were therefore the shorter to cure the effect.

But as a thief, when he entereth into a house to rob first putteth out the lights, according to that, *Qui male agit, odit lucem* – he that doth evil, hateth light – so these imps that live in the gunshot of devilish assaults go about to darken and disgrace the light of such as are toward and virtuous, and make the night the instrument to contrive their wicked purposes. For these witches, having so long and covertly continued to do much mischief by their practices, were so hardened in their lewd and vile proceeding that the custom of their sin had quite taken away the sense and feeling thereof. And they spared not to continue the perplexity of this old servant both in body and mind, in such sort that his friends were as desirous to see death rid him from his extremity as a woman great with child is ever musing upon the time of her delivery. For where distress is deep and the conscience clear, *Mors expectatur absque formidine, exoptatur cum dulcedine, excipitur cum devotione* – death is looked for without fear, desired with delight, and accepted with devotion.

As the acts and enterprises of these wicked persons are dark and devilish, so in the perseverance of this fellow's perplexity, he being in his distraction both of body and mind, yet in bed and awake, espied Mary Sutton (the daughter) in a moonshine night come in at a window in her accustomed and personal habit and shape, with her knitting work in her hands, and sitting down at his bed's feet, sometimes working and knitting with her needles and sometimes gazing and staring him in the face, as his grief was thereby redoubled and increased. Not long after, she drew nearer unto him and sat by his bedside (yet all this while he had neither power to stir or speak) and told him if he would consent she should come to bed to him, he should be restored to his former health and prosperity.

Thus the Devil strives to enlarge his kingdom and upon the neck of one wickedness to heap another. So that *Periculum probat transeuntium raritas, pereuntium multitudo*: in the dangerous sea of this world, the rareness of those that pass the same over safe, and the multitude of others that perish in their passage sufficiently prove the peril we live in. In the ocean sea, of four ships not one miscarries. In the sea of this world of many sowers, not one escapes his particular cross and calamity. Yet in our greatest weakness and debility, when the Devil is most busy to tempt us and seduce us from God, then is God strongest in the hearts of his children and most ready to be auxiliant, and helping to save and uphold them from declining and falling. God's liberality appears more than his rigour, for whom he draws out the Devil's throat by faith, he would have to trample him down by virtue lest he should only have fled, not foiled his enemy.

This is made shown in his miraculous working with this fellow, for he that before had neither power to move or speak had then presently by divine assistance free power and liberty to give repulse to her assault and denial to her filthy and detested motion, and to upbraid her of her abominable life and behaviour, having before had three bastards and never married. She upon this (seeing her suit cold and that God's power was more predominant with him than her devilish practice) vanished, and departed the same way she came.

She was no sooner gone but, as well as he could, he called for his master, told him that now he could tell him the cause of this vexation: that Mother Sutton's daughter came in at the window, sat knitting and working by him, and that if he would have consented to her filthiness he should have been freed from his misery, and related all that had happened. His master was glad of this news, for that the means found out, the matter and manner of his grief might be the easier helped and redressed. Yet was he distrustful of the truth, and rather esteemed it an idleness of his brain than an accident of verity. Nevertheless he resolved to make proof thereof.

The next morrow he took company along with him and went into the fields, where he found her working and tending her hogs. There Master Enger speaking to her, she was a very good housewife and that she followed her work night and day. "No sir," said she, "my housewifery is very slender; neither am I so good a follower of my work as you persuade me." With that, he told her that she was, and that she had been working at his house the night before. She would confess nothing, but stood in stiff denial upon her purgation [oath], insomuch as the gentleman by fair entreaties persuaded her to go home with him to satisfy his man and to resolve some doubts that were had of her. She utterly refused, and made answer she would not stir a foot, neither had they authority to compel her to go without a constable. Which Master Enger perceiving and seeing her obstinacy to be so great, fell into a greater dislike and distrust of her than he did before, and made no more ado, but caused her to be set upon a horseback to be brought to his house.

All the company could hardly bring her away, but as fast as they set her up, in despite of them she would swerve down, first on the one side, then the other, till at last they were fain by main force to join together and hold her violently down to the horseback and so bring her to the place where this perplexed person lay in his bed. Where being come and brought by force to his bedside, he (as directions had been given unto him) drew blood of her and presently began to amend and be well again. But her assiduity and continual exercise in doing mischief did so prevail with her to do this fellow further hurt, that watching but advantage and opportunity to touch his neck again with her finger. It was no sooner done and she departed, but he fell into as great or far worse vexation than he had before.

The report of this was carried up and down all Bedfordshire, and this Mary Sutton's wicked and lewd courses being rumoured as well abroad as in Master Enger's house. At last it came into the mouth of Master Enger's son (being a little boy of seven years old), who not long after espying old Mother Sutton going to the mill to grind corn, and remembering what speeches he had heard past of her and her daughter, followed the old woman, flinging stones at her, and calling her witch. Which she observing conceited a rancour and deadly hatred to this young child, and purposed not to suffer opportunity pass to be revenged. As soon, therefore, as she had dispatched at the mill, she hastened homewards, and could not be quiet till she had grumbled to her daughter what had happened, and how the child had served her. Then, conferring how Master Enger had used Mary Sutton the daughter, and how her little son had used the mother, they both resolved and vowed revenge. This conference and consultation of villainy was had and concluded in the presence and hearing of Henry Sutton (the bastard of Mary Sutton), little thinking that his fortune should be to give in evidence to break the neck of his own mother and grandmother.

To effect their devilish purpose to the young child of Master Enger, they called up their two spirits, whom she called Dick and Jude, and having given them suck at their two teats which they had on their thighs (found out afterwards by enquiry, and search of women) they gave them charge to strike the little boy and to turn him to torment. Which was not long in performing but the child, being distract, was put to such bitter and unsupportable misery, as by his life his torments were augmented, and by his death they were abridged. For his tender and unripe age was so enfeebled and made weak by that devilish infliction of extremity as in five days, not able longer to endure them, death gave end to his perplexities.

The gentleman did not so much grieve for the loss and hindrance he had in his cattle (which was much), nor for the miserable distress that his servant had endured (which was more), as that the hopeful days of his young son were so untimely cut off (which touched his heart most of all). Yet did his discretion temper his passions with such patience that he referred the remembrance of his wrongs to that heavenly power that permits not such iniquity to pass unrevealed or unrevenged.

As he was thus wrapped in a sea of woes, there came a gentleman, a friend of his forth of the North, that travelling towards London sojourned with him all night. He perceiving Master Enger to be full of grief, was desirous to know the cause thereof, and he was as unwilling by the discourse of his misfortunes to renew his many sorrows, till at last his friend's urgent importunacy persuaded him not to pass it over with silence. Upon Master Enger's relation of what had happened, the gentleman demanded if he had none in suspicion that should do these wrongs unto him? "Yes," quoth Master Enger, and therewithal he named this Mary Sutton and her mother, and told him the particulars of his losses and miseries. His friend understanding this, advised him to take them, or any one of them, to his mill dam, having first shut up the mill gates that the water might be at highest, then binding their arms cross, stripping them into their smocks, and leaving their legs at liberty, throw them into the water. "Yet, lest they should not be witches, and that their lives might not be in danger of drowning, let there be a rope tied about their middles, so long that it may reach from one side of your dam to the other, where on each side let one of your men stand, that if she chance to sink they may draw her up and preserve her. Then, if she swim, take her up and cause some women to search her. Upon which, if they find any extraordinary marks about her, let her the second time be bound, and have her right thumb bound to her left toe and her left thumb to her right toe, and your men with the same rope (if need be) to preserve her, and be thrown into the water, when if she swim, you may build upon it that she is a witch. I have seen it often tried in the North country."

Figure 9.1 Woodcut image from *Witches apprehended, examined, and executed, for notable villainies by them committed*, 1613. This image depicts a "trial by water," the method commonly used to determine whether a woman was a witch. Men on either side of the river hold a rope that is used to drag the woman from the water after the test. The image also shows various scenes from the chapbook in which it appears, including a wagon damaged by the witch's familiar, an animal that performed evil deeds in the witch's name.

Source: Reproduced with permission of the Bodleian Library, Oxford University.

The morrow after, Master Enger rode into the fields where Mary Sutton (the daughter) was, having some of his men to accompany him, where after some questions made unto her they assayed to bind her on horseback. When all his men being presently stricken lame, Master Enger himself began to remember that once [be]rating her about his man he was on the sudden in the like perplexity. And then taking courage and desiring God to be his assistance, with a cudgel which he had in his hand he beat her till she was scarce able to stir. At which his men presently recovered, bound her to their master's horse, and brought her home to his house, and shutting up his mill gates did as before the gentleman had advised him. When being thrown in the first time she sunk some two foot into the water with a fall, but rose again and floated upon the water like a plank. Then he commanded her to be taken out and had women ready that searched her and found under her left thigh a kind of teat, which after the bastard son confessed her spirits in several shapes, as cats, moles, etc., used to suck her.

Then was she the second time bound cross her thumbs and toes, according to the former direction, and then she sunk not at all, but sitting upon the water turned round about like a wheel or as that which commonly we call a whirlpool. Notwithstanding Master Enger's men standing on each side of the dam with a rope tossing her up and down to make her sink but could not.

And then being taken up she, as boldly as if she had been innocent, asked them if they could do any more to her. Master Enger began to accuse her with the death of his cattle, the languish of his man who continued in sorrow both of body and mind from Christmas to Shrovetide, as also the death of his son. All which she constantly denied and stood at defiance with him till, being carried towards a justice, Master Enger told her it was bootless to stand so obstinately upon denial of those matters, for her own son Henry had revealed all, both as touching herself and her mother, and of the time and manner of their plotting to torment his little boy. When she heard that, her heart misgave her, she confessed all, and acknowledged the Devil had now left her to that shame that is reward to such as follow him. Upon which confession the mother also was apprehended, and both being committed to Bedford Gaol, many other matters were there produced against them, of long continuance (for they had remained as before, about twenty years) in the prosecute of these lewd and wicked practices. But, for this matter of Master Enger, at the last Assizes, the evidence of the bastard son and the confessions severally taken both of old Mother Sutton and her daughter Mary, found them guilty in all former objections. So that arraigned at Bedford on Monday the thirtieth of March last past, they had a just conviction, and on Tuesday the next day after they were executed.

Notes

1 Very likely today's Milton Ernest, located about 8km north of Bedford.
2 Pliny the Elder, *Natural History* (circa AD 77–79).

10 The gentlewoman's unnatural crimes

The murders committed by Margaret Vincent against her own children were particularly heinous, in large part because Margaret was known to be a sober, civil, witty, and educated gentlewoman. As a gentlewoman, she was supposed to be a paragon of virtue in a society that respected rank and looked to the upper orders to learn how to behave with propriety and modesty. After her crime, Margaret was "now deserving no name of gentlewoman." Her crimes were also heinous because they involved the killing of her own children. (Technically, this is not infanticide, which involved the killing of babies under one year old, whereas the children Margaret strangled were toddlers.) The author could only conclude that Margaret had been bewitched, else no woman could commit so unnatural an act as to murder her own children. Indeed, after her crime, not only was Margaret no longer worthy of being called a gentlewoman, she was a "creature not deserving mother's name," and (rather like John Arthur and Martha Scambler discussed in Chapter 8) was "more unnatural than pagan, cannibal, savage, beast or fowl." Finally, Margaret's crimes were horrible because they deprived her husband of his family and his happiness. Through these murders, therefore, Margaret lost the three things that best classified her in early modern English society: her status as a gentlewoman, a good wife, and a loving mother.

According to the anonymous author of this chapbook, Margaret's crimes were motivated by her conversion to Roman Catholicism. As we have already seen, and will see in subsequent tales, this is a common theme in the crime chapbook genre, in which "papists" are often depicted as deceitful anti-Christs thirsting after the blood of true Christians. Here, the author is almost sympathetic to Margaret: like the Devil's ease of enticing "the female kind" and the "weak sex" to witchcraft, so too were Catholics so persuasive that even an honest gentlewoman could easily be ensnared by their charms, like a bird caught in a trap. Her husband, Jarvis, was not so "easily removed" from his faith, and accounted Margaret "vain and frivolous" for attempting to bring about his conversion. Thus denied her chance at converting her family, Margaret became convinced that she had to end the lives of any Protestants who opposed the Catholic faith. She targeted her children for these murders because they had been "hoodwinked . . . from the true light" by her husband.

While in prison awaiting death, she became repentant of her actions, and the author is convinced that, despite "the blood of her two innocent children so willfully shed," her sins were washed away "by the mercies of God." More than anything, this book is a warning to women, and especially "good gentle-women," to be careful around Catholics, and to be good wives and mothers, all of which were familiar themes in the crime chapbook genre.

***

A pitiless mother, that most unnaturally at one time murdered two of her own children, at Acton within six miles from London, upon Holy Thursday last 1616, the ninth of May. Being a gentlewoman named Margaret Vincent, wife of Mr. Jarvis Vincent of the same town. With her examination, confession and true discovery of all proceedings in the said bloody accident. {London, 1616?}

How easy are the ways unto evil, and how soon are our minds (by the Devil's enticement) withdrawn from goodness. Leviathan,[1] the archenemy of man-kind, hath set such and so many bewitching snares to entrap us that unless we continually stand watching with careful diligence to shun them, we are like to cast the principal substance of our reputation upon the rack of his ensnaring engines. As for example, a gentlewoman, ere now fresh in memory, presents her own ruin amongst us, whose life's overthrow may well serve for a clear looking-glass [mirror] to see a woman's weakness in, how soon and apt she is won unto wickedness, not only to the body's overthrow but the soul's danger. God of his mercy keep us all from the like wilfulness.

At Acton, some six miles westward from London, this unfortunate gentle-woman dwelled, named Margaret Vincent, the wife of Mr. Jarvis Vincent, gentleman, who by unhappy destiny marked to mischance I here now make the subject of my pen and publish her hard hap unto the world, that all others may shun the like occasions by which she was overthrown.

This Margaret Vincent before named, of good parentage, born in the county of Hertford at a town named Rickmansworth, her name from her parents Margaret Day, of good education, graced with good parts from her youth that promised succeeding virtues in her age, if good luck had served. For being discreet, civil, and of a modest conversation, she was preferred in marriage to this gentleman Master Vincent, with whom she lived in good estimation, well beloved and much esteemed of all that knew her for her modest and seemly carriage. And so might have continued to her old age, had not this bloody accident committed upon her own children blemished the glory of the same.

But now mark (gentle reader) the first entrance into her life's overthrow, and consider with thyself how strangely the Devil here set in his foot and what cunning instruments he used in his assailments. The gentlewoman being witty and of a ripe understanding desired much conference in religion, and being careful, as it seemed, of her soul's happiness, many times resorted to divines to have instructions to salvation, little thinking to fall into the hands of Roman wolves (as she did) and to have the sweet lamb, her soul, thus entangled by their persuasions.

Twelve or fourteen years had she lived in marriage with her husband well beloved, having for their comforts diverse pretty children between them with all other things in plenty, as health, riches, and such like, to increase concord and no necessity that might be hindrance to contentment. Yet at last there was such traps and engines set that her quet[2] was caught and her discontent set at liberty. Her opinion of the true faith (by the subtle sophistry of some close Papists) was converted to a blind belief of bewitching heresy. For they have such charming persuasions that hardly the female kind can escape their enticements, of which weak sex they continually make prize of and by them lay plots to ensnare others, as they did by this deceived gentlewoman. For she, good soul, being made a bird of their own feather, desired to beget more of the same kind and from time to time made persuasive arguments to win her husband to the same opinion, and deemed it a meritorious deed to charge his conscience with that infectious burden of Romish opinions, affirming by many false reasons that his former life had been led in blindness, and that she was appointed by the Holy Church to shew him the light of true understanding. These and such like were the instructions she had given her to entangle her husband in and win him if she might to their blind heresies.

But he, good gentleman, over-deeply grounded in the right faith of religion than to be thus so easily removed, grew regardless of her persuasions, accounting them vain and frivolous, and she undutiful to make so fond an attempt, many times snubbing her with some few unkind speeches, which bred in her heart a purpose of more extremity. For having learned this maxim of their religion that it was meritorious, yea, and pardonable, to take away the lives of any opposing Protestants were it of any degree whatsoever, in which resolution or bloody purpose she long stood upon and at last (only by the Devil's temptation) resolved the ruin of her own children, affirming to her conscience these reasons: that they were brought up in blindness and darksome errors, hoodwinked (by her husband's instructions) from the true light, and therefore to save their soul (as she vainly thought) she purposed to become a tigerous mother, and so wolfishly to commit the murder of her own flesh and blood. In which opinion she steadfastly continued, never relenting according to nature but casting about to find time and place for so wicked a deed, which unhappily fell out as after followed.

It so chanced that a discord arose between the two towns of Acton and Willesden about a certain common bordering between them, where the town of Acton, as it seems, having the more right unto it, by watching defended it a time from the other's cattle. Whereupon the women of the same town, having likewise a willingness to assist their husbands in the same defence, appointed a day for the like purpose, which was the Ascension Day last past, commonly called Holy Thursday, falling upon the 9th of the last past month of May. Which day (as ill chance would have it) was the fatal time appointed for her to act this bloody tragedy, whereon she made her husband fatherless of two as pretty children as ever came from woman's womb.

Upon the Ascension Day aforesaid, after the time of divine service, the women of the town being gathered together about their promised business, some of them came to Mistress Vincent and according to promise desired her company. Who having a mind as then more settled on bloody purposes than country occasions, feigned an excuse of ill at ease and not half well, desired pardon of them, and offering her maid in her behalf, who being a good, apt, and willing servant was accepted of, and so the townswomen, misdoubting no such hard accident as after happened, proceeded in their aforesaid defences. The gentlewoman's husband being also from home, in whose absence, by the fury and assistance of the Devil, she enacted this woeful accident in form and manner following.

This Mistress Vincent, now deserving no name of gentlewoman, being in her own house fast locked up only with her two small children, the one of the age of five years, the other hardly two years old, unhappily brought to that age to be made away by their own mother, who by nature should have cherished them with her own body, as the pelican that pecks her own breast to feed her young ones with her blood. But she, more cruel than the viper, the envenomed serpent, the snake, or any beast whatsoever, against all kind, takes away those lives to whom she first gave life.

Being alone (as I said before) assisted by the Devil, she took the youngest of the two, having a countenance so sweet that might have begged mercy at a tyrant's hand, but she regarding neither the pretty smiles it made nor the dadling [wobbling] before the mother's face, nor anything it could do, but like a fierce and bloody Medea[3] she took it violently by the throat, and with a garter taken from her leg, making thereof a noose and putting the same about her child's sweet neck, she in a wrathful manner drew the same so close together that in a moment she parted the soul and body. Without any terror of conscience she laid the lifeless infant, still remaining warm, upon her bed and with a relentless countenance looking thereon, thinking thereby she had done a deed of immortality. Oh, blinded ignorance! Oh, inhumane devotion! Purposing by this to merit Heaven, she hath deserved (without true repentance) the reward of damnation.

This creature not deserving mother's name, as I said before, not yet glutted nor sufficed with these few drops of innocent blood, nay, her own dear blood bred in her own body, cherished in her own womb with much dearness full forty weeks. Not satisfied, I say, with this one murder but she would headlong run unto a second and to heap more vengeance upon her head. She came unto the elder child of that small age that it could hardly discern a mother's cruelty nor understand the fatal destiny fallen upon the other before, which as it were seemed to smile upon her as though it begged for pity, but all in vain, for so tyrannous was her heart that without all motherly pity she made it drink of the same bitter cup as she had done the other. For with her garter she likewise pressed out the sweet air of life and laid it by the other upon the bed sleeping in death together, a sight that might have burst an iron heart asunder and made the very tiger to relent.

These two pretty children being thus murdered, without all hope of recovery, she began to grow desperate and still to desire more and more blood, which had been a third murder of her own babes, had it not been abroad at nurse and by that means could not be accomplished. Whereupon she fell into a violent rage, purposing as then to shew the like mischief upon herself, being of this strange opinion that she herself by that deed had made saints of her two children in Heaven. So taking the same garter that was the instrument of their deaths and putting the noose thereof about her own neck, she strove therewith to have strangled herself. But nature being weak and flesh frail, she was not able to do it. Whereupon in a more violent fury (still animated forward by instigation of the Devil) she ran into the yard purposing there in a pond to have drowned herself, having not one good motion of salvation left within her.

But here, good reader, mark what a happy prevention chanced to preserve her in hope of repentance, which at that time stayed her from that desperate attempt. The maid, by great fortune, at the very instant of this deed of desperation returned from the field or common where she had left most of the neighbours. And coming in at the backside, perceiving her mistress by her ghastly countenance that all was not well and that some hard chance had happened her or hers, demanded how the children did.

"Oh Nan," quoth she, "never, oh never, shalt thou see thy Tom more," and withal gave the maid a box upon the ear. At which she laid hold upon her mistress, calling out for help into the town. Whereat diverse came running in and after them her husband, within a while after, who finding what had happened were all so amazed together that they knew not what to do. Some wrung their hands, some wept, some called out for neighbours; so general a fear was struck amongst them all that they knew not whether to go nor run.

Especially the good gentleman her husband, that seeing his own children slain, murdered by his wife and their own mother, a deed beyond nature and humanity, in which ecstasy of grief at last he broke out in these speeches: "Oh Margaret, Margaret, how often have I persuaded thee from this damned opinion, this damned opinion that hath undone us all."

Whereupon with a ghastly look and fearful eye she replied thus, "Oh Jarvis, this had never been done if thou hadst been ruled and by me converted. But what is done is past, for they are saints in Heaven, and I nothing at all repent it."

These and such like words passed betwixt them till such time as the constable and others of the townsmen came in and according to law carried her before a justice of the peace, which is a gentleman named Master Roberts of Willesden, who, understanding these heinous offences, rightly according to law and course of justice made a *mittimus* for her conveyance to Newgate in London, there to remain till the Sessions of her trial. Yet this is to be remembered that by examination she voluntarily confessed the fact how she murdered them to save their souls and to make them saints in Heaven, that they might not be brought up in blindness to their own damnation. Oh, wilful heresy, that ever Christian should in conscience be thus miscarried. But to be short, she proved herself to be an obstinate papist, for there was found about her neck a crucifix with other relics which she then wore about her, that by the justice was commanded to be taken away and an English Bible to be delivered her to read, the which she with great stubbornness threw from her, not willing as once to look thereupon, nor to hear any divine comforts delivered thereout for the succour of her soul.

But now again to her conveyance towards prison. It being Ascension Day and near the closing of the evening, too late as then to be sent to London she was by commandment put to the constable's keeping for that night, who with a strong watch lodged her in his own house till morning, which was at the Bell in Acton where he dwelled. Shewing the part and duty of a good Christian, with diverse other of his neighbours, all that same night they plied her with good admonitions, tending to repentance, and seeking with great pains to convert her from those erroneous opinions which she so stubbornly stood in. But it little availed, for she seemed in outward shew so obstinate in arguments that she made small reckoning of repentance, nor was a whit sorrowful for the murder committed upon her children but maintained the deed to be meritorious and of high desert.

Oh, that the blood of her own body should have no more power to pierce remorse into her iron natured heart, when pagan women that know not God nor have any feeling of his deity will shun to commit bloodshed, much more of their own seed. The cannibals that eat one another will spare the fruits of their own bodies; the savages will do the like; yea, every beast and fowl hath a feeling of nature, and according to kind will cherish their young ones. And shall woman, nay, a Christian woman, God's own image, be more unnatural than pagan, cannibal, savage, beast, or fowl? It even now makes a trembling fear to beset me to think what an error this unhappy gentlewoman was bewitched with, a witchcraft begot by Hell and nursed by the Romish sect, from which enchantment God of Heaven defend us.

But now again to our purpose. The next day being Friday and the tenth of May, by the Constable Master Dighton of the Bell in Acton, with other of his neighbours, she was conveyed to Newgate in London. Where lodging in the master's side, many people resorted to her, as well of her acquaintance as others and as before, with sweet and comfortable persuasions practised to beget repentance and to be sorry for that which she had committed. But blindness so prevailed that she continued still in her former stubbornness, affirming (contrary to all persuasive reasons) that she had done a deed of charity in making them saints in Heaven that otherwise might have lived to destruction in Hell, and likewise refused to look upon any Protestant book as Bible, meditation, prayer book, and such like, affirming them to be erroneous and dangerous for any Romish Catholic to look in. Such were the violent opinions she had been instructed in, and with such fervencies therein she continued that no dissuasions could withdraw her from them, no, not death itself, being here possessed with such bewitching wilfulness.

In this danger of mind continued she all Friday, Saturday, and Sunday. The Sessions drawing near, there came certain godly preachers unto her, who prevailed with her by celestial consolations, that her heart by degrees became a little mollified and in nature somewhat repentant for these her most heinous offences. Her soul, a little leaning to salvation, encouraged these good men to persevere and go forward in so godly a labour, who at last brought her to this opinion, as it was justified by one that came from her in Newgate upon the Monday before the Sessions: that she earnestly believed she had eternally deserved hellfire for the murder of her children, and that she so earnestly repented the deed, saying that if they were alive again not all the world should procure her to do it. Thus was she truly repentant, to which (no doubt) but by the good means of these preachers she was wrought unto.

And now to come to a conclusion, as well of the discourse as of her life, she deserved death, and both law and justice hath awarded her the same. For her examination and free confession needed no jury: her own tongue proved a sufficient evidence, and her conscience a witness that condemned her. Her judgment and execution she received with a patient mind, her soul no doubt hath got a true penitent desire to be in Heaven, and the blood of her two innocent children so wilfully shed (according to all charitable judgements) is washed away by the mercies of God. Forgive and forget her, good gentlewomen. She is not the first that hath been blemished with blood nor the last that will make a husband wifeless. Her offence was begot by a strange occasion but buried, I hope, with true repentance.

Thus, countrymen of England, have you heard the ruin of a gentlewoman who, if Popish persuasions had not been, the world could not have spotted her with the smallest mark of infamy but had carried the name of virtue even unto her grave. And for a warning unto you all, by her example, take heed how you put confidence unto that dangerous sect, for they surely will deceive you.

Notes

1 The Leviathan is a menacing sea monster mentioned several times in the Old Testament (Job 41:1–34, Psalms 74 and 104, and Isaiah 27:1).
2 A quet was a small bird, commonly known as a guillemot or pigeon, for which traps were often set. In this case, it refers to Margaret Vincent being ensnared by Catholics.
3 A goddess of Greek mythology known for being a vengeful murderess and sorceress.

11 The unhappy litigant

The murder of Sir John Tindall caused a great stir in 1616. After losing a lawsuit in the notoriously slow and disreputable Court of Chancery, septuagenarian John Barterham (elsewhere his name is spelled "Bertram") determined to murder the master who decided against him, on the grounds that he was ridding England of a corrupt official who was prone to bribery and bias. (Technically, masters made recommendations to the lord chancellor and common law judges, who made the final decision.) The murder quickly came to the attention of Sir Francis Bacon, the attorney general, who was so alarmed at the murder of one of the king's judges that he interrogated Barterham personally. There is some evidence that Bacon commissioned this chapbook in order to send a clear message to readers about how disputes of this nature should be handled. Even though Barterham lost his suit in Chancery, which the author admits might well have been a result of corruption or bribery, the unhappy litigant had the opportunity to petition the king's Privy Council for better treatment at law, or to appeal to the king, who was the fount of justice and the ultimate arbiter of the law. Magistrates were subject to human frailties, made errors in law, and were sometimes corrupt, but instead of resorting to the mechanisms that existed to resolve his dispute, and showing patience and forbearance, Barterham took the law into his own hands and then took his own life, rather than showing the "selfsame stoutness of mind" and "masculine fortitude" to "defend his act" in court and die with "his former courage." The author makes it clear that no amount of judicial error or corruption authorized Barterham (or anybody reading this story) to take the law into his own hands. Yet the chapbook is also a warning to those who adjudge legal matters that they must avoid bias, corruption, or bribery, because they held a sacred trust, and might end up the same way as Sir John.

***

A true relation of a most desperate murder, committed upon the body of Sir John Tindall, knight, one of the masters of the Chancery. Who with a pistol charged with 3 bullets, was slain going into his chamber within Lincoln's Inn,[1] the 12th day of November, by one John Barterham, Gent. Which Barterham afterwards hanged himself in the King's Bench in Southwark on Sunday being the 17th day following, 1616. *London: Printed by Edw{ard} Allde, for L. L. dwelling in Paul's Churchyard at the Sign of the Tiger's Head, 1617*

These days of ours are so busy, and offer so many wondrous occurrences to fill the mouth of rumour, that it seems almost a thing impossible that any novelty should happen in any Christian kingdom more strange and remarkable than those which have lately fallen out in this of our own. The states of countries are stages upon which all degrees of men play their parts (by God's appointment), after several manners of action, and with various events. Kings fill their scenes with glory and admiration, if they sit in the thrones of virtue, or come to confusion and tragical ends, if their scepters be advanced out of wickedness. Lords and great personages are like chessboard men, moved and removed from place to place, according to his pleasure who sets them, and are taken or maintain their dignities as the fortune of the game goes with or against them. Poor men are fortune's tennis balls, bandied with bounds and rebounds, sometimes aloft, struck up with windy prosperity, and sometimes under the line, into the hazard of wants and misery.

England had never so much work for a chronicle, never such turnings, tossings, and mutabilities in the lives of men and women and the streams of their fortunes. More eclipses have been seen within few years than our ordinary almanac-mongers did set down in their calendars, being such as came not within the reach of Ptolemaical[2] prediction. Thus of the celestial bodies (the sun and moon), are common interpositions of this lower globe, between their great lights and them.[3] But these sublunary, terrestrial adumbrations [foreshadowings] in our State, as they are extraordinary fatal, so are they extraordinary fearful. Fame hath now talk enough for her thousand tongues; and the babbling of them, ministers speech to all the kingdoms in Europe.

But not diving therefore into this ocean, wherein an argosy [formation of warships] may with all her sails meet with danger, if not suffer wreck, let us stand upon the shore and content our eyes only to behold the encounters, fights, grapplings, and overthrowings of two meaner vessels, which upon our English coast (by disastrous winds) have been both lately cast away.

Of which, to set down the truth to the life, you must understand that one Master John Barterham was the principal agent. A man so stricken in age that so much hair as was upon his head (it being exceeding bald) with a long and comely beard, were all turned white, for threescore and ten [70] years at least sat upon his stooping shoulders. His dwelling was at Westminster, his living had been good in former times, but when it was at best, it was by him weakened, wasted, yea, and almost utterly consumed in tedious and expensive suits of law, in which the cunning which he had gotten by experience made him more covetous in prosecuting of such contentions. Omitting all other courses of his life, as his breach of wedlock, by being sundered [separated] from his wife, and such like, needless here (as black imputations) to be laid upon him, sithence [since] in this last deed of his, he hath left himself infamous enough and impious enough to the world. Let us behold him only acting his part in the bloody tragedy of another and himself.

A long time had he had suits depending in the Chancery,[4] in which the law not running with so even and calm a stream as he did expect or persuade himself that the justice of his cause did deserve. One Sir John Tindall (one of the Masters of the Chancery, a man grave for his age, reverenced for his wisdom, knowledge, and authority) giving and awarding this Michaelmas[5] term, by a certain report (having had the hearing of this business for Barterham, as of others for him before), a sum of money to the value of 300 marks[6] or three hundred pounds, or thereabouts, by judgment of the court as a full satisfaction. Yet Barterham, being of a haughty, turbulent, and disdainful spirit, full of rage, fury, and headlong indignation, propounding to himself that Sir John Tindall was the only caltrop[7] thrown under his feet to prick him and cast him down, sealed a damnable vow betwixt Hell and his soul to be revenged only there, where (to his judgment) he found his injuries to stick. Therefore, as his state (he said) was confounded by Sir John Tindall, Sir John Tindall should be by Barterham confounded likewise in his.

The means to make this vengeance sure much tossed and troubled his working cogitations. After many hammers beating on that damnable anvil, at last the Devil (a ready schoolmaster to a quick scholar) stood whispering in his ear this word, "Report, Report, etc." Upon which, starting out of his melancholy thoughts, it did him good at heart to think that as he found himself undone by the report of a lawyer's pen, so now, by another report[8] of his own devising, he should overthrow the lawyer. He provides himself therefore of a pistol, which charging with three bullets, nothing wanted now but place and opportunity. He made choice of Westminster for the place, and the returning of Sir John from the hall, should in the open street, be the fatal hour of this desperate execution.

But whether the glass of his life was appointed to run a little longer yet, or whether crossed by numbers of people still walking up and down, so that Barterham could not stand conveniently to bring his purpose to pass, it is unknown. But howsoever, he, constant in his resolution, followed close the

A

TrueRelation of a moſt

deſperate Murder, committed vpon
the *Body* of Sir IOHN TINDALL
Knight, one of the Maiſters of the
Chancery;

Who with a Piſtoll charged with 3. bullets, was ſlaine
going into his Chamber within *Lincolnes-Inne*, the 12.
day of Nouember, by one *Iohn Barterham* Gent:

Which *Barterham* afterwards hanged himſelfe in the
Kinges-Bench in *Southwarke*, on Sunday being the
17. day following. 1616.

LONDON

Printed by *Edw: All-de*, for *L. L.* dwelling in *Pauls* Church-yard,
at the ſigne of the Tygers head. 1617.

Figure 11.1 Title page from *The true relation of a most desperate murder*, 1616. The woodcut
image depicts the murder of Master of Chancery Sir John Tindall by John
Barterham.

Source: © The British Library Board C.27.c.21. title page.

old knight, until he came to Lincoln's Inn, where alighting out of his coach and spying Barterham, who (according to his custom, and vexation of spirit) growing into uncivil language with Sir John, upbraiding him to be the utter undoer of him and his and crying after him (even to the knight's chamber door) for new compromise, arbitrements [arbitration], and a great deal of frantic talk, which Sir John slighted, bidding him to trouble him with his clamours no more. At this in disdain so to be cast off, Barterham out with his pistol, shot and killed him, his last farewell to the world being only a deep-fetched groan.

At which his servants about him crying out, "Murder, murder!" On a sudden Barterham was laid hold on, and being hauled away to be led to some judge to be examined, and they who plucked him along, with reviling language (for the love they bore to Sir John) and odiousness of the fact, terrifying Barterham with threats of hanging, etc. He, glorying in the deed and no way repenting it but scorning to stand to the mercy of any more lawyers, on a sudden stabbed at himself. But his hands being held and the wound (though it bled much) not being dangerous, he was examined before the Judge and (his wound being dressed) committed to the King's Bench prison in Southwark, there to be kept close prisoner with a keeper attending upon him. A Roman [steadfast] resolution, but accompanied with the desperate fury of a barbarous infidel. Here (in his killing the knight) his losses and wants suffered and his courage sung. But in the last act (which hereafter is set down) his soul suffered and the Devil danced, the pains of Sir John Tindall's wound being nothing so great as the wounds of Barterham's conscience.

Oh, bloody hand! To snatch up vengeance when it was not thine. Was there not a king to complain to? A king wise in judgement, upright in justice, pitiful in relieving the compassionable wrongs of his poorest subject? A king that abhors bribery, hates cruelty, loves mercy, and cares not for the proud and wicked but can throw them down, be they never so high exalted? Was there not a council table[9] to fly unto as a sanctuary for men pursued by violence of men never so great? Are there not reverend judges? Was all law, justice, and religion shut up in the whole kingdom's bosom that Barterham (like a madman) must run desperately up and down and strike the next he bear malice to?

The law is a dumb king; the king a speaking law.[10] All subordinate judges are but organ-pipes, to sound forth such notes of concord as the king sets to keep his kingdoms in tune. So that if anyone jar [disagree], no subject is to take upon him to mend or correct, but to tell the fault to him who is chief master of that music, and to let his ear distinguish the tunes. Rulers and magistrates are gods upon Earth, yet are they mortal gods, and being destined to die carry about them human frailties. Errors in them, in judges, in counsellors, in men lifted up to authority, are eclipses in the sun, fearful and fatal. Mean men's oversights are faults and flaws in images of clay, but those of eminent persons are blemishes in statues of gold.

The seeds of such lawyers (and so of all other men) who have no defects are sown in Heaven; Earth is too cold a country to bring forth that harvest.

What of all this? Must every common hand (as the Puritan would do the like in the Church) be lifted up to pluck down all chairs of justice unless they who sit in them plead only his cause, be it right or wrong? God forbid. If upon Earth there were no remedy for wrongs, yet we are sure there's a just judge in Heaven. No man in punishing must be his own carver. Thousands may wonder that such a courage and settled resolution could take fire from the cold bosom of a man so aged. But the Devil being a second in any quarrel, what coward dares not venture into the field? Besides, he that is desperate of his own life may adventure to kill Julius Caesar in the Senate, albeit he fought fifty & two pitched fields and still came home safe.

But clasping up the leaves of this discourse, let us now take the pains to go visit Barterham at the King's Bench, where he lay prisoner.

The wilful murder of Master Barterham, done upon himself by a piece of bed-cord in the chamber where he lay close prisoner within the King's Bench in Southwark, which fact was committed on Sunday the 17th of November, 1616

The said Barterham, being committed for the former murder of Sir John Tindall, to the King's Bench, it was his lot to be lodged in a chamber, either fatal, for that many have been kept there for offences of the same, or like nature, or else memorable for their departing out of that chamber to public execution. An officer was in this room continually attendant on him, except at such times when he went down to fetch in such things as he wanted or called for. Which (to man's opinion) he might do safely because at his first coming in he was searched, and ever after narrowly watched, from having about him either knife, garter, or ought else by which the Devil might put him in mind to catch an advantage to endanger his life.

Two several days (with two or three keepers at least waiting on him) was he sent for by the judges to be examined. At the first going, he was called to the Bar and an indictment read to him for the murder aforesaid, to which he pleaded not guilty. At his passing along the streets, his presence so full of age and his face so full of sorrows, together with the rumour of his wrongful undoing, which quickly spread itself amongst the people, moved them to such consideration that they shed tears to see what misery he was fallen into. They prayed for him and cursed the other.

Upon the Saturday before the Sunday in the which he cast away himself did he thus go abroad, and returned about four o'clock in the evening with a slow and dull pace fitting to his years. He seemed in his chamber rather vexed than dejected. His thoughts appeared and made shew to be more troubled than tormented, and the rather because he did expect within a day or two, at the most, to be fetched to his trial, and the next day after to be sent to execution. Which, as some say, he fearing that it should have been to hang alive in chains,[11] struck with so strong impression into him that to avoid that shame and that torture he purposed to lay violent hands upon himself, if he could but meet opportunity.

Upon Sunday morning therefore (the seventeenth of this present November), Barterham getting out of his bed, and seeming to have his head busied and full of some matters which he purposed with all speed to write and send to the judges, he called for a Bible. It was brought to him, and opening the book he turned to the 59th chapter of Isaiah, which he read, intending to make use of it by writing of some part thereof, beginning at the 14th verse:

> "Therefore judgment is turned backward and justice standeth far off, for truth is fallen in the streets and equity cannot enter. Yea, truth faileth, and he that departeth from evil maketh himself a prey: and the Lord saw it, and it displeased him that there was no judgment, etc."

With more to the same effect in four or five verses following, which applying to his own interpretation of himself and the injustice (as he said) done unto him, he requested to have pen, ink, and paper brought him. Seeming to be in a very good mind, his keeper went for such things.

This was somewhat before ten (for the prisoners were new-set to hear a sermon), but before the keeper could come up again, this wretched creature, shutting up the Bible which lay on the table, did, with a small piece of a cord fastened to a weak tenterhook, strangle himself. The tenterhook being so loose that after he was cut down and only the knot of the cord being still at the tenterhook, a prisoner but lightly touching it, it fell out of the post into his hand. Besides this, so near did mercy stand at one elbow (though the Devil jogged him by the other) that he might with much ease and quickness have saved himself. For that as he hung the one foot stood on the very ground, and one knee touched a joined stool, which he had turned down to get up upon. But he was to fall under a judgement that could not dally.

His keeper coming up, amazed to see his prisoner made away, cried out he was undone. His wife called in people who suddenly cut down the body, being yet warm in all parts, good heat in his hands and a very fresh colour in his face. They rubbed him, beat the soles of his feet, chafed his wrists, poured aqua-vitae [liquor] into his mouth, at which his lips being opened, the nether [lower] jaw gaped so from the upper, that great hope there was to have revived him. To hasten which the second time was aqua-vitae poured into him, which went down, when presently all his mouth appeared full of blood, bubbling at his lips as it seemed out of his first wound by the bowing and forcing his body. But after much labour spent upon him to no purpose, he was given over, being in a short space cold as clay. And after two other days spent in examining witnesses before a sufficient jury, and to give them and the world satisfaction, he was on Tuesday in the evening, by men hired for that purpose, carried away and buried in the common highway passing by Saint George's fields, where now the body lies with a stake of wood driven quite through it.[12]

Thus (reader) have I delivered unto thee the truth of these two lamentable occurrences, fearful to the times present as they will be a terror of judgment to those to come. The fatal and sudden ruin of that aged gentleman (Sir John Tindall) is much to be lamented, in respect of his place, because happily upon him did depend the deciding of many men's causes, which peradventure are now new to begin again. Then in regard of that reverence which is due unto the law: it appearing very horrid that in a state so governed as ours is (where small offences are punished to their deservings, and great ones with death) any subject durst have the courage, first to resolve to watch a magistrate new risen from the seat of justice, to kill him, and then either failing there or else being frighted from doing it, yet to pursue him to his very chamber door, and there most barbarously to dispatch him. Had not the murderer been his own justicer, condemning and executing his own self, the example had been prodigious, and as full of danger as it is of wonder. But to terrify others from imitation of such damnable attempts, God, out of his divine vengeance, drew an arrow to smite him to the heart who had shed the blood of another. Barterham had either great wrongs done him or else supposed that such were offered. If his wrongs were true, then you see the revenge was fearful, striking down an officer of the law, a man of worship, authority, learning, and wisdom, when he had gone far in years and overtaken a reverend age, when he was in the fullness of riches, of command, of attendance by servants, suitors, and clients.

Far be it from my thought to accuse the gentleman of any injustice, for in this he was far from it, as hath since been sufficiently made manifest. Yet his fall (like the father's skin flayed off for taking bribes and covering a judgment seat wherein the son was placed as a judge[13]) may terrify others (if at least any such be in our kingdom) from laying the hand of their own greatness on any poor suppliant, oppressing him either for lucre, self-will, partiality, revenge, or any other private respect, doing violence therein to the sacred rites of equity. For God sometimes, when sin is grown mellow and ready to fall to the ground, can make the weak hand of the poorest creature an instrument to beat into the earth the wickedness of men far more mighty.

Let those, therefore, who are put in trust (being lifted up into the seats of justice as God's deputies and stewards) to deal in law-differences between subject and subject, take heed that they lean neither to the right hand, nor to the left. Nor, according to the old tale, to open the oyster, eating up the meat themselves which belong to others and to give the shells to their clients. The least corruption in a lawyer turns his ink to poison and his paper to many a poor man's winding sheet [burial shroud]. Bribery in him is a tetter [skin disease] which begins a little at first, but if it be suffered to run till it grow round it will blemish the beauty of his very soul. And ink will hardly kill it, especially in him, because (when such a thing doth happen) it comes for the most part by writing with an ill pen.

But leaving the law to her own purity, and those that defile the same to the punishment of their own consciences, which is everlastingly to be thrown over the bar, out of the court of God's mercy to fall into his terrible judgment. Let us a little look back upon miserable Barterham: wretched every way in loving law contentions, which utterly undid him in his estate, and lastly in destroying himself after he had confounded another, to the extreme hazard (if not certain ruin) of his own soul.

Fool that he was, to avoid a hanging he hung himself. To shun one shame of a public gallows, where (happily) God might have sent him the grace of repentance, and with the good these saved him, even at the last hour, he ran desperately to a more infamous execution. He fled out of a storm to fall into a voluntary shipwreck. Barbarous man, he had done bad enough before in killing another, but to kill himself was the basest cowardice. Wolves and serpents never make away themselves, and shall man (a creature of the noblest resolution) descend into that poverty of courage which brute beasts contemn as the basest? He is held a villain that sheds another man's blood, but what may we call him that desperately lets out his own?

Men may heap up to themselves much honour by one act of virtue, as a jewel comprehends great treasure in a little room, and as that nutshell which held all Homer's Iliads smally written in vellum. But what worth soever Barterham had in him (all his life time), how just soever his cause and work of revenge might by his own arguments have been made to the world, yet this last act, so base, so dishonest, so dishonorable, wipes out the glory of all former goodnesses, if any were in him.

A moral there is, that Saturn, for one whole year, was tied up in bands made of wool to shew with what patience he did forbear his indignation.[14] And so this bloody executioner (of two lives) had a woolly hand laid upon him for some thirty or forty years together in his turbulent suits of law. But in the end, that wool turned into hard hemp, and it paid him home for all.

As our pace upon Earth is, so stand we steady or with steps uncertain. As the ship of life meets with a good or bad pilot, so doth she nobly escape all rocks of danger or else is violently split upon them. The departure of every good man out of this world is unto him as an entry into a city where he is entertained with honors, and his funeral is as glorious as a king's coronation. But of a wicked man, it is to fall amongst thieves and murderers who rob and spoil him of all his riches provided for that journey. And such was the wretched estate of Barterham.

To conclude, let no man think that if his complaints of wrongs had been just, and having taken so sharp, so sudden, and so public a revenge upon the doer as he did suggest, that ever he would have fallen into that misery to wreck both soul and body for fear of a little temporal punishment. But rather that he should, with the selfsame stoutness of mind, with a masculine fortitude, have defended his act to the last gasp and have even labored for both quick trial and a full circle of spectators at his death (whatsoever he had been doomed to suffer) to the end, that his last and latest constancy might have given credit to his former courage. But his fact was foul, his quarrel ignoble, his defence unmanly, his conscience seared, his hands full of bloody guiltiness, his heart of shame, his soul of terrors, and his end damnable.

Notes

1 Lincoln's Inn is one of four Inns of Court (along with Gray's Inn, the Middle Temple, and the Inner Temple) that trained and housed barristers since the middle ages.

2 At this time, the theories of Claudius Ptolemy (AD 90–168) were the leading ideas about mathematics, astronomy, astrology, and geography.

3 This is based on the common belief, informed by Ptolemy's notion of geocentrism, that the "superlunary" sphere (that which was beyond the moon) was perfect and could be observed and interpreted to foreshadow and bring to greater perfection that which was "sublunary" (beneath the moon).

4 The Court of Chancery was an English equity court that heard cases not appropriate for the strictures of the common law. Trials were heard by the lord chancellor, common law judges, and masters.

5 One of the four annual law terms, running from October to December.

6 An English mark was valued at two-thirds of a pound. Thus, 300 marks was 200 pounds and the author is uncertain whether the award was 300 marks or 300 pounds.

7 A caltrop was a weapon used in warfare. It was made of iron nails and was positioned on the ground points up to slow the advance of horses and soldiers.

8 The sound of a pistol being fired.

9 Petitions were commonly presented to the Privy Council, with the petitioner standing hat in hand at the front of the table used for council meetings.

10 This is based on a common legal maxim *rex est judex et lex loquens*, or "the king is judge and speaker of the law," and is thus an authority above the normal courts to which an appeal could be made.

11 Barterham expected a long and tortuous death at the gibbet because he killed one of the king's appointed servants.

12 For those who committed self-murder (suicide), a stake was sometimes driven through their heart in order to pin the soul to the body. This was based on the belief that the self-murderer's desecration of his body meant that his soul could not go to Heaven, and thus his ghost could otherwise return to Earth to plague the living unless it was held down. Most of the time, however, suicides were buried in the parish churchyard without being staked down.

13 Book III of Herodotus's *Histories* (circa 450–420 BC) recounts that in order to punish a corrupt judge who accepted bribes, King Cambyses II (circa 525 BC) had the judge flayed (his skin was removed in strips) and appointed the judge's son to replace his father. The bench on which the son sat as judge was upholstered with his father's flayed skin.

14 The Roman god Saturn is usually depicted bound in wool for most of the year. During Saturnalia (the week beginning December 17), Saturn's bonds are loosened and he is allowed to rule again before being rebound. In Christian societies, Saturn became associated with agriculture, and his binding and release was analogized to wheat being bound to the earth most of the year, and released during the autumn harvest. He is, thus, a symbol of patience being rewarded. In Barterham's case, he had been bound by the law for decades, exhausting his patience.

12 The life and death of a churlish knave

Griffin Flood was one of the few professional criminals we will meet in this collection. His story is part of a familiar trope that we will also see later in the stories of "The penitent apprentice" and "The wicked life of Captain Harrison." Beginning young adulthood as a respectable apprentice, Flood quickly descended into knavish behaviour. He made his living by threatening to report foreign workers to the courts, unless they agreed to provide him with a sum of money, either in exchange for his silence, or so that he would bring a slow legal action that prevented other informers from bringing their own suits. In the early seventeenth century, a number of refugees from Catholic countries – particularly the Low Countries – travelled to England in order to practice as Protestants without risk of persecution. However, to ensure that Londoners and members of craft and trade guilds had the opportunity to work, these foreigners – who had often completed apprenticeships and become master craftsmen in their birth countries – were forbidden from working and owning property unless they had completed an apprenticeship and been admitted into a guild, or had otherwise earned the official right to work. Informers were encouraged to report illegal foreign workers by bringing a suit (or action) to court. In exchange for their information, the informer would receive a fee, typically one-half of the fine levied against the foreigner.

Flood thus directed his criminal enterprise toward blackmailing and informing on the type of professions most likely to be performed by foreigners, including tapsters, ale-wives, chandlers, flax dressers, and shear-grinders. These were either jobs performed by artisans who should belong to a guild, or were unskilled jobs that could easily have been performed by English commoners. Eventually, Flood's criminal behaviour escalated to the attempted murder of a constable and the murder of a vintner he was trying to extort. Even in prison awaiting trial for murder, Flood was quarrelsome, and his refusal to accept the power of the law or his social superiors resulted in his death by *peine forte et dure*. As the author notes, "Never was there (I think) the like audacious and shameless fellow living in this city, nor any of a more impudent carriage before his betters." Even Flood would have agreed with this assessment, if there is any truth to the claim that he wrote his own epitaph: "Here lieth Griffin Flood full low in his grave, which lived a rascal and died a knave."

***

The life and death of Griffin Flood, informer, whose cunning courses, churlish manners, and troublesome informations molested a number of plain dealing people in this City of London. Wherein is also declared the murder of John Chipperford, vintner, for which fact the said Griffin Flood was pressed to death the 18th day of January last past. *London: Printed for J. T. and are to be sold at the Sign of the Bible without Newgate, 1623*

Of the bad condition, foul speeches, and ill demeanour of Griffin Flood, and how he became first to be an informer

Now first to make a character or description of this Griffin Flood. He was a fellow of mean birth, rude bringing up, ill instructed in either learning or good manners, harsh in speech, and churlish in condition, full of quarrels, stubborn and unruly, and in brief, of a most debauched condition, as by the sequel may appear.

But omitting these, and to come to particulars: he was in his younger days bound apprentice with a currier or dresser of leather. In which time of his service he picked such quarrels among his fellow servants and followed them with such cunning, as they being over-awed with his shameless lying, were forced to submit to whatsoever he pleaded against them, insomuch that sometimes they were fain to buy their peace with their purses. And thus by his cunning informations of falsehoods to his master and mistress, in which he commonly prevailed, he learned to tread the first step to this troublesome course of life, now named an informer, where after being made a freeman[1] of this city, he followed the same ways and became a great troubler of diverse other servants and apprentices dwelling near him, where if he found any that he knew, either in tavern, alehouse, bowling alley, or play house, or else going abroad in service time when they should have been at the church to the service of God with their masters, he would be sure to pick some feeling of money from them, or make it known to the displeasure of their parents or masters, all which these poor servants and apprentices would do before their names and credits should come in question.

Of the manner of his informations against tapsters, hostelers, chamberlains, and such like

After this, entering further into this kind of life and perceiving some small gain to come thereby, he began to haunt alehouses, inns, hostelries [hotels], cellars, and such like, where if he found either foreign tapster, hosteler, chamberlain, or any other party that was no freeman of this city, to him would he privately come and thus make his gloss:

"My friend," quoth he, "you being no freeman, but live here by sufferance under your master, I understand that there be certain informers which I know that mean to trouble and sue you by action, and bring you in question for the wronging of the customs of this city, wherein no man must make his living by way of trading but such as have served seven years an apprentice, or else made freeman by adoption or purchase.

"Now if you will," quoth Flood, "prevent this trouble and be my client, I will for a small matter defend you from the same, and clear you from all informers whatsoever, for I am an enemy to all such knaves whose purpose is to wrong such honest meaning men as you are, for my conscience draws me to it, and I will prove honest therein."

The poor country fellow being thus honeyed and loath to leave his master's service, hath Flood down into the cellar, makes him drink, lends him money, and becomes so pliable to his conditions that he is led up and down as with a twine thread, till a part of his means falls into this Flood's purse. But "no longer penny, no longer paternoster,"[2] the fellow grows weary and is no longer able to feed Flood's desires, but leaves him off, and submits himself to the trial of his action, where Flood, as a cunning jack on both sides, follows him so close that after much money spent he is forced to forsake his service and to leave the city, and the master of the same foreigner is likewise brought to composition [legal action] to be rid of this crafty informer.

Another way of information that Flood used against foreigners and such like

This Flood also comes to another fellow being no freeman, where after the like conference as before, he takes upon him with the man's consent to bring him into action, and so to prevent all others of the like, declares against him by merit, and so it hangs in court many years unfollowed by Flood for a monthly stipend received from the fellow thus sued. And so all other informers were prevented for bringing him in question, for one of them by order of law cannot take another's case in hand. And thus Flood, to his great benefit, dealt with many poor people in London.

How he troubled an honest alewife not far from Cripplegate, and how finely she requited him

There was an honest alewife, whose name and dwelling I omit, not far from Cripplegate, well-known and reputed of among her neighbours, who kept in her house good lodging and orderly diet for entertainment of strangers and wayfaring [travelling] men. Amongst others that resorted to her house, there was a foreign tailor, a very poor man, who ran more on the score for lodging and diet than he was able to pay. Therefore to come out of her debt, he desired to work out the same, either in making new apparel or mending of old, whereupon this ale-wife put an old petticoat of hers to mend, which got the poor man but six pence. Which matter this Flood having notice of, warned both her and her husband into the court for setting this foreigner on work: where, do what either he or she could, it cost them forty shillings, and so came home without any other comfort, for Flood had shared his part of the money, of which he made no little brags amongst his companions.

But it fell out after a certain time this Flood came again to the said ale-wife's house, thinking to find out another like prize, where casting his knavish eye up and down, he espied the good wife run down into the cellar with a black pot or two (measures contrary to the city's custom[3]). After follows Flood and thinking to attach [seize] them, the woman having a ready wit and now thinking to be revenged, caught up a pewter quart pot, and lustily laid it upon Flood's pate [crown of the head], and most grievously broke both his head and face, and withal cried out with a loud voice, "Oh help! Murder, murder!" The noise being heard not only up into the house but abroad into the streets, caused many people come running in and inquiring the matter, she with feigned tears cried out he would have ravished her and forced her against her will, and that she to defend herself had with a pewter pot broke his face. Whereupon all the beholders knowing Flood to be a very knave, and believing the woman by her tears to tell true, called for a constable who carried both Flood and the ale-wife before a justice, where she standing stiffly in her accusation, he was committed to prison, where he lay with his broken pate and face until such time as he had given the woman a good sum of money in composition [compensation] for the supposed wrong he had done her.

How Flood churlishly handled two informers, and of his hatred against all firkin-men

After this, Flood becoming a little kinder to poor ale-wives, and using much to resort to a cook's house a widow, which often gave him a breakfast to stay his knavish stomach, whereupon (as the Devil is good to somebody) so this Flood stood close to this woman in courtesy and promised to defend her from all actions whatsoever. For indeed as then there were a couple of informers had her in chase, and by no means could she be rid of them, for commonly they came once a month to her house and got money of her. But it so happened whilst Flood was talking with this woman that these two aforesaid informers came to her house, according to their accustomed manner, which Flood perceiving and being a little potshaken [intoxicated], took up a broom-staff and fell a-bombasting them, and being all together by the ears down in the kennel, Flood like a cunning knave all begraveled and bedirtied his own face, crying out they would murder him, and by that means so cunningly used the matter that his fellow knaves were carried both to the Counter [Compter], whilst he being the third and worst, escaped imprisonment.

But now mark the jest, as they were going to prison there comes by a lusty lubberly firkin-man,[4] bearing out drink to his customers, a familiar friend and acquaintance of one of these informers thus beaten, and hearing of these wrongs done by Flood, falls upon him and most bravely behangs [hangs about] him, and so amongst the tumult of people gets him away unknown, and leaves Flood behind with the amends in his own hands, seeking for he could not tell whom. Whereupon in mortal hatred, he sought revengement against all firkin-men, and for this one man's sake vowed to be a plague to all the rest, and so after that there could not be a firkin-man step out of doors, but he would be on their jacks, especially all those that were foreigners. Insomuch, were he but in the shape of a firkin-man it was enough for him to set his knavish wit on work. By this means many of them were enforced to buy their freedoms, to their great charges. Others that were of the poorer sort, he with his cunning framed actions affrighted from London, where they lived as before in much poverty.

How he troubled a poor shear-grinder for relieving his own father

Flood still following these pitiless courses, came upon a time to a shear-grinder's[5] shop, where he saw a very poor country old man turning the stone, which old man was the shear-grinder's own father, and in love to his son took that pains to save him from hiring one to do the same work. All this Flood noted, and with a harsh and commanding language, said, "My friend," quoth he, "how darest thou be so bold as to set a foreigner on work, knowing that Flood stands here as a witness? I tell thee I will make thee repent it." These, and such like threatening words, not only amazed the poor shear-grinder, but much grieved the old man. But to be short, in question was he brought and censured by order to give satisfaction to Flood for his information, and the old man was discharged from any further labour therein, but lay upon his poor son to be kept in charity, and thus was the cruelty of this Flood expressed to his shame and disgrace.

How his harsh and churlish dealing caused a poor flax-maid to hang herself

I must not here omit his harsh dealing against a poor flax-maid in London, who after she had served twelve years prentice, and wearied with that servitude, took shop for herself and set up. Of which flax-maid when Flood had notice, he came unto her, from whom he oftentimes got much money, and still to buy her own quietness (being not free but a foreigner) provided still for his cunning bribery, and had still her money in readiness, so long that in time she grew weary of him, and not able to hold out any longer, she revealed it unto a friend of hers, who counseled her to get her freedom, which she might easily do having served twelve years prentice. Which counsel she followed and was made free of a worshipful company, but not of the city, which was thought sufficient for a woman's security to follow flax-dressing.[6]

Hereupon Flood perceiving his wonted benefits to fail, hammered in his knavish pate another trick of information against her. So watching his time, he espied a country chapman buying a certain parcel of flax of her, and giving her some earnest thereof [giving her money in exchange], as Flood took hold of by witness he presently took possession thereof, as goods foreign bought and foreign sold, and recovered them by way of action, which was a great hindrance both to the flax-maid and to the country chapman. But to be short, the maid was still haunted with the informations of this Flood, which drove her (as some reported) to such a melancholy that she took no comfort in her business, and as it was known afterward, she hanged herself in her own girdle. The cause I will not say was Flood's, but let such as understood the manner of her life and carriage, in discretion, judge and censure thereof rightly.

How Flood troubled an honest man only for asking him a question

The debauched carriage of this Flood was such, that if any but gazingly looked upon him, he would be sure to pick quarrels with him, and if he used not his speeches with advisement, this Flood would take advantage on his words, for the least occasion was sufficient for him to make an action of, whose troublesome courses are verified as followeth:

There was an honest man, belonging to Blackwall Hall, who as he stood in Guildhall[7] yard, saw Flood come forth with a pair of tailor shears in his hand. Of whom this man demanded what they cost?

"Why fellow?" quoth Flood, in a clownish manner. "Dost thou think I stole them?"

"Why no," quoth the other, "yet I may ask a question."

"A question," quoth Flood, "I pray thee what art thou?"

"I am a man," quoth he.

"A man," said Flood, "I will have money from thee then."

"Money from me?" quoth the other. "Do thy worst, I care not for thee."

Such like words were passed betwixt them, and so they departed. But within a while after, Flood brought this honest man in question about the Statute for Buildings, which was about a little shop that he kept to sell flax in, not, as Flood alleged, so sufficiently plastered with lime and hair,[8] of which he made such a long declaration to the Court, that he so puzzled the man that he knew not well how to answer the same. And though Flood little prevailed in his suit, yet by his harsh roaring language, and foul words, which he so clamoured against this honest man, that for quietness sake, he was forced to give some satisfaction to be rid of him.

How Flood deceived an officer, and cunningly made him arrest his own master

Upon a time this Flood comes to one of the city's officers, and tells him he hath a writ to serve upon a freeman for setting a foreigner on work. Of which this officer was glad to hear of, and thinking thereby to get money, as he had oftentimes before so done by Flood's means, goes with him. Where coming together to a worshipful gentleman's [house] of this city, they found a foreign painter, new colouring the gentleman's house walls.

Which gentleman (to speak truly) a worshipful knight, though not named, seeing Flood and the other officer in the yard, comes forth and demanded "What news?"

"Mary," quoth Flood, "here is a writ to serve on your worship for maintaining foreigners," and thereupon gives the same to the officer to do his duty.

At which the officer looks very blank, considering it was his own master on which he should serve it. Yet notwithstanding, according to his oath so done it was, and his master was forced to compound with Flood. Who after took a pride in such treacherous actions, making himself merry at the officer, whom he had cunningly brought to arrest his own master.

Of Flood's ingratitude for a Dutch chandler's benevolence to him lying in the Compter

This Flood, in acting of many of these his arch knaveries, was at length outstripped by a fellow cunninger than himself, and being overthrown in an action and condemned in a round sum of money, for want of sureties was laid in the Compter.[9] Where lying in prison in much necessity, there was a Dutch chandler,[10] I will not say dwelling near unto Newgate, that in pity oftentimes sent him much relief as meat and drink from his own table both at dinner and supper, and now and then some small pieces of money to comfort him, with an intent after his imprisonment to draw him to his friendship, and that Flood should be a trusty staff to defend him from all informations that any other informer should have against him, for commonly these Dutch chandlers are much troubled with those kind of people, and therefore this Flood he purchased to make his pillar to lean on. This passed on and many courtesies were sent to him lying in prison by the Dutch chandler, which were all as butter melted in the sun, for after when Flood had got his liberty and followed again his former courses of life, this Dutch chandler was the first man he brought in action, and for all his forepassed favours received at his hands, he was the party he made most prize of.

How Flood came to search a tavern in service time, and how finely the vintner requited him

Flood growing malicious against a tavern-keeper of London, whose name I omit, came upon a Sabbath day in service time, and brought the church-wardens to his house, where finding certain good fellows taking their morning draught fought to have him presented. But the vintner having a ready wit, wrought as cunning a trick to bring both Flood and the church-wardens into the same trespass. So the foresaid tavern-keeper, seeing himself fallen into the danger of the law, said as followeth: "Master churchwardens, and you Master Flood, I pray you be good unto me. I am a young beginner, and a little trouble will much hinder me, therefore I pray you stand my good friends and in kindness take a cup of wine," and withal called for a slice of roast beef, which the plain-dealing churchwardens well accepted of, and withal Flood being a hungry fellow was nor behind in the same given breakfast.

Which being finished, quoth Flood, "this shall not serve your turn, for I must have money from you, and it is not your bribing breakfast shall satisfy my turn."

"Why knave," replied the vintner, "thou art as deep in the fault as I, or any of these my customers, for the churchwardens and thyself also have both eaten and drunk here in my house in service time, of which I now take witness. Therefore do thy worst, I care not for thee." At which words Flood grew a little pacified and was contented to let the vintner go unpresented for that time, and ever after those churchwardens much favoured the said tavern.

How Flood out-braved a citizen with a red nose

Upon a time, Flood being railing and roaring in Guildhall, as his manner was, a citizen who had a red nose, a very substantial man, rebuked him, calling him brazen faced fellow to be so audacious in so reverent a place as that was. "Brazen faced fellow," quoth Flood, "if your copper nose, sir, were set on my brazen face, it would make a very rich show." Which words not only daunted the citizen, but made him silently pass away much abashed. For rogue, rascal, slave, and renegade were as common in Flood's mouth, as "how do you sir" to a man of courtesy.

Of his churlish keeping the walks in Moorefields

To speak yet further of churlish condition, he was chosen (being fit for a trou-blesome office) to oversee the walks in Moorefields, and like the Pinder of Wakefield[11] to prevent the intercourse of people over the grass, and not to suf-fer them to make other paths beside the walks. To which office being chosen, he got him a sturdy brown bill,[12] and like a valiant champion intercepted all inroads over the field, favouring neither old nor young, rich nor poor, gentle-man or other, in such sort that he had many roaring combats and much mis-chief was done by his harsh behaviour. He not only broke many a man's pate, but set tenterhooks under the rails whereby sundry people (stooping under the rails) tore their cloaks, bands, and apparel, and so spoiled their clothes in such sort, that he was not without many bitter curses, and now and then he caused sundry of the ruder and unrulier sort of people to sit in the stocks for their stubbornness in crossing the walks. And many other pranks he there played, which though he were not ashamed to act, your modesty forbids me relate, in which he showed himself rather a beast than a man, so far he forgot Christianity and honesty, that he lost all humanity. And for that cause he was very deservedly put from that means, which had been sufficient (if honestly used) to have maintained a man to live well upon.

Of his shameless bragging and boasting of base conditions

Never was there (I think) the like audacious and shameless fellow living in this city, nor any of a more impudent carriage before his betters, for to some, to whom he was far unequal, would he most upbraidingly say with a full mouth, "What, know you not Griffin Flood and bring I not the most milk to your pail, is it not I that bring sacks to your mill? I tell you Griffin Flood (by his informations) shall make men quick." Furthermore, to my knowledge I saw him once stand in the middle of Guildhall, with his arms akimbo on both sides, with a number of people about him, where he being not ashamed, boastingly said, "I think in my conscience I am the veriest knave in all England, and when I am buried this shall be my epitaph: 'Here lieth Griffin Flood full low in his grave, which lived a rascal and died a knave'."

Of his manners and troublesome carriage in the time of his imprisonment

Return we now to his imprisonment in Newgate, where since his coming thither, the other prisoners have been so troubled with his railing language that they accounted him rather a monster than a man, and such quarrels he bred amongst them that they many times fell together by the ears, so that day nor night could they be quiet for him, for what with his cursing, banning, roaring, and blaspheming he showed himself rather an atheist than a Christian, and little remorse of conscience possessed him, and all his former offences came little to his remembrance, especially these petty abuses before rehearsed. But the main ground of his imprisonment, which was for the murder of John Chipperford, vintner, something terrified him and a little troubled his conscience, for blood lies heavy on a murderer's soul, and the revenge thereof hourly thunders in his ears. So by this Flood was it here verified, for upon a night in Newgate as he lay in his bed, in his dream a fearful vision appeared unto him, which was (as he thought) the ghastly shape of the man he had murdered with a bleeding wound in his breast gaping wide open, threatening as it were a speedy revengement. At which Flood in his sleep cried out most fearfully, "The Devil! The Devil pursues me! Help, help, he will tear me in pieces!" With such like words of terror and amazement that many of the prisoners, affrighted, rose from their sleeps and came to pacify him in this his distracted agony. For such were his fits in Newgate, and so distempered was his brain that he continued there in great discontent without any patience.

Of a revenge certain tapsters took upon him in Newgate

A man he was that few loved, neither in prison nor without, and therefore came many thither to vex and torment him. Amongst the rest in a merry vain came certain tapsters to him in prison, belike some which he had wronged by his troublesome informations, who instead of comforts brought him flouts and instead of reliefs gave him griefs. For everyone called for his can of beer, saying to him in mockage, "Here Mr. Flood, I drink to you! Here Mr. Flood, a health to you!" And such like severally, each of them tossing off [drinking down] his beer, giving him only the empty cans but therein never a drop of drink, whereupon Flood grew so enraged that he enstyled them with no better than "slaves and rogues," and for their sakes vowed a revenge (if ever at liberty) against all other tapsters.

And to put the same in practice, he presently sent for a debtor of his which was a tapster that owed him a certain sum of money. Which fellow, in pity, by reason of his imprisonment, brought him a part thereof, thinking therewith in that his extremity to content him. But Flood as his churlish custom ever was, so kept he his old order, and would not receive less than his whole debt. Whereupon the fellow goes his ways and bids him recover it by action, which Flood with a stern look threatened to do, but afterward considering how his case stood and how that (in prison) he lay much impoverished, sent for some part of his money before promised. "Not so," quoth the tapster, "for I am otherwise minded," returning him this answer, according to the proverb: *He that will not while he may, when he would he shall have nay*.[13]

So was it with Flood, when he might have lived well and in good government, the want of grace and serving God, cut him off with a nay, where then being tempted by the Devil, he ran himself so deep into the danger of the law that his life answered it with an untimely death.

How after all these his troublesome courses of life, he was for a murder pressed to death

Now to come to the last period of his shame and devilish manners, in an agony of wrath (furthered on by Satan) he most wickedly stabbed a constable and withal a vintner both at one time, whereof the vintner, after he had long laid languishing, died as a man murdered by willful violence, for which this Flood was attached, imprisoned, arraigned, and put to trial. But by no persuasions would he commit himself to the law, but most obstinately stood to the severe justice of the bench, who according to custom, censured him to the press, where he received his deserts by being bruised in terrible manner to a most fearful death, whose execution was performed in the pressing yard at Newgate upon the 18th of January this present year.

The Life and Death ⁴⁴⁰

OF

Griffin Flood Informer.

Whofe cunning courfes, churlifh manners, and
troublefome Informations, molefted a number of
plaine dealing people in this City of *London*,

Wherein is alfo declared the murther of *Iohn Chipperford* Vintner,
for which fact the faid *Griffin Flood* was preffed to death
the 18. day of *Ianuary* laft paft.

L O N D O N,
Printed for *I. T.* and are to be fold at the figne of the Bible
without New-gate. 1 6 2 3.

Figure 12.1 Title page from *The life and death of Griffin Flood*, 1623. The woodcut image
depicts Flood, an infamous criminal, being pressed to death as a result of his
refusal to plead to an indictment for murder.

Source: © The British Library Board 1132.a.45, title page.

Notes

1 That is, Flood had completed his apprenticeship and been admitted into his trade's guild. This freed him from his indenture and entitled him to work in his trade.

2 This common proverb meant, in essence, "no pay, no pray." In this case, the unwillingness of the foreigner to continue paying Flood meant that the informer would no longer hold off his legal action.

3 Various legislative acts and city bylaws, known as "victualing laws," regulated the prices and measures for units (usually pints, quarts, and gallons) of beer, wine, etc. Thus, using incorrectly-sized containers could result in the customer being cheated.

4 A man who sold casks (firkins) of beer to tapsters, ale-wives, and hoteliers for sale to customers.

5 A man who sharpened scissors on a stone wheel.

6 The complex preparation of flax fibers so that it can be spun into yarn and used to make coarse linen.

7 The building that serves as the ceremonial and administrative centre for the corporation of the City of London.

8 Buildings at this time were often sided with a plaster of sand, water, lime, and horsehair. The lime and hair made the plaster strong and allowed it to adhere to wooden laths, which framed the building. Without sufficient lime and hair, the plaster would have been weak and the building at risk of collapse.

9 Flood was placed into debtors' prison until he could pay the judgment.

10 An artisan who made and sold candles.

11 A pinder was a person put in charge of impounding stray animals before they destroyed the town's crops, and ensured in common fields people did not create new pathways, which could also ruin crops. The Pinder of Wakefield was a character from Robin Hood lore who refused to allow Hood's party to pass, then became part of the outlaw gang.

12 A curved blade commonly used to clear brush, but also as an offensive weapon usually in warfare.

13 An old English proverb, recited in John Heywood, *Proverbs* (1546).

13　The witches of Faversham

While this chapbook exemplifies the mass hysteria about witches that occasionally ran through the English countryside, two particularly interesting points arise in the case of the Faversham witches. The first is the willingness of the women accused of witchcraft to admit to their relationship with the Devil. They seemingly believed that they in fact signed a contract with the Devil and that his imps suckled from them, provided for them, and satisfied their desire for revenge. Although many people living in early modern England believed that witches and the Devil existed, to a modern eye it is nonetheless difficult to understand how these women could so willingly accept that these events truly occurred. It is also quite interesting how willing these women were to name the other women whom they believed to be witches. Especially given the probable fate that awaited the various women involved, this was a particularly poor show of neighbourliness. Perhaps in both cases, the women thought they would gain some advantage, or wanted to use this opportunity for one last chance at empowerment in a society that generally saw women as inferior. Of course, we must filter these confessions through the pen of the reporter, in this case the mayor (and for that reason, chief magistrate) of Faversham, whose reportage was almost certainly designed to convince his readers of the guilt of these witches, and of the justness of their executions. It is unlikely that these examinations were as straight-forward as is suggested in this account.

***

The examination, confession, trial, and execution of Joan
Williford, Joan Cariden, and Jane Hott, who were executed at
Faversham in Kent, for being witches, on Monday the 29th of
September, 1645. Being a true copy of their evil lives and wicked
deeds, taken by the mayor of Faversham and jurors for the
said inquest, with the examination and confession of Elizabeth
Harris, not yet executed. All attested under the hand of Robert
Greenstreet, mayor of Faversham. *London: Printed for J. G., 1645*

*The confession of Joan Williford, September 24, 1645, made before the
mayor and other jurates*

She confessed: That the Devil about seven years ago did appear to her in the
shape of a little dog and bid her to forsake God and lean to him. Who replied
that she was loath to forsake him. She confessed also that she had a desire to
be revenged upon Thomas Letherland and Mary Woodrose, now his wife. She
further said that the Devil promised her that she should not lack, and that
she had money sometimes brought her she knew not whence, sometimes one
shilling, sometimes eight pence, never more at once. She called her Devil by
the name of Bunne. She further saith, that her retainer Bunne carried Thomas
Gardler out of a window, who fell into a backside. She further saith, that near
twenty years since she promised her soul to the Devil. She further saith, that
she gave some of her blood to the Devil, who wrote the covenant betwixt
them. She further saith, that the Devil promised to be her servant about
twenty years, and that the time is now almost expired. She further saith, that
Jane Hott, Elizabeth Harris, Joan Argoll were her fellows. She further saith,
that her Devil told her that Elizabeth Harris, about six or seven years since,
cursed the boat of one John Woodcott, and so it came to pass. She further
saith, that the Devil promised her that she should not sink, being thrown into
the water. She further said Goodwife Argoll cursed Mr. Mayor and also John
Mannington, and said that he should not thrive, and so it came to pass. She
likewise saith, that the Devil sucked twice since she came into the prison; he
came to her in the form of a muse.

She, being brought to the bar, was asked, "Guilty or not guilty?" She
answered, "Guilty." When she came to the place of execution Mr. Mayor
asked her if she thought she deserved death? To whom she answered that
she had, and that she desired all good people to take warning by her and not
to suffer themselves to be deceived by the Devil, neither for lucre of money,
malice, or anything else, as she had done, but to stick fast to God, for if she
had not first forsaken God, God would not have forsaken her.

*The examination of Joan Cariden, widow, taken September
25th, 1645*

This examinant saith, that about three quarters of a year ago, as she was in
the bed about twelve or one o'clock in the night, there lay a rugged soft thing

upon her bosom which was very soft, and she thrust it off with her hand. And she saith, that when she had thrust it away she thought God forsook her, for she could never pray so well since as she could before, and further saith, that she verily thinks it was alive. This examinant saith, that in the same year that this mayor was formerly mayor, the Devil came to her in the shape of a black, rugged dog in the night-time and crept into the bed to her and spake to her in mumbling language. The next night it came to her again, and required this examinant to deny God and lean to him, and then that he would revenge her of anyone she owed ill will to, and thereupon this examinant promised him her soul upon those conditions. And that about that time the Devil sucked this examinant and hath diverse times since sucked her, and that it was no pain to her.

Confessed, upon the examination of Joan Cariden before Mr. Mayor, that Goodwife Hott told her within these two days that there was a great meeting at Goodwife Pantery's house and that Goodwife Dadson was there, and that Goodwife Gardner should have been there but did not come, and the Devil sat at the upper end of the table.

The examination of Jane Hott, widow, taken before the mayor and jurates, the 25th of September, 1645

This examinant confesseth that a thing like a hedgehog had usually visited her and came to her a great while ago, about twenty years ago, and that if it sucked her it was in her sleep and the pain thereof awaked her and it came to her once or twice in the month and sucked her, and when it lay upon her breast she struck it off with her hand, and that it was as soft as a cat.

At her first coming into the gaol, she spake very much to the others that were apprehended before her, [urging them] to confess if they were guilty, and stood to it very perversely that she was clear of any such thing, and that if they put her into the water to try her she should certainly sink. But when she was put into the water and it was apparent that she did float upon the water, being taken forth, a gentleman to whom before she had so confidently spake and with whom she offered to lay twenty shillings to one that she could not swim, asked her how it was possible she could be so impudent as not to confess herself, when she had so much persuaded the others to confess? To whom she answered, that the Devil went with her all the way and told her that she should sink, but when she was in the water he sat upon a cross-beam and laughed at her.

These three were executed on Monday last.

The examination of Elizabeth Harris the 26th of September, 1645, before Mr. Mayor

This examinant saith, that about 19 years ago the Devil did appear to her in the form of a muse. She further saith, that she had a desire to be revenged, and the Devil told her that she should be revenged. She called the Devil her Imp. She further saith, Goodman Chilman of Newnham said that she stole a pig, then she desired that God would revenge her of him, and the man pined away and died, and she saw it apparent that her Imp was the cause of that man's death. She further saith, that the Devil bid her to forsake Christ and lean to him. Whereupon she saith that she scratched herself with her nails and fetched blood from her breast, and she wiped it with her finger and gave it to her Imp, who wrote the covenant with it. She further saith, that a fortnight, after the Devil sucked her but she felt no pain. Being demanded how many witches were in town, she answered that were a heavy sentence. She further saith, that Goodwife Dadson, Joan Argoll (William Argoll's wife), Goodwife Cox, have very bad tongues. She further saith that her Imp did suck her every three or four nights. She further saith, that her son being drowned in Goodman Woodcott's high [boat] she wished that God might be her revenger, which was her watchword to the Devil, and this high was cast away, and she conceives that her wish was the cause of its being cast away. She further saith, that Joan Williford told her that her Imp said on Wednesday last, that though the boat (she now knowing what boat) went cheerfully out, it should not come so cheerfully home. She saith further, that Goodwife Pantery did many times make meetings with Goodwife Williford and with Goodwife Hott. She further saith, that Goodwife Gardner hath a very ill tongue.

All these are true copies of examination, one whereof is not yet executed, and were taken before me, Robert Greenstreet, mayor.

14 The baronet at the bar

This trial of Sir Edward Mosely for an allegation of rape involved issues of rank, wealth, gender, reputation, and credibility, all criteria that juries commonly took into consideration when deliberating on their verdict. Mosely was a baronet, a senior member of the English gentry, and with an income of £3000 per year, which rivalled some of the richest of the nobility, was very wealthy. He admitted to having mistresses, among whom he, and several of his witnesses, included Mistress Anne Swinnerton. Even Master Swinnerton was suspicious of his wife's behaviour, to the point where he asked her explicitly whether or not the sex was consensual, and then deliberately sought out Mosely in order to pose the same question. This testimony prompted the court to query why Swinnerton would more likely believe Mosely than his own wife, which suggests that her reputation and character were under scrutiny. This suspicion was heightened when Master Kilvert testified that Mistress Swinnerton was after Mosely's money. She allegedly expected the exorbitant sum of £2000 for her silence. This may have suggested to the jury that Mistress Swinnerton was maliciously using the court system in order to force a settlement. If true, this strategy did not work in Swinnerton's favour. Testimony that Swinnerton was complicit in the sexual act and a person believed to be of loose sexual morals, the woman's generally combative attitude toward the court and its witnesses, and the entire absence of any discussion of the elements common to rape charges – coercion, crying out, and penetration – compelled the jury to acquit Mosely. This was possibly an issue of gender politics, or simply the court's expectation that it, and its proceedings, should be accorded due respect by all participants.

***

The arraignment and acquittal of Sir Edward Mosely, baronet, indicted at the King's Bench bar for a rape, upon the body of Mistress Anne Swinnerton, January 28, 1647. Taken by a reporter there present, who heard all the circumstances thereof, whereof this is a true copy. *London: Printed by E. G. for W. L., 1647*[1]

Sir Edward Mosely, baronet,[2] indicted for felony and rape upon the body of one Anne Swinnerton (wife of Mr. Swinnerton, a gentleman of Gray's Inn[3]).

This trial was taken the 28th day of January, in the 23 year of King Charles, An[no]. Dom[ini]. 1647. Before Master Justice [Francis] Bacon[4] and Master Justice [Henry] Rolle in hilary term[5] in *Banco Regis* [King's Bench].

First, Sir Edward Mosely appeared at the bar and pleaded not guilty. Then Master Swinnerton and his wife appeared to give evidence. Then the court demanded of Master Swinnerton what counsel he had ready to open the indictment.[6] Master Swinnerton answered that there had been such tampering with him and his witnesses to stop the prosecution that he could get no lawyers to open his wife's case. The court asked him whether he had spoken with any lawyers to be of his counsel. He said he had, but none would undertake it – only Master Cooke had promised him that he would open the indictment for him, but he appears not. So that by the tampering of Sir Edward Mosely, Master Lowder, Master Ja[mes] Winstanley, Master Blore, and Master Brownell and twenty more, none would assist him in the maintaining of the indictment. These gentlemen before named appeared in court and did not deny but that they did use what means they could (in a fair way) to put the business betwixt Sir Edward Mosely and Mistress Swinnerton, which they conceived they might lawfully do believing it could not possibly be a rape, having had intelligence of some former passages in it.

Then the court said, "Master Swinnerton if you had desired counsel, the court would have assigned you counsel."

Then Master Swinnerton proceeded with his evidence, saying, "Coming home to my chamber about six o'clock in April 1647,[7] I found Sir Edward Mosely came rushing out of my chamber. I, entering, saw my wife thrown upon the ground with all her clothes torn, the bedclothes torn and hanging halfway upon the ground, my wife crying and wringing her hands, with her clothes all torn off her head, her wrist sprained, Sir Edward Mosely having thrown her violently upon the ground. Whereupon (seeing her in this condition) I asked her what was the matter, she said Sir Edward Mosely had ravished her."

Master Swinnerton further informed the court that Sir Edward Mosely, two or three days before he did the rape, said that "he would ravish my wife though he were sure to be hanged for it."

Then Mistress Swinnerton began her evidence, saying, "Upon my oath here I swear that he said he would force me to my bed, and then he swore, 'God damn him, he would lie with me though he were sure to die for it.' Then he takes me and carries me to a narrow place betwixt the wall of the bed and with his hands forced my hands behind me and lay with me whether I would or no."

Then Sir Edward Mosely interrupted her, saying, "Did not your husband come to the chamber door at that time you pretended you were ravished and knocked at the door, and I would have opened the door for him, whereupon you said, 'it is my husband, let the drunken sot stay without,' and would not suffer me to open the door," and asked her whether she did not say so, she said it was false.

Then the court demanded of Master Swinnerton what he said to his wife when he found her in this manner. Master Swinnerton answered, "I said that if she were ravished as she said she was, she must take her oath of it and indict him for it. And if she did not [I] would believe that she had played the whore with him and [I] would turn her off and live no more with her, and she should be Sir Edward Mosely's whore altogether. But," said he, "being desirous to be further satisfied in the business, I often sought for Sir Edward Mosely but could not find him, for he had fled away from his chamber. One day I met him accidentally in Holborn and desired to speak a word with him. He said he knew my business, but he was in haste and could not stay. Then I told him I had earnest business with him and I must speak with him. He told me he suspected I had some design to arrest him and would not be persuaded to stay. Then I pressed him that if he would go and drink a cup of ale with me he should come in no danger concerning any arrest at all, and if he then would give me satisfaction I would not prosecute the law against him."

The court demanded of him what he meant by satisfaction. Master Swinnerton answered, "Only to know what he could say to excuse himself."

The court said, "Why would you believe him before your wife?"

Master Swinnerton answered, "My meaning was, if he could satisfy me that my wife was consenting to it, I had rather waive the prosecution than bring my wife and myself upon the stage, and this was my intent and no other."

Then the court asked Sir Edward Mosely how Master Swinnerton's wife came to be so with her clothes torn and ruffled in this manner (none but he and she being in the room). Sir Edward Mosely answered, "She always went very ill-favouredly in her apparel."

Then the court asked Mistress Swinnerton whether there were any in the room but Sir Edward and herself. She answered, "A little before there was my maid, but I had sent her to the baker's house for bread for my children, and in the meanwhile he lay with me against my will."

Then the court asked the maid what she could say. She said, "When I came from the baker's and entering into the chamber I found my mistress crying and wringing her hands, saying she was undone. Also I heard Sir Edward Mosely say, before I went to the baker's, that 'he would lie with my mistress though he were sure to be hanged for it,' and at all times he was wont to be very uncivil and rude when he came into the chamber. Once he came into the chamber when I was there alone. Truly I durst not stay in the chamber for I always observed he was so lecherously given that any woman, were she never so mean, would serve his turn. At this time he came into the chamber a little before I went to the baker's. I observed he would fain [gladly] have thrown my mistress upon the bed when I was there, but my mistress would not yield to it but grew very angry with him and said he was a rogue and spit in his face. Yet he would not let her alone. Whereupon I told him, if he would not be more civil I would call my master, and if he came he would crack his crown for using my mistress so uncivilly. Sir Edward Mosely answered he cared not a fart for my master, and that for me I was a base jade [hussy] and he would make me kiss his . . . "

"What?" said the court, but the maid having some modesty could not bring it out.

Then said her mistress, "He said she should kiss something that was about him."

"What was that?" said the court again.

Master Swinnerton answered, "He said he would make her kiss his arse."

Then the court said to the maid, "You must not be so nice in speaking of the truth, being upon your oath."

Mistress Swinnerton said, "Then came Master Ja[mes] Winstanley to tamper with me from Sir Edward Mosely and told me if I pleased to accept a hundred pounds I should have it, if I would be reconciled to Sir Edward Mosely."

Then the maid said, "My mistress made this answer: she cared not for money."

Mistress Swinnerton said, "It is true I said so, and this I said: If Sir Edward Mosely would [fall] down upon his knees and confess that he had wronged me I would not prosecute him. But also I resolved that he should wear a paper upon his breast or upon his hat, acknowledging the injury he had done unto me. If he would do so I would forgive him. Then," said she, "Master Ja[mes] Winstanley desired to know where the place was in the room where I was ravished, whereupon I showed him. Master Ja[mes] Winstanley answered, 'this was such a place for such a business that if I had the strongest woman in England I could ravish her here whether she would or no.'"

Then the prosecutors for the king having ended their evidence, the court asked Sir Edward Mosely what he could say for himself. He said he had many witnesses and desired that they might be examined what they could say in his behalf.

Then Master Kilvert was called in, who appeared. The court said, "Master Kilvert, though you be not upon your oath, you must speak the truth in the fear of God."[8]

Master Kilvert answered, "I know it my lord. What I shall say here I speak it in the presence of God, and I shall speak no more than what is truth."

Mistress Swinnerton seeing of him said, "I hope nobody will believe what this knave Kilvert will say, for he is a knave known to all the court and all that hear him."

Then Master Kilvert went on with his evidence, saying, "I thank God this is the second time I ever came in[to] this woman's company. The first time was at the Fleece Tavern in Covent Garden, where she came to a dinner to meet with Sir Edward Mosely. As soon as she had set down at the table she said that this room had been a very lucky room to her, for once before in this room she had received three hundred pounds for the composition [settlement] of a rape which she charged a reverend divine withal. I shall not stick to name the man, she said it was Doctor Belcanquell. This doctor, I knew him to be a reverend man and to my knowledge is long since dead and in Heaven. And for this rape, she said then, she would not take under two thousand pounds for a composition of Sir Edward Mosely, which she said was little enough, he having three thousand pounds a year."

Mistress Swinnerton hearing of this clapped her hands at him and said he was a knave and a rascal and all was false which he said.

Then the court said to her, "Mistress Swinnerton, you should carry yourself soberly and moderately, otherwise you will disparage all your witnesses." Then the court asked her whether she did meet at this tavern (having affirmed before that she never was in Sir Edward Mosely's company but in her own chamber), whereupon she staggered at it a little and [was] loath to confess it. At last she answered, true, she was there, but this rascal Kilvert had bewitched her to come thither.

Master Kilvert said further, "After she had sat awhile at the table, she takes her stool and removes it to sit next to Sir Edward Mosely, and there falls hugging and embracing him. Whereupon," said he, "'Surely lady, whereas you say Sir Edward hath ravished you, I do believe rather you have ravished him, otherwise you would not make so much of him.'" So Master Kilvert made an end of his evidence.

Then Master Wood, another witness, said he met her at Islington in Sir Edward Mosely's company, and there she confessed to him that Sir Edward Mosely had many times left the key of his chamber with her to go to him when she pleased, and she said she had often made use of it. Then said this witness, "After I had seriously looked upon her and seeing of her a woman of that strength and body, I said I wondered Sir Edward Mosely should ravish her. She said, 'Do you wonder at that, why? Do you take me behind the bed there (there being a bed in the room) and see whether you may not do it.'"

Another witness said that she had confessed to him that Sir Edward Mosely had once lay with her with her consent. Afterwards she asked him, "Now what will you give my maid, you must give her something?" He answered, "I'll give her forty shillings," whereupon she said "forty shillings, that's base, you cannot give her less than 10 pounds and a silk petticoat. But," sayeth she, "when he went forth of doors she said he gave her nothing but a groat[9] and so basely went his way."

Another witness said he heard her say (that it being generally known that Sir Edward Mosely ravished her) she was like to lose many of her best customers in town.

Another witness said he heard Swinnerton say that if she would not take her oath that she was ravished by him she should never be no wife of his. Afterwards Mr. Ja[mes] Winstanley was called into the court. He said, "'Tis true she took me and showed me the place where she was ravished." He wondering how Sir Edward being but a little man and she such a lusty woman should be ravished by him! "'Why,' said she, 'should you wonder at that?' Then she put her leg between my legs, and put her other leg setting her foot against the wall, saying now, 'in this posture as you see me here, I myself could ravish any woman whatsoever.'"

Another witness said, the night before she went to prefer [initiate] the Bill of Indictment against Sir Edward Mosely, she confessed she had like to have been distracted and run mad, for fear the Grand Jury should find the bill [true].

Two other witnesses affirmed upon their credit, whereas it was said by Master Swinnerton and his wife that Sir Edward Mosely fled from his chamber immediately after the act was done, they said they had daily recourse to his chamber and walked to and fro with him, sometimes in Gray's Inn walks, sometimes to Westminster, and to other places in the town for six weeks together after this pretended rape, and many times they saw Mistress Swinnerton stand at her own door looking upon him as he passed by (which was but six steps from Sir Edward's chamber door) and never questioned about it. But oftentimes (they said) seeing her stand watching there, they feared she would go up to him and tempt him to wickedness.

Then, evidence being given on both sides, the jury went from the bar and returned and gave their verdict that Sir Edward Mosely was not guilty. Then the court said, "Sir Edward Mosely, take heed what company you keep hereafter. Let this be a warning to you, you see in what danger you bring yourself to in keeping ill company."

Notes

1 This chapbook was reprinted in *The Harleian Miscellany; or, A Collection of Scarce, Curious, and Entertaining Pamphlets and Tracts . . . found in the late Earl of Oxford's Library*, Vol. IV (London: Robert Dutton, Gracechurch Street, 1810), pp. 46–50.
2 The rank of baronet was admitted into the English gentry by James I in 1611 as a revenue-gathering scheme. A baronet was senior to a knight and, unlike a knighthood, was hereditary, but unlike members of the titular aristocracy (beginning with baron), the holder was not entitled to sit in the House of Lords. Baronets were entitled to the honorific "Sir" before their names, unless they were lords by virtue of another title.
3 Gray's Inn is one of the four Inns of Court that trained and housed lawyers.
4 Though they shared the same name, this was not the same Francis Bacon mentioned in Chapter 11.
5 Hilary is one of the four law terms, between January and March.
6 Although lawyers were rare in the criminal courtroom, they were sometimes allowed on the prosecution side to "open," or help reveal the facts of the indictment. In this case, because no lawyer would take the case, Mr. Swinnerton became "prosecutor for the king."
7 Until 1752, the year began in England on Lady Day, March 25. Thus, April 1647 came early in the new year, and the case was heard in January 1647, nine months later.
8 This statement had become formulaic by the mid-seventeenth century when addressing defence witnesses, who were not allowed to testify under oath.
9 An English coin worth 4 pence, or 1/3 of a shilling.

15 The child-killer of St. Olave

A number of gruesome murders are described in this chapbook and the story of the title character, Abigail Hill, does not appear until the final third. The author describes the instruments of judgment used by God to reveal wicked murders that had remained hidden to the knowledge of man. One man was tormented by his conscience, and others were followed by crows, ravens, dogs, and apparitions, which eventually led to the murderers being discovered and brought to justice. Yet, interestingly, in the story of Abigail Hill that follows this lengthy digression, the murderess felt no such torment for her multiple and horrendous crimes of child-killing. It took the suspicion of her neighbours to reveal the truth, and Hill's conscience never weighed on her enough to confess the fact of more than one killing, which she described as merciful. Not only did she kill several orphan children under her charge, she also borrowed children each quarter in order to receive her entitlement from the parish charity, thus making a "trade" of her crimes. The story of Abigail Hill is preceded by a misogynistic rant, in which the author marvels at the ability of a woman who should have been made "tender by nature" to commit crimes so horrid, especially to children under her direct charge. Like so many other chapbooks, this one ends with a reminder of the author's central purpose: to warn other bloody-minded men and women to take heed, lest their crimes be found out, and they suffer the same punishment as the murderers described therein.

***

A true relation of the most horrid and barbarous murders, committed by Abigail Hill of St. Olave, Southwark, on the persons of four infants, parish children, whom she undertook to nurse. For which most cruel murders, being convicted and condemned at the Sessions held at the Old Bailey, Wednesday, December 15th, she was accordingly executed on Wednesday, December 22nd in Cheapside near unto Woodstreet. Together with a true account of the strange and stubborn end she made, and her jeering of her executioner at the hour of her death. And a caveat to all other women that are suspected for the like unnatural and most unmerciful practices. *London: Printed for F. Coles, 1658*

The first sin remarkable in the posterity of Adam was a crying sin. The blood of Abel cried unto Heaven for vengeance. No doubt, but Cain before committed many actual transgressions. "Sin lieth at the door," sayeth God.[1] Mark what hast sin and the punishment thereof do make to overtake the sinner. We shall find sin lying at the door when there was scarce a door in the world.

The shedding of innocent blood is a sin that lieth at the door of the conscience and knocketh thereat as loud as thunder, but custom in sinning doth take away the sense of sin. In a man or woman of a bloody spirit, one murder makes way for another. Her conscience was seared as was this wicked woman's who is the subject of our present discourse. There are some who delight in murder and the ruin of the world and these persons, though they thirst after fame and immortality and after their deaths have monuments raised to eternalize their names, yet they go in an indirect and cross way both to God and nature. It is the endeavour of nature to preserve itself. Now, what can be more contrary to this endeavour than to destroy one another, which is the way to destroy nature?

And we shall find God so tender in shedding of blood that his commandments are always and altogether express against it. David was not permitted to build the temple unto God because he had in his [hands] blood, although it was red only in the blood of his enemies and the enemies of God.[2] The children of Israel were forbidden to eat anything in which was the blood and the same mandate was given also the Christians.[3] Although St. James and the elders of Jerusalem determined that the converted Gentiles should not observe the laws of the Jews, yet they were expressly commanded to keep themselves from blood, and from that which is strangled they should be so far from the shedding of the blood of one another that they should refrain from the blood of the creatures allowed by God for the nourishment of men that was shed.[4] And this shedding of the blood of one another hath been so odious to God that he always left some tokens of his high displeasure against it and the murderer hath seldom escaped undiscovered or unpunished.

For besides the checks of the conscience which flasheth forth terror and flies in the face of the murderers, we shall find that it hath pleased God, oftentimes in a miraculous manner, to make discoveries of murders committed sometimes by birds, sometimes by beasts, and sometimes by the apparition of the person murdered, of which histories can furnish us with abundant examples and no ages have been exempted from giving many remarkable demonstrations of it.

We need not go into foreign countries to fetch examples to prove this truth. It is not yet two years since the notorious murder was committed by Nathaniel Butler on the person of his dearest friend and companion, John Knight. The bloody design being put in execution, how was his conscience tormented with the horror and apprehension of his guilt. We shall find it was so much startled that he was not able either to tarry at home or to fly abroad, what a deep impression did the blood of his friend leave upon his soul. How many tears did he shed to purge it? How unquiet was his soul, how perplexed was that body which could find no rest but by death only? This so startled him that he could enjoy no intermissions, no respites of any comfort but by death only, and in this manner many being tormented in their consciences do need no further discoveries, it being impossible for them to be at quiet until they do discover themselves and offer themselves as sacrifices to that justice which they have violated.

Sometimes murderers have been discovered by the fowls of the air. In the same manner a gentleman in Norfolk, Ralph Suckey by name, having murdered one who, as he said, had done him great injury, could not afterwards be satisfied within himself. Walking one time in the field he beheld a company of crows flying by him and making such a noise, as they are accustomed when they go in flocks. The noise they made was but ordinary, but the guilt of this murderer was extraordinary, for reflecting on the horror of his act and applying all things to himself, he believed that the crows did particularly reprove and tar [accuse] him for his murder. Walking not long afterwards at a town called Burnham, he beheld three or four more crows flying by him and making the like noise. The apprehension thereof working upon the guilt of his conscience did so much affright him that he expressed words of great suspicion, of which notice being taken by a standerby he was presently had before a justice to whom he confessed his long concealed murder and said, moreover, that if his tongue should deny it, yet his conscience would proclaim it. Having confessed it he seemed to be at great ease, having discharged himself of a burden that did so greatly oppress him and seemed to be than death unto him, the pains whereof, being condemned by justice, he willingly did undergo at Thetford the Assizes following.

If you please to descend into the theater, it will present you with a history more rare and remarkable than this. It will give you the sight of a cruel and a covetous young man, who to enjoy the rate[5] of his brother's son did, under the pretense of hunting, draw him into a neighbouring wood, where most inhumanely he bereaved him of his life and buried him under a great tree. This being done, he divulged it forth abroad that his kinsman, having a great mind to see novelties and the government of foreign countries, was travelled beyond the seas and in his absence had ordained him to be overseer of his estate, being very sorry that he could no ways dissuade him from such rash and heady counsels. This report was entertained into the belief of all his kinsmen and continued current for certain years. At the last he caused it to be spread forth abroad that his kinsman was dead beyond the seas, and being the only heir that was left, he for many years without any disturbance did inherit his estate, but not without some visible judgment, for his children died. It was the wit of justice that he should be left childless himself who had destroyed his brother's child to enrich his own family.

In the process of time, walking in the fields which so unjustly he had possessed and thinking himself secure and free from all dangers whatsoever, beheld where two ravens soaring over his head did stoop lower to it as they came nearer to him. This sight was strange unto him, but the noise they made was more terrible. He used all the means that possibly he could to fright them from him, but neither the shouts which he made nor the noise of his gun would prevail, for the ravens still hovered over his head or were near unto him either on the one side of him or the other. Entering into [his] house they made a great noise and soaring upward they wheeled about the house and then perched on the top of it. He caused them to be shot at but they were not hurt, and if they rose from the top of the house they presently again would alight upon it.

Night coming on, the master of the house entertained a hope that they would be gone, and commanding horses to be made ready he withdrew himself with his ordinary train of servants to another place. But all in vain, for these two dreadful and black-winged summoners did still attend him. On the morning following he offered a round sum of money to anyone that could kill those ravens, which although it was often attempted as before, yet could never be effected. At the last, his hope and his heart fainted and caving with despair, he confessed the murder he had committed. His words at the first were taken as proceeding from a man that had lost his senses and his health. But the place being searched wherein the wood he acknowledged that he had buried his brother's son, after a little digging in the ground the spade grated against the skull and several bones were taken up, which no sooner were brought unto the house where the murderer was but the two ravens (having done the business in which the divine providence did employ them) did fly away and they were seen no more about the houses. The murderer being dragged to the jail was brought not long afterwards before the court of justice, where being condemned for his murder, he answered for the guilt of his fact with the forfeit of his life.

Sometimes we shall find that dogs have been made instruments to bring to light murders that have been committed, sometimes inanimate things have been made instrumental in it, and the judgment of God upon murderers have amongst the heathen been so remarkable that we shall find they have seldom escaped unpunished.[6] The censure of the Barbarians when they saw the viper to leap out of the fire and to hang on the hand of Paul is most considerable.[7] "Surely," said they, "this man is a murderer whom though he hath escaped the sea, yet vengeance will not suffer him to live."

But to proceed to our subject in hand, it is an ancient proverb in this nation that seldom any notorious murder is committed but a woman hath a hand in it. To this the several gaols in this land and places of execution have given many testimonies. How merciless were those female furies who came over from Ireland with recruits for the late king.[8] Their knives were more bloody than were the swords of their companions. It is not much regarded, but very true it is, that the finest and softest tempers being depraved do grow most obdurate, the purest natures do prove most vicious. Had not Lucifer been the son of the morning it is possible that he had never been the Prince of Darkness. Had not the complexions of some women been so tempting and their inclinations so tender by nature, it is likely they had never been such devils as they are. It is a principle in philosophy that *Corruptio optima est pessima*, the best corruption is the worst, and it holds true as well in the inclinations of the mind as in the constitutions of the body. Who would have thought that love and tenderness should be corrupted into cruelty? Who would have thought that the nurse of children should become the murderer of children? O horrid fruits of unruly avarice, and O the wickedness of a woman's heart hardened into the practice of all manner of villainy.

This woman, Abigail Hill, was looked upon by all her neighbours for a woman inclined to much compassion. She seemed much to pity young children that were in distress and according to her power to relieve them. She was therefore supposed to be a good nurse, into whose charge and care the nursing up of young children should be committed. She lived many years in the parish of St. Olave in Southwark with her husband, who is yet living, and some children she brought up carefully and returned them after the time was out unto the parish who paid her for them, thinking her to be a careful and good woman. And this was the reason that many children were brought unto her, and if at any time any child forsaken by the wicked mother was left upon the parish, she would be ready to receive and undertake to bring it up, being a nurse as wicked and more cruel than the mother.

Seven years thus she lived and no notice was taken of what became of her children if any were missing, it being believed that they died by sickness or having too many of them lying on her hands she had delivered the charge of them to some other poor woman to be careful of them. It was oftentimes murmured indeed amongst her neighbours that such and such a child was conveyed away and much suspicion there was amongst them because they could not tell what was become of it, and the suddenness of the removal of the child without any noise of sickness or discontent did add much unto their jealousy. At the last, it pleased God that this wicked woman and her husband did fall out, where in the heat of his passion he did upbraid her with the children she had made away.

This presently was taken notice of by the neighbours, who affirming it was pity that such a wicked creature should live upon the Earth, did acquaint the constable with it. Who, carrying her before a justice of the peace (she having but little to say for herself), was sent to Newgate, and at the Sessions following, which began on Wednesday, December 15th, her indictment was read for murdering of four children. And she being not able to say anything for herself, as to give answer what became of the children or, if they were dead, to satisfy where they were buried, the jury found her guilty, not only for that horrid murder, but for the charge against her that she had made a trade of it, and that at the Quarter Day[9] she would borrow children of her poor acquaintance and bring them to the masters of the parish as if they were those she had taken into her custody to nurse, and having received her pay for them she would return them again unto those of whom she had borrowed them.

All the confession which she made at the bar was that indeed once one of her children lying sick and but little hope of life, she did wring it by the neck and killed it to put it out of its pain. For this and her other horrid murders she was condemned to suffer death and be hanged at Cheapside, which accordingly was performed on Wednesday, December 22nd, 1658. Being come to the place of execution, either the stubbornness of her resolution or the desperateness of her condition had made her almost senseless, for she made no confession at all and being advised of the shortness of her life and to meet with God by repentance, she would return no answer to the admonitions of the divine nor of any other that did give her any saving counsels. It is observable that being on the ladder, as the executioner was fitting the fatal rope about her neck, she turned suddenly unto him as if she had been in some passion and said unto him, "What! Do you make account to choke me?" She had time given on her to make her confession, but the people perceiving that she abused their expectation the hangman at the last turned her off the ladder and she died miserably, as she died mercilessly.

We hear of some women, the one in Shoreditch and the other in Shoe Lane, who, although they have made no trade of Cain of it, have brought their children or their apprentices to the like untimely ends. These are sad stories, but I hope not true. But this woman may be an example unto all to take heed how they run into the same guilt, lest they partake of the same public punishment.

Notes

1 Genesis 4:7.
2 I Chronicles 22:8.
3 Leviticus 3:17; Leviticus 17:12; Deuteronomy 12:23.
4 The decisions of the Council of Jerusalem are described in Acts 15.
5 The land and goods.
6 The text up to this point also appeared in an alternate version of the story of George Strangwayes, the next chapbook in this collection (British Library shelfmark 1244.a.7). This demonstrates how commonly certain material, particularly that which opened many of the chapbooks, was reused to help fill out the stories.
7 Paul was a devout Jew who had persecuted Christians before his own dramatic conversion on the road to Damascas. In Acts 28, a viper rose out of a fire and bit Paul on the hand, thus identifying him as a murderer.

8 The female furies were warrior godesses from classical mythology who punished wrongdoers. This context refers to Catholic women who travelled from Ireland to England in the 1640s in support of Charles I's war with the House of Commons.

9 In England, Quarter Days were days when servant contracts began and ended, and when rent was due from tenants. They occurred on Lady Day (25 March), Midsummer Day (24 June), Michaelmas Day (29 September), and Christmas Day (25 December). On these days, Hill was allowed to seek her charitable entitlement from the parish for taking care of orphan children, whom she was required to bring to the parish officials.

16   The cavalier killer gets pressed

This tale of Major George Strangwayes is the longest and most detailed in this collection. Strangwayes's estate in Mussen (or Mullen) was rented by his sister, Mabel, who borrowed a sum of money from him to stock and operate the farm, a loan Strangwayes was happy to provide because he expected to inherit his sister's property and wished to see it improved. All went well until Mabel decided to marry John Fussel, who would therefore inherit her chattel property; she then denied her debt to Strangwayes, which compelled him to consider a legal remedy. Feeling that he could not succeed in court because Fussel was a talented attorney, Strangwayes killed his brother-in-law by shooting him through the window of his London lodging. Perhaps the most interesting aspect of this chapbook is that the author clearly shows a great deal of respect for George Strangwayes. He describes Strangwayes as a gentleman of "honour and gallantry," who had a "brave and generous soul" and a "stout and active body." The author is also sympathetic to the fact that Strangwayes had been aggrieved by his sister and was not receiving fair treatment at law because of Fussel's profession, factors that helped to explain why George was forced to commit his crime. Even Strangwayes's death, which took only eight or ten minutes of pressing (it was not uncommon for this to take hours or even days), is described as merciful, and the author believes that despite his crimes Strangwayes will receive God's grace and salvation. In comparison to most of the other murderers in this collection, who are likened to uncivil, sub-human creatures, this author treats Strangwayes with a great deal more courtesy and empathy than is common in the crime chapbook genre.

***

The unhappy marksman, or a perfect and impartial discovery
of that late barbarous and unparalleled murder committed by
Mr. George Strangwayes, formerly a major in the king's army,
on his brother-in-law Mr. John Fussel, an attorney, on Friday
the eleventh of February. Together with a full discovery of the
fatal cause of those unhappy differences which first occasioned
the suits in law betwixt them. Also the behaviour of Mr.
Strangwayes at his trial. The dreadful sentence pronounced
against him. His letter to his brother-in-law, a member of
parliament. The words by him delivered at his death, and his
stout, but Christian-like manner of dying. Published by a faithful
hand. *London: Printed by T. N. for R. Clavell at the Stag's Head in
St. Paul's Churchyard by St. Gregory's Church, 1659*[1]

Since the various relations of this sad and horrid act (even in the city where
it was committed) are so many that the illegitimate births of those corrupted
parents must of necessity fill more distant places with so spurious an issue,
that when it comes to be nursed with those usual adjuncts, which either envy
or love will extort from most relaters, it may possibly grow to so monstrous
a form that all the vestiges of verity must of necessity be lost in its variety of
disguise. Wherefore it was thought fit by one that is not only a lover of truth
but an honourer of both the parties deceased, ere a farther travel hath warmed
her with impudence, to unveil report in so clear and impartial a discovery as
may neither deform the truth nor disgust their relations.

Mr. George Strangwayes (commonly known in the country where he
chiefly resided by the name of Major Strangwayes, an office which he had
with much honour and gallantry performed in the first unhappy war[2]) was
second son to Mr. James Strangwayes of Mussen[3] in the county of Dorset. A
gentleman of an ancient and unblemished family whose virtues this unhappy
son of his, till sullied by this rash act of ungoverned fury, did rather seem to
illustrate by a constant course of worthy and manly actions, than any ways
to degenerate from the best achievements of his most successful predeces-
sors. He was now about the five or six and fortieth year of his age, a person
that had a brave and generous soul included in a stout and active body. He
was of stature tall and framed to the most masculine proportion of man. His
constitution such as rather fitted him for the active employments of busy
war than the more quiet affairs of peace-affecting studies. Yet was he not so
much a stranger to those arts, which are the adorning qualifications of a gentleman, but that he had sacrificed to Minerva whilst in the Temple of Mars,[4]
and in the most serious consultations had always a judgment as dexterous
to advise, as a heart daring to act. What he appeared most unskilled in was
love's polemics, he having spun out the thread of his life without twisting it
in matrimony.

He was in some trivial actions performed since the time of his imprisonment, condemned for a parsimonious sparing too low for the quality of

a gentleman, which if true, I much wonder that he whose former frugality was but the child of discretion, being now so near a supersedeas[5] from all the afflicting wants mortality trembles at, and having none of his relations whose necessities craved a subsistence from what he left behind, should near his death save that with dishonour which in his life he spent with reputation.

But to detain thee no longer with the character either of his person or qualities, which probably some of his many enemies may unjustly censure for partiality, I will hasten to as full a relation, both of the original ground of their unhappy difference and the fatal conclusion of his implacable wrath, as it hath been possible by the most diligent inquisition to obtain, both from the nearest in acquaintance to both parties and such ocular informations as were observable in much of the time from his sentence to his execution.

The father of Mr. Strangwayes, dying about some ten years since, left him in possession of the farm of Mussen, leaving his eldest daughter Mistress Mabel Strangwayes, since wife to Mr. Fussel, his executrix. The estate being thus left, Mrs. Mabel, being then an ancient maid,[6] rents the farm of her brother George and stocks it at her own cost, towards the procuring of which stock she engaged herself in a bond of £350 to her brother George. Who, presuming on her continuance of a single life and by consequence that her personal estate might in time return to those of her then nearest relations, of which himself had a just reason to expect (if not the whole) the greatest share, he not only entrusted her with the forementioned bond but likewise with that part of the stock and such utensils of the house as by his father's will properly belonged to himself, which he presumed she could better secure, passing under the notion of hers, than he whose whole estate was liable to the dangerous hazard of sequestration,[7] a disaster so epidemical as many thousands besides himself by sad experience know that honesty, the common preservative against other calamities, was the principal means that made them obnoxious to this.

His estate being (as he then conceived) thus in a fair probability of preservation from those vultures of a commonwealth, sequestrators, by the calm neutrality of a discreet sister, they for some time lived very happily together, he making the farm of Mussen the common place of his residence. But on a sudden the scene alters and she whom he thought age and a long continued single life had imprisoned too fast in her virgin-ice, ere to be thawed with the thoughts of a matrimonial life, began to express some resentments [sentiments] of affection towards Mr. Fussel, a gentleman of good esteem in the country where he lived and of much repute for his eminent abilities in matters of law. He had formerly bore arms under the same royal standard which Major Strangwayes did, in which troublesome time of action he always proved himself a very useful member of that unfortunate army, serving them faithfully till their sad declination with many other noble sufferers, enforced him a long time to mourn both his and their calamities in an uncouth gaol. His ordinary place of residence was now in Blandford,[8] an eminent town in Dorsetshire, in and about which place, through some that feared his vigorous proceedings in the law, may seem glad to have their weakness protected by the absence of so able a prosecutor. The major part, especially such as had the happiness to experiment his honesty and ability in soliciting their causes, will with a far greater weight both of reason and religion, have a just cause to repent so considerable a loss.

But not to dismantle too many of those unhappy differences which were the prodigious monsters that first hatched this horrid murder – it looking too much like a crime to pollute the ashes of the dead with the sins of the living, wishing all the enmity, that like Hydra's fruitful heads may spring up between the friends of both the deceased parties, were sepulchered [entombed] in their graves – we will only insist upon what appears to be the first and most fatal argument of their quarrel. Mrs. Mabel Strangwayes, now no longer disguising her affections to Mr. Fussel, being then a widower, lets her resolutions discover themselves in so public a way that it soon arrives to the ear of her discontented brother. Though not apparently for any former hate between them, yet (as is most likely) doubting those abilities of Mr. Fussel's which (since in relation to the law) he, with many others, were pleased by an easy metaphor to term subtlety, might, if not prejudice him in part of his own estate, yet wholly deprive him of that part of his sister's, which before hope (grounded on fair probabilities) told him he was of all men most likely to enjoy.

To prevent this approaching storm, he lets his sister know his disgust of her intended marriage, and being farther exasperated by his unmovable constancy (as it is affirmed by the friends of Mr. Fussel) broke out into such exuberant expressions of passion that to her terror he affirms, if ever she married Mr. Fussel, to be the death of him, either in his study or elsewhere. Which bloody resolution since the time wherein those black thoughts developed themselves by action, she hath under her hand confirmed (as is reported by the relations to Mr. Fussel) by several letters, but such as since they contain little (besides this asseveration [declaration]) concerning our present purpose I shall omit the inserting of them, presuming all wives (especially good ones) need not a pattern by which to be taught to mourn such losses as these.

To trouble thee no further with a digression, whilst this paroxysm [fit] of his passions continues in such a dreadful vigor, he and his sister are parted, at which time (as she pretends) he unjustly detained much of the stock belonging to the farm, which either by her father's will or her own purchase was properly hers. Withal she denies any such thing as the sealing [of] the fore mentioned bond, pretending it only a forgery of her brother's. On the other side, he complains of injuries done to him of no less extent than the endeavouring to defraud him of a part of his estate, besides the money due by bond.

These were the differences which first fomented a rage not to be quenched but by blood, over which part unspotted Justice spread her wings,[9] who groaned under the burden of afflicting wrongs or who had the greater unhappiness to be the oppressor of the innocent, since the law hath left it undermined. I think it not only an audacious presumption but savouring very much of partiality and a soul biased by a self-interested affection than of an even and equal tempered friend, in whoever should so peremptorily affirm the justice of one cause as to brand the other with an ignominious scandal of forgeries and oppression.

Their bodies are both at rest in their silent dormitories, their souls no doubt triumphing in eternal joys. Shall we, we whose uncertainty of life and certainty of sin and its consequence death, which we know not in what shape the eternal disposer of the universe will send to assault us, with uncertain censures, sully their memories, the only and that doubtful remainder of swiftly fading mortality? No, let their fames rest as peaceable as we know their bodies and hope their souls do. If thou hast been a friend to either, be not so much an enemy to thyself as to abuse the other, but let thy resentments of love or sorrow rather develop themselves in a sober and silent pity than loud and clamorous censures. That being the dress in which I can assure thee it will appear most lovely to the view of those which having to neither party any more of concern than what pity extracted from the goodness of their natures, look upon the action with a general sorrow, upon the parties deceased with a charitable remorse and upon their surviving friends with the wishes of a hearty reconciliation.

And here (though I would not have it look like flattery), he being a person I have little acquaintance with and one that probably may never know me as author of these papers, I cannot choose but commend the calm and equal temper of Mr. John Fussel, eldest son to the gentleman that was slain, who as well by the public report as by my own private experience (I having been since sometime in his company), I find to behave himself with that comely discretion, that though he did violently prosecute him as his father's murderer he hath not been at any time heard to let fall any indecent language concerning his uncle Strangwayes, but such as appears to express more sorrow for the offence than envy to the man. A temper which by preserving will gain him (whilst living) the love of all, whom the common invitation of a general pity or the nearer call of relative respects summons as mourners for either of the lamented dead.

I have now done with the introduction to this tragic and dismal story, having unraveled as many of those almost occult causes, by which being first propagated it since hath been made horridly public, as civility or necessity in enucleating [revealing] the truth requires. For he that would see more, it is his best course to confer with their counsel and look over the large impertinencies of litigious courts, than to expect them in this piece, whose small bulk by as much of their sense as in an ordinary dialect might be expressed in two lines, when stuffed with their farragoes[10] of tautologies, would be swelled beyond its intended growth. Wherefore, to leave that to those it more concerns I shall hasten to reveal how he carried on the design, since any discovery on his confession argues, he intended to murder him.

Mr. Fussel, both for the better prosecuting his own suits against his brother Strangwayes as likewise for the following of several causes for many others, he being a man of very great employment, being in this city on hilary term last, had his lodging one story high at the sign of the George and Half-Moon, three doors farther, without the bar, than the Palsgrave's Head Tavern, opposite to a pewterer's shop. He being retired to his lodgings between nine and ten (not having been in it above a quarter of an hour before the fact was done), he sitting writing at his desk with his face towards the window, the curtain belonging to it being so near drawn that there was only left room enough to discern him, two bullets shot from a carbine struck him, the one through the forehead and the other in about his mouth, the third bullet or slug stuck in the lower part of the timber of the window. The passage where the other two came in (since in the corner of the window) being so narrow that little more than an inch over or under had saved his life by obstructing their passage. But: *Nemo tam divos habuit faventes, crastinum ut possit sibi polliceri* – Sen[eca][11] [Nobody has ever found the gods so much his friends that he can promise himself another day]. His appointed time was come, and those eternal decrees by which all men are ordained once to die had stinted the farther progress of his life to this fatal minute.

In that *punctilio* [minute period] of time wherein the bullets struck him, ere giving warning by a dying groan or being tortured by those almost inseparable concomitants [accompaniments] of death, convulsive motions, he is in an instant disanimated, the swiftness of the action not giving warning to his clerk, though then in the room, to assist his murdered master. Till, perceiving him lean his head on the desk and knowing him not apt to fall asleep as he wrote, conceiving that some more than ordinary distemper was the cause of it, he draws near to assist him. Being suddenly terrified with the unexpected sight of blood such an amazing horror seizes him that for the present he is in a dreadful ecstasy lost to action. But speedily recollecting himself, he with an hasty summons calls up some of the household, by whose assistance he discovers what sad disaster had bereaved him of his master.

They speedily make down into the street but found there nothing that might light them with the least beam of information, all (as if directed by those evil angels that favour such black designs) appearing, as they conceived, more silent and still than is usual in this popular city at that time of night. Officers are raised and Mr. Fussel's son acquainted with the sad news, who ere he could spare time to mourn his father's unexpected death must with more active passion (as near as those dark suspicions which only directed them could give leave) prosecute his revenge.

Several places are troubled with a fruitless search, the first that was apprehended being a barber, whose lodging being in the same house with Mr. Fussel's and he that night absent, gave them very pregnant causes of suspicion, all being aggravated by the wild humour of his wife and she exasperated by the extravagancy of her husband, as if she had done it purposely to foment their suspicion. Besides that constant torrent of her passion which ran with the usual current of ordinary scolds, had some collateral streams of expressions, that had not the hidden providence of the Almighty, protector of innocence, by as much of miracle as this latter age hath heard of, discovered the author of the murder, it had without doubt wafted her husband to a gibbet. But presuming that for what she did then in the hot intemperance of a jealous rage she hath long since made a calm recantation, I will here give no farther occasion of continuing a difference betwixt them but go on in the prosecution of my story, which proceeded thus.

Having yet apprehended none that they had on former differences any important reasons to suspect, young Mr. Fussel calling to mind those irreconcilable quarrels which had of long time been between his father and his uncle Strangwayes, and knowing him to be a man whose impetuous rage had formerly been so often allayed in blood that though then the motive to it, being a legitimate war, made the action not only honest but honourable; yet being so well versed in that killing trade he might still retain enough of the sharp humour to actuate his anger into so vindictive a guilt, that he might be prompted to act what weaker spirits would tremble to think.

Upon which considerations he propounds to the officers the apprehending of him, which motion, finding a general approbation, is suddenly prosecuted and he apprehended between two and three in the morning, being then in bed at his lodging in the Strand, over against Ivy Bridge at one Mr. Pims, a tailor, a door on this side the Black Bull. He being now in the officer's custody is had before Justice Blake, by whom, although with an undaunted confidence denying the act, he is committed to Newgate. Where remaining till the next morning, he is then by a guard conveyed to the place where Mr. Fussel's body lay, where, before the coroner's jury he is commanded to take his dead brother-in-law by the hand and to touch his wounds, a way of discovery which the defenders of sympathy highly applaud. On what grounds, here is no place to dispute. But here the magnetism fails and those effluviums [secretions], which according to their opinion being part of the *anima media* [middle soul] tenaciously adheres to the body till separated by its corruption, being the same that by united atoms becoming visible composes those spectrums that wander about the cenotaphs and dormitories of the dead, and doth, when hurried from the actions of vitality by a violent death, as endeavouring to revenge its wrongs, fly in the face of the murderer, and, though in such minute parts as are too subtle for the observations of sense, keeps still hovering about him. And when he is brought to touch the murdered body which was its former habitation, by the motion of sympathy calls from those sally-ports [entryways] of life some of those parts of her life which yet remains within it, who that they may flow forth to meet it are conveyed in the *vehiculum* [transport] of the blood. They illustrate this by dogs and several other animals, which with a violent impetuosity assail those that make a custom of murdering things of the same species.

There having been nothing discoverable by this experiment, he is returned back to the prison and the jury (though but with little hopes of satisfaction) continue their inquest. When now, to the amazing wonder of future ages and the farther confirmation of those continued miracles by which the all-discerning power of the eternal and everliving God pleases often to manifest itself in the discovery of black and secret murders, which though acted in the silent region of the night and plotted with all the deep obscurity that Hell and the black spirits of eternal darkness can lend to the assistance of such dismal and horrid designs, yet are disveloped [discovered] by ways so unthought-of even by those which torture their wits for discovery. That man, though adorned with all the knowledge, the world's first transgressors ravished from the forbidden tree, instead of an angel-illuminated paradise finds his fancy clouded in a chaos of confusion, black and obscure as that, which ere penetrated by Heaven's segregating breath, spreads its gloomy curtains over the first unformed matter.

Several questions are propounded amongst all by the foreman of the jury, one which (though not to the disparagement of the gentleman) succeeding ages will count more fortunate than wise. It was this: That all the gunsmiths shops in London and the adjacent places should be examined what guns they had either sold or lent that day. This being a question in the apprehension of most of the jury, so near approaching to an impossibility as not without much difficulty to be done, one Mr. Holloway, a gunsmith living in the Strand, then one of the jury, makes answer. It was a task, in his opinion who knew how numerous men of that profession were in and about the city, not to be done. Withal replying that for his own part he lent one and made no question but several others had done the like.

This answer of his being by the apprehensive foreman speedily took notice of, he is demanded for the satisfaction of the rest of the jury to declare to whom he lent the gun. He after some small recollection answers, "To one Mr. Thomson, living in Long Acre, formerly a major in the king's army and now married to a daughter of Sir James Astons." Upon this a speedy search is made after Major Thomson, who being abroad, as some say fled, though most moderate men conceive about his ordinary occasions, it being unlikely any man would discover [reveal] a guilt by flight, which (if culpable of), though by all charitable people the contrary is generally hoped, he might rationally expect more security in a confident stay than in a betraying absence. Besides, being of no former acquaintance with Mr. Fussel there was no probable cause to render him suspected. But with our charitable prayers for his freedom, referring our censures either of his innocence or guilt to his further trial at the next Sessions, we will return to our relation.

Major Thomson not being found, his wife is took in hold, who though clearing herself from the knowledge of any such thing as the borrowing of the gun, yet is continued a prisoner till her husband shall be produced. Who being then about some urgent occasions in the country, on the first news of her confinement suddenly hastens to London, where being examined before a justice of peace he confesses he borrowed a carbine that day of Mr. Holloway and that he borrowed it at the desire of Mr. George Strangwayes, who acquainted him with no farther use he intended to make of it than for the killing of a deer. For which use he charged it with a brace[12] of bullets and as some say a slug, which I believe not, there being but two orifices where they entered his head and one bullet sticking in the window. If any object two bullets may enter at one orifice, though it be something unlikely we will not stand to dispute it, the number not being so uncertain as their fatal errand was certainly performed.

Being thus charged and primed, between the hours of seven and eight at night he meets Mr. Strangwayes in St. Clements Churchyard, to whom he delivers the gun. Where he spent that interval of time between the reception of it and the execution of the murder is uncertain, he having left in that kind no satisfying relation. It is most like traversing the streets near the place, that so he might take advantage of the fairest opportunity, which now unluckily offers itself.

Mr. Fussel, in the manner as is declared before, was retired into his chamber. He that shot the gun, as some report, stood on a bulk[13] belonging to a pewterer living overright [beside] Mr. Fussel's lodging. But it is something unlikely, the bulk being of such a shelving form as not to admit a firm standing place unless he stood on that end of it next to Temple Bar, which if so, the situation of the window would have enforced him to shoot much sloping. Wherefore I rather conceive (which hath been to some confirmed by Major Strangwayes his own confession) that he which shot stood on the ground, which hath the most probable appearance of truth, the window not being so high as to impede his aim nor the distance so great for the shot to lose its force, though the carlip[14] is but short, wanting some inches of a yard in the barrel, as is affirmed by young Mr. Fussel, in whose hands it now is.

To give you a certain relation who fired the gun is that which I believe no man living can do, except there be (which I hope not) some such unhappy person yet alive, Mr. Strangwayes carrying that great secret with him to his grave, denying to reveal it at the Sessions here, as reserving it for the general Assizes hereafter. But joining with the common opinion of most men, I think it to be himself, knowing him to be a person that through the whole course of his life, in those actions that deserved the name of discreet showed too great a want of that. In this where a wicked subtlety was as requisite, as ever in his former actions a noble policy had been to commit his life, which lay exposed to the danger of every engagers discovery, into the hands of many in the performing an act which might with more facility be done by one. When he had fired it, the streets were so empty that he passed unnoted by any. Between the hours of ten and eleven he brought back the gun to Major Thomson's house, where leaving it he retires to his lodging, where in his absence he had left one to [im]personate him. That piece of policy being thus performed, he comes (according to his usual custom) into his lodging about seven in the evening and going up into his chamber made some small stay there, from whence taking the advantage of a time in which he found the employments of the household such as not to have the leisure to take much notice of his actions, he secretly conveys himself down the stairs and having a private way of opening the door, conveys himself out and his disguised friend in. Who, by those of the family being oft heard walking about the chamber, occasions that mistaken deposition of theirs concerning his being in the house.

Having now concluded that act of darkness he went about, he is once more returned to his lodging and secretly discharges his disguised friend. Hast[en]ing to bed, he lay there (though in all probability with no very quiet night's rest) till three in the morning, at which time the officers sent to apprehend him enter the house and hast[en]ing to his chamber, make known their dreadful errand, an act enough to have frighted a timorous [nervous] soul to a present confession. But he, with a resolved constancy slights those terrors of the law, and without any such reluctancy as argued the least depression of spirit, goes with them before Justice Blake, by whom (though carefully examined) there was nothing discoverable that could render him any ways suspected, more than the former enmity betwixt them. However, he is on suspicion committed to Newgate, where remaining with a countenance that appeared no ways clouded with guilt, he continued constant in the denial of the fact. In the interval between the time he was first committed and his confession, he fell violently ill of a sharp and dangerous pleurisy.[15] In which acute distemper, though summoned by the approaches of death, he continued in a resolute denial of the fact. But God, whose judgments here in this appeared but the road to his mercies hereafter, freed him from that less ignominious death that dying by the formalities of law, the burdening of his body might in confession disburden his soul. This was the time in which some of the Church of Rome and those of the more learned sort of their clergy, gave him frequent visits and (as they have caused it to be reported) converted him to their church. What of truth there is in this, which what the opinion generally received is, you shall hear toward the conclusion of our story.

On the Monday following the time of his being apprehended, being the one and twentieth of February, Major Thomson, to hasten the enlargement [release] of his imprisoned wife, being returned to London makes a full discovery before an officer on what occasion he borrowed the gun and in what manner and at what time he delivered it to Mr. Strangwayes in St. Clements Churchyard, who on this happy discovery is brought before Justice La Wright, he that took the examination of Mr. Thomson. Here it being demanded of him on what occasion he caused the gun to be borrowed, and brought to him charged at that time of the night, with such other questions as most immediately concerned the business in hand. And withal seeing Major Thomson there, whose discovery he had so little cause to doubt, that now seeing it performed and not being able to apprehend the manner how, he in an amazed terror after some minutes of a deep and considerate silence, in a most pathetical manner, acknowledging the immediate hand of God to be in this wonderful detection, he no longer veils his guilt with confident denials but in a humble and submissive lowliness of spirit, such as rather strove with the tears of a penitential Magdalene to expunge the rubric characters of his guilt than with the brazen impudence of a despairing Cain, by a sullen and surly denial to fly the mercies of that God whose vengeance will pursue him. He hath now confessed the fact, he stands now a contrite penitent with the excellent Seneca acknowledging, that: *Maxima peccantium pena est peccasse.*

(Epist. 97.)[16] [The greatest punishment for those sinning is to have sinned.] Yet though a convicted murderer, he is the compassionated object of all the beholders, whose heads he now makes fountains of tears by having so lately made his brother's a fountain of blood.

This doleful scene, with the pity of most but the wonder of all, being thus passed over he is now returned again a much lamented prisoner to Newgate. From whence February the four and twentieth he was brought to his trial at the Sessions house in the Old Bailey, where appearing with a countenance that carried in it a mixture of courage and contrition, being such as rather seemed dejected for offending the law of God than any ways terrified for any torments that could be inflicted upon him by the laws of man. Being demanded to plead he answers, that if it might on his being tried be admitted to him to die by that manner of death by which his brother fell, he would plead. If not, by refusing to plead, both preserve an estate to bestow on such friends for whom he had most affection and withal free himself from the ignominious death of a public gibbet.[17]

Many arguments (and those urgent and pressing) were used by the Lord Chief Justice [John] Glyn and the rest of the bench to induce him to plead, as laying before him the sin he committed in refusing to submit to the ordinary course of law, the terror of the death his obstinate silence would enforce them to inflict upon him. These with many other motives were used but all invalid, he remains impenetrable, refusing either to plead or to discover who it was that fired the gun, only affirms (which he continued till his death) that whoever fired it, it was done by his directions but with no intent to be the death of his brother-in-law, but only (as he was pleased to say) to let him know that a life made odious by so many pressing acts of unjustice as he had received from him, though by their politic contrivance defended from any punishment the law could inflict, yet was not safe where the person offended hath spirit enough to revenge an injury.

This (not to be justified resolution) cherished a long time by his hot and haughty spirit, had often on the sight of Mr. Fussel raised in him impetuous storms of rage, such that often broke out into that intemperance as both by word and letter he several times challenges him. And in consideration of his being something more impaired by age than himself, offers him what odds in length of weapon he could with reason and honour demand. This encountering naught but a silent and slighting repulse, he one day meeting him in Westminster Hall accosts him with this compliment: "Brother Fussel, it argues not discretion in us of either side, we being both Cavaliers [royalist officers], to submit our causes to this present course of law, where the most of our judges are such as were formerly our enemies. Calais Sands were a fitter place for our dispute than Westminster Hall."[18]

These affronts finding a man too subtle to seek any other revenge than what lay safe under the sure guard of the law, he rather seeks from thence to do him a certain mischief, than by the uncertain managing of a duel to run the hazard of being mischieved himself. So that he not only refused that way of deciding the quarrel, but indicts his brother Strangwayes as a challenger, which adding more fuel to his former conceived rage puts him upon this dangerous way of satisfying his vindictive passion. And though he by a constant asseveration [declaration] affirms that the firing of the gun was only intended to terrify him, he affirming, that had not the hand of him who fired it fell lower than was intended, it had been impossible for the bullets to have so unhappily hit the mark. Yet its being charged with three bullets, whereas small shot (if only intended to affright) would have been a more certain terror with less hazard of danger, is an argument so prevalent with most men, that the action carries no fairer a face than a horrid and willful murder.

But not to engulf too far in censuring the act, we hasten to declare (as far as concerns our business in hand) the demeanor of the actor, who persisting on his first resolution not to plead hears from the offended court this dreadful sentence:

"That the prisoner be sent to the place from whence he came, and that he be put into a mean house stopped from any light, and that he be laid upon his back with his body bare, saving something to cover his privy parts. That his arms shall be stretched forth with a cord, the one to one side of the prison, the other to the other side of the prison, and in like manner shall his legs be used. And that upon his body shall be laid as much iron and stone as he can bear, and more. And the first day shall he have three morsels of barley bread, and the next day shall he drink thrice of the water in the next channel to the prison door, but no spring or fountain water: And this shall be his punishment till he die."

This thunderbolt of judgment levelled at his life, he yet with a passive valour (high as ever was his active), with a constancy which might cast a blush on the ghost of an ancient Roman hearse, but continues his resolution. Being returned to the prison, from thence [he] writes this sad letter to his brother-in-law Major Dewie, a member of parliament and a gentleman that had married another of his sisters:

Dear Brother,

I hope these lines and pressing death, will so far expiate my crime as to procure your and my other friends' forgiveness. For my conscience bears me witness, I was provoked by many of my brother-in-law's insufferable wrongs. After diverse parleys, finding his inveterate spleen[19] so implacable as to indict and inform against me at the open bench, my flesh and blood held no longer patience but sought to usurp the revengeful attribute which God appropriates to himself, when he would not answer me in single combat, though I offered him advantage in length of weapon. Yet this I will assure you, that I did not intend his death but by the discharging of a warning piece to have only terrified his heart from practicing litigious suits, and thereby to let him know that he was at another man's mercy if he contemned the same.

In a word, each man oweth a death, I two, by this untimely fact: the one to my maker, the other to the law, which invokes to pay the one the more willingly, being confident that the other is cancelled by the all-seeing eye of divine mercy and justice. These in short are the last words of

> Your dying brother,
> George Strangways

From the Press Yard in Newgate,
23 February, 1658

This being one of the last scenes he was to act on the stage of mortality, he now retires by divine contemplation to dress his soul in those robes of repentance wherewith she was suddenly to meet her celestial bridegroom. In which pious action he hath the frequent assistance of divines, some of excellent abilities as Dr. Wilde and Dr. Warmsley. There was also with him Mr. Jenkins, Mr. Watson, and Mr. Norton, to all of which by a repentant acknowledgement of the foulness of his crime, by a detestation of all those thoughts that had formerly fomented his malice, and by a solemn and serious invocation of his redeemer for the increasing of those rays of mercy which (even in that dark and dismal agony the apprehension of guilt might have plunged her into) he yet found irradiate the darkest apprehensions of a soul clouded with sin and sorrow.

To some whose zeal (if meriting the name) was more in that act than their discretion, when with the harsh and unseasonable rigid means of the law they appeared rather as if they came to fright his soul into a distracting despair than to fortify her with comforts fit to undergo so sad a conflict. He desiring them to proceed no further in so unseasonable a discourse, with an exalted height of Christian confidence affirming that through the powerful operation of mercy, whose restoratives he felt even in the grasp of death, he doubted not but his scarlet sins were washed white as wool. And that (though through the red sea of his brother's blood) he should safely arrive at the Celestial Canaan [Heaven]. Thus spending that narrow stock of time allowed him for the levelling his accounts with Heaven, as if his soul, which before travelled with a snail-like slowness towards her Celestial home, were now in her full career, the fatal day arrives.

On Monday the last of January, about eleven o'clock in the morning, the sheriffs of London accompanied with diverse officers came to the press yard, where after a short time of stay Major Strangwayes was guarded down. He was clothed all in white: waistcoat, stockings, drawers, and cap, over which was cast a long mourning cloak, a dress that handsomely emblemed the condition he was then in. Who though his soul wore a sable robe of mourning for her former sins, it was now become her upper garment and in some few minutes being cast off, would discover the immaculate dress of mercy which was under it.

From hence is he guarded to the dungeon, the sad and dismal place of execution, being accompanied by some few of his friends, amongst which was the Reverend Dr. Warmsley, whose pious care intended now to be near as inseparable to him as life itself. Having asked the executioner for a place to kneel in, and being answered that there was none of more conveniency than the bottom of the dungeon. "Well," said he, "this place must then serve him who is forced immaturely to fall, for there can be no greater vanity in the world than to esteem the world which regardeth no man, and to make slight account of God who greatly respected all men. For only, gentlemen, let me tell you, had I served my God as faithfully as I served my lord and master, my king, I had never come to this untimely end. But blessed be God for all, I shall willingly submit and earnestly implore your prayers for the carrying me through this great work."

Then turning to Dr. Warmsley, he said, "Sir, will you be pleased to assist me with your prayers?"

Doctor: "Yes Major, I come to officiate that Christian work, and the Lord strengthen your faith and give you confidence and assurance in the merits of Jesus Christ."

After they had spent some short time in prayer, Dr. Warmsley taking him aside had with him some small time of private conference concerning the clear demonstration of the faith he died in and about receiving the sacrament,[20] they appeared something to differ in opinion, which renders the world much unsatisfied as, in point of religion, whether he died a Protestant or not. Those of the Church of Rome affirming that whilst he lay sick of his pleurisy he was visited by several Catholics that are in orders [priests], some of whose names I have heard, and that they proved so prevalent with him that they had wrought him to an absolute conversion, and that they were confident, though he had not long lived so, in that faith he died. Whether this be true I leave every judicious reader to judge by the succeeding circumstance.

When he had left off his conference with Dr. Warmsley, in which he desired him not to press at that unseasonable time matters of controversy, it being a matter full of danger to disturb that calm the soul ought to wear when she comes to encounter death, and then applying himself to the company in general, with a voice something more elevated than ordinary, speaks these words:

"For my religion (I thank my God) I never had thought in my heart to doubt it, I die in the Christian religion," but never mentioned the Protestant, "and am assured of my interest in Christ Jesus, by whose merits I question not but my soul shall ere long triumph over these present afflictions in eternity of glory, being reconciled to the mercies of my God through my Saviour Jesus Christ, into whose bosom I hope to be gathered, there to enjoy that eternal, infinite, and boundless happiness wherewith he rewards all the elect. So the Lord bless you all, bless you in this world till he brings you to a world ever blessed. And bless me in this last and dreadful trial. So let us all pray: Jesus, Jesus have mercy on me."

Having said this, he takes his solemn and last leave of all his lamenting friends, and now prepares for that dreadful assault of death he was speedily to encounter. His friends placed themselves at the corners of the press, whom he desired when he gave the words to lay on the weights. His hands and legs are extended, in which action he cries out, "Thus were the sacred limbs of my ever-blessed Saviour, stretch forth on the cross, when suffering to free the sin-polluted world from an eternal curse." Then crying forth with a clear and sprightful voice, "Lord Jesus receive my soul," which was the promised signal, those sad assistants perform their dreadful task and laid on at first-weight, which finding too light for a sudden execution, many of those standing by added their burdens to disburden him of his pain. Which notwithstanding for the time of its continuance, as it was to him a dreadful sufferance, so was it to them a horrid spectacle, his dying groans filling the uncouth dungeon with the voice of terror. But this dismal scene soon finds a quiet catastrophe, for in the space of eight or ten minutes at the most his unfettered soul left her tortured mansion, and he from that violent paroxysm falls into the quiet sleep of death.

His body having lain some time in the press, he was brought forth, in which action, ere coffined, it was so much exposed to the public view, that many standers by beheld the bruise made by the press, whose triangular form, being, placed with the acute angle about the region of the heart, did soon deprive that fountain of life of its necessary motion, though he was prohibited that usual favour in that kind to have a sharp piece of timber laid under his back to accelerate its penetration. The body appeared void of all scars and not deformed with blood, but where the eminencies [weights] of the press touched on the middle parts of the breast and upper of the belly. His face was bloody, but as it appeared to the most inquisitive spectators, not from any external injury but the violent forcing of the blood from the larger vessels into the veins of the nose and eyes, whose smaller branches forced open by so sudden a compression, as if they mourned in the colour of his crime, had their last tears composed of blood. And now committed to that sable cabinet, his coffin, he is in a cart that attended at the prison door conveyed to Christ Church, where his ashes shall sleep till time herself be dissolved to eternity. And as it is our Christian duty to hope hath made good in every part this excellent saying of an ancient philosophical poet,

> *Cedit item retro, de terra quod fuit ante,*
> *in terram, & quod missumst ex aetheris oris*
> *id rersum caeli rellatum temple receptant.*

> (Lucretius Lib. 4)[21]

[Then, too, that which was of the earth returns
to earth, and that which was sent from the regions of the firmament
the shining temples of Heaven welcome returning.]

Thus did they leave the busy world, the one,
So swiftly from all mortal trouble gone;

As if his soul practiced at first to fly,
With the light motions of eternity:

Gone with such silence, as his hasty breath,
By a few groans disdained to parl with death,
Which fatal swiftness did the other lead,
A sad slow road to the grave; his soul to read.

Repentant lectures, being taught before,
It in a storm of tortures did pass o'er,
The rubric sea of life, whose high-swollen flood,
Passions hot dictates doubly died in blood.

When scarce this nation e're saw son of hers,
That wrote revenge in such red characters,
Can she but mourn, her offspring should inherit,
With English valour an Italian spirit?

Such as is, by a hot intemperate rage,
Become the shame, and wonder of the age,
No, let her mourn; the sad expression runs,
In the same strain with what her true-born sons.

Disrobe their thoughts in; But me-thinks I hear
A sort whose separation would appear,
As if refined with purer flames of zeal,
Than other Christians are; by no appeal.

Made to the throne of mercy to be won,
From harshly censurings: but such acts being done,
By men, whose different judgments not embrace,
Their tenants in the whole, defects of grace.

Not humane lapses; But take heed thy proud,
And Pharisaic heart speak not too loud,
Where Heaven commands a silence. Since none knows,
To what mysterious destiny he owes.

A debt to nature, in whose gloomy cell
Life's fairest transcripts have too often fell,
By sad untimely deaths. Then with the free
And Christian candour of white charity,

Forbear to cast thy sable censure on
This sanguine guilt; And since that both are gone

Beyond the verge of mortal knowledge, let
Not thy harsh censure aggravate the debt,

Which (if they nature's Common Laws obey)
Just sorrow teaches all their friends to pay.

Notes

1 This chapbook was reprinted in *The Harleian Miscellany; or, A Collection of Scarce, Curious, and Entertaining Pamphlets and Tracts . . . found in the late Earl of Oxford's Library*, Vol. VII (London: Robert Dutton, Gracechurch Street, 1810), pp. 9–24. There, the name "Strangeways" is used throughout, rather than the original "Strangwayes."

2 The English Civil War, especially the first phase (1642–46).

3 The text clearly reads "Mussen" (with long-s's) in several locations and is reprinted as such in the *Harleian Miscellany*. As no Mussen will be found in Dorset today, it is possible the author wrote "Mullen" (today's Corfe Mullen?) and the printer confused the handwritten l's as long-s's.

4 Minerva was the Roman goddess of wisdom, and Mars the Roman god of war. The author is suggesting that, though more warlike than wise, Strangwayes was not devoid of wisdom.

5 A *supersedeas* is a legal writ used to delay punishment pending an appeal; in this context, Strangwayes's pending execution will put an end to the other incident, but the author feels Strangwayes should have paid his debt ("parsimonious sparing"), since he would no longer have need for money.

6 A woman who had never been and was likely never to be married.

7 As an officer who was loyal to King Charles during the Civil Wars, Strangwayes was concerned that parliamentary forces would take his land if it was in his name.

8 Blandford Forum today.

9 Lady Justice, a medieval composition of the Greek goddesses of justice, Themis and Dike, and the Roman goddess, Justicia, was sometimes depicted with wings.

10 The text actually reads "fucagoes" but the author almost certainly meant "farragoes," which means a "confused mixture" or "hotchpotch." This was probably an error by the printer, who might have misread the author's handwriting, which likely misspelled the word as "faragoes" or "furagoes."

11 From Seneca the Younger's play, *Thyestes* (circa AD 65).

12 The original reads "lease" (with a long-s) but the author almost certainly wrote "brace" (likely with a long-s in place of the "c"). Thus, the printer could easily have misread this word. A "brace of bullets" is a common phrase suggesting multiple rounds were loaded or fired.

13 A framework extending from a building, such as as a balcony.

14 An obscure type of firearm.

15 An illness of the lungs associated with sharp pain while breathing.

16 Seneca the Younger, *Epistles to Lucilius*, letter 97 ("On the Degeneracy of the Age"), paragraph 14, sometimes translated as "the punishment of crime lies in the crime itself."

17 Strangwayes wanted to be shot to death, or, if this was not allowed, he would refuse to plead and suffer pressing in order to protect his estate from forfeiture and avoid the shame of being hanged.

18 Calais Sands refers a spit of land attached to the beachfront in Calais, France, which from Dover, England, is the shortest route across the English Channel. Duels were often fought

in this location both because they were illegal in England and France, and because Calais Sands was deemed to be neutral ground, and thus outside the reach of the law. Westminster Hall was the location of the three main common law courts. Thus, Strangwayes would rather settle the dispute through honourable fighting than through the courts.

19 The phrase "inveterate spleen" was commonly used to mean rage or violent temper.

20 The Catholic sacrament of extreme unction, one of the last rites administered to those in immediate danger of death, which was disavowed in Protestant faiths.

21 Although the extract is correct, this passage comes from Lucretius, *On the Nature of Things*, book II, not book IV as stated by the author.

17 The gardener's gallows reprieve

There is evidence that malicious prosecution, such as appears to have been the case in this story, was a common occurrence in the early modern period. At a time when apprentices and servants – typically, teenaged boys and girls – had limited legal authority and freedom, false accusations of crimes such as rape and sodomy were frequent, particularly against their masters or somebody else in their households. Malicious prosecution typically occurred when the accuser wished to gain some benefit from the accused, such as when girls who had become pregnant through an assignation wished to secure financial support, or when servants wished to get out of their legal contracts, which is possibly the situation in this story. In this case of alleged buggery, the youth Henry Wells was obviously deemed to be credible, likely because of the earnestness and consistency of his story over several retellings (and it is possible that despite his ultimate retraction, he was telling the truth). As described in quite exciting and fast-paced prose, the gardener's reprieve happened at the brink of death, when Wells, after much pressure and separated from his family of supporters, recanted his statement. This was followed by a hasty audience with no less than the person of the king himself, Charles II, who authorized the gardener's reprieve and encouraged the news of it to precede the formal pardon, for fear that in the meantime an innocent man might be executed. Most commendable in this case are the actions of the ordinary and keeper, who tirelessly fought for the exoneration of a man they believed to be innocent. This case reminds us that, even in the face of serious allegations of sexual misconduct – buggery being considered one of the greatest affronts against the laws of God and nature – the participants of the criminal justice system did not simply let those accused of serious crimes be punished without due consideration.

***

Innocency reprieved, or the gardener at the gallows, for buggery, laid to his charge. Being a true narrative of a strange and admirable passage of God's providence in the reprieve of Thomas Rivers, gardener, living at St. Giles in Southampton buildings, who, being indicted for buggering his apprentice Henry Wells, a lad about 15 years of age, was condemned on Friday the 13th of this instant December at the Old Bailey Sessions and drawn to Tyburn the Wednesday following, about 10 o'clock. Where being tied up, the lad and his mother being present, they declare the wrong they had done him, who thereupon was reprieved. Also the passages between the master and servant when brought back. Written by one who was an eye and ear witness. {*London, 1667*}

I cannot stand to make any preface to the ensuing narrative, in regard I am confined in my time and to one sheet of paper. I shall therefore apply myself to inform the reader of what I had from his own mouth who is the subject of this ensuing discourse. Thomas Rivers, gardener, aged about 27 years, dwelling in Southampton buildings in Vine Street, took an apprentice or servant whose name is Henry Wells, a lad about 15 years old. The said Rivers had married a wife above two years before and brought her out of Ireland, who is a woman of an honest and simple behaviour. This boy ran away from his master about three months ago, and being a lad of a prompt wit and confidence, spent much of his time about birds, which Mr. Rivers's wife also delighted in and occasioned her, when he was with them, to allow him something for the keeping of them and would range up and down the fields to take his pleasure.

But the said Rivers, about two months after this lad ran away, understanding he was with his mother, obtained two warrants to apprehend him[1] and bring him home again, the last whereof he served upon him with his own hands about three weeks or a month ago, and had the boy before a justice. Where being come, he swore *That the occasion of his running away from his said master was because he had several times buggered him.* Upon which oath, the said Rivers was committed to the Gatehouse,[2] where he remained about 16 days. And when the last Sessions was in the Old Bailey, December 11, 1667, he was brought from thence to Newgate, and from thence to his trial at the Old Bailey. There came this lad and swore against him *That his said master Thomas Rivers, did one time when his mistress was forth, invite him, the said Henry Wells, into bed to him and asked if he were cold, which he said he was, and then and there he buggered him and entered his body. And that after that he took him in the cellar and tied him up by the two wrists and there abused him, and also that upon a Sunday after, the said master took him out into the fields and did the like unto him after he had bound him.*

There came in behalf of Mr. Rivers the gardener two or three witnesses, viz. the constable, the beadle,[3] and a neighbour. The two former did assert *That they were present when the master apprehended the boy and had him before the justice, and that then the boy swore he had buggered him eight times.* The other spake to his conversation and living, *which*, he said, *was harmless and innocent, the said Rivers being of a very softly disposition and nature.* But all this took not away the boy's evidence, which he declared with so much confidence and answering all objections that the said Thomas Rivers was brought in guilty on Friday the 13th day of this instant December, 1667, and accordingly, was condemned to be hanged at Tyburn (the common place of execution) for the said fact.

Between the sentence and the execution, the minister of the place, Mr. Welden, was often with him and, after many serious exhortations, did persuade [encourage] him to confess his fact, and thereby give glory to God, whose justice had brought him to that signal punishment. But Mr. Rivers still persisted on his innocency, and the burden of all still was *That he was as innocent from the fact as the child unborn.* And notwithstanding his remorse and repentance, which was kindly and good, for all his former sins, but observing that this had no impression at all upon him, put Mr. Welden, the minister (whose prudent industry in this thing is much to be commended), upon a more strict examination of the boy. Which accordingly he did, having sent for him on Sunday and at other times, found the boy still in the same story. Some of the keepers also taking the lad to task, yet could not find him vary one word from what he had sworn at the court.

And now the fatal day of Mr. Rivers's execution is come, which was on Wednesday the 18th day of this instant December, 1667. He, being prepared to die, was put into the cart that morning, about 10 o'clock, and so guarded away to Tyburn. But still God was pleased to put it upon the heart of Mr. Welden, the minister of Newgate, to send one of the keepers again for this boy, who was brought accordingly and carried to the White Hart Tavern in Smithfield and there again examined and exhorted in the fear of God, that if he had sworn falsely against his master, that he would then and there declare it. But still the boy persisted in his report. And it was observed before by the minister and the keeper that the boy's mother, whose name is Wells, and also others of his kindred did used to whisper to him, either before or after they had examined him. Mr. Welden singles him out from them and takes him into a coach with himself and the keeper, and so he accompanied his master to the gallows. Yet all this while, he did not discover the least remorse of heart.

Being all come to the place of execution, Mr. Rivers is tied up to the gallows, and here having made his last speech and prayer, he now waited for the fatal turn [execution] that should turn him into eternity. And now was the last time that this lad had to confess his error, which accordingly he did, being in the same cart where the prisoner was to be turned over. The minister told him, *That now was the last time he had to declare his conscience and the truth of the fact.* The lad, seeing his master now upon the brink of death and his cap ready to be pulled down over his eyes, cried out, *That he had wronged his master and sworn falsely against him.* The minister hearing that bid him direct his speech to the people, which accordingly he did and declared to them that were spectators that he was foresworn, which the boy's mother also did at the place of execution.

Upon which, the ordinary (having order before, if the boy did deny it) taking notice, presently dispatched one of the sheriff's officers with one of the keepers to the King's Majesty, who immediately riding to Whitehall, he found His Majesty at dinner. They declared to His Majesty the whole business, whereupon His Majesty was graciously pleased to order them forthwith to return back with all haste and reprieve the prisoner and not stay for methodizing [authorizing] it, lest it should be too late. And now the messenger of life being come to the place, which is to the prisoners as a resurrection from the dead, where he was untied from the gallows and brought back again on horseback behind one of the officers, with halter about his neck, the officer having the end of it in his halberd [right] hand.[4] They alighted at the tavern with the guard, where came into him again the boy and his friend, who again asked him forgiveness, to whom he meekly said *the Lord forgive you, for I do*. And being desired to drink a glass of wine, he took only one glass and reflected again upon some passages of his own life, repeating what he thought had been amiss in himself. He could not call to mind any pleasure he had been else [otherwise] addicted unto, unless it were ringing,[5] which being still with the rope about his neck and the noose under his ear, as it was put by the executioner, some of the company thought that might put him more than ordinary in mind of it.

From thence he was conveyed unto Newgate where he now remains, and several of his friends and neighbours being with him the next morning and discoursing with him about diverse things as concerning the fact, unto which he answered, he thanked God he was never so much as tempted to it. Also concerning his death, and what thoughts he had when he thought he should be turned off, he answered, that he had thoughts of dying but withal a very great impress upon his mind that his innocency, as to that thing, would be cleared up before or at his death, which he saith he was persuaded to from a dream that happened to him the night before he was carried to be executed, which was this:

> He thought he beheld himself in a field of wheat, and whilst he was beholding the goodliness of the corn there were abundance of turtledoves come flying about him, and others stood before him staring him in the face, which he looks upon as emblems of innocency, and the wheat to be near the harvest but yet not wholly ripe for the sickle.[6]

Notes

1 As an apprentice or indenture contract was a binding agreement, Rivers had the legal right to force the return of Wells to his service.

2 A prison physically adjoining Westminster Abbey that was torn down in 1776.

3 A minor town or church official who carried out civil, educational, and ceremonial duties, and served as the "town crier."

4 Although Rivers escaped the gallows, he was still considered to be a prisoner because he had received a stay of execution pending his formal pardon from the king, which still required proper "methodizing."

5 Bell ringing was a popular pastime that came under attack during the Protestant Reformation because it was popularly believed to possess spiritual power in relation to the dead and

dying, and was derided as a Catholic ritual. In this content, it was perceived to be a vice, like gambling, drinking, and sabbath-breaking.

6 At this time, dreams were commonly believed to predict the future through metaphorical and analogous revelations. In this case, turtledoves conferred innocence and the wheat, which metaphorically represented Rivers, was not yet ready to be harvested by the sickle, a symbol of death. As the anonymous author well knew, early modern readers would have little difficulty understanding the importance of this dream.

18 The murderous siblings of Monmouth

This short chapbook describes a murder committed against an innocent and supportive mother by her avaricious son and his servant. The background is familiar. A young man of good upbringing was placed into an apprenticeship with an attorney, which set him up for a decent life until he should inherit his deceased father's estate. Unwilling to wait for nature to take its course, Henry Jones expected his mother to give up the estate, which brought her a good annual income, and which by law and right were hers for the remainder of her life. Henry thus got his mother alone and shot her in the head before his servant, George Briggis, cut her throat. Mary Jones was an accomplice to the murder because she had foreknowledge of her brother's intentions and because she tried to hide the crime by laundering his bloody clothing. It is interesting that each of the three criminals suffered a different form of death, demonstrating that the manner of execution was as important as the outcome. Henry refused to plead and was pressed to death over the course of two torturous days. George was hanged by the neck until dead. He was lucky that he was Henry's servant and not the victim's, else he might have been convicted of petty treason and been subjected to the brutal punishment of drawing and quartering. Mary was burned at the stake. This was the standard punishment for a woman convicted of petty treason, which, in this case, applied to a daughter who murdered her mother. Presumably, had Henry Jones pleaded and been convicted, he, too, would have suffered the fate of a petty treasoner – being hanged, drawn, and quartered. Unlike nearly every other chapbook in this collection, the anonymous author did not offer moral commentary about the decrepit state of a society that saw children turn against a mother purely for greed. In some ways, this makes the murder of Mrs. Grace Jones very straightforward, and for that reason, all the more terrible.

***

A most barbarous murder, being a true relation of the trial and
condemnation of Henry Jones and Mary Jones at the Assizes
held for the town and county of Monmouth, before the judges
appointed for that circuit on Thursday the 7th of March, 1671. For
murdering of their own mother, Mrs. Grace Jones of Monmouth,
in the county of Monmouth, on the eleventh day of October last,
1671. With the particulars of the murder and the wonderful
discovery of the murderers. Also their confessions and speeches at
the places of execution on Saturday the 16th of this instant March,
1672. With allowance. *London: Printed for E. Horton, 1672*

Henry Jones of Monmouth, in the county of Monmouth, by his late father
Thomas Jones of the said town, was very carefully brought up in his youth.
And when he came to maturity, put by his said father to an attorney, and after
he had served his time with his master, did return home to his said mother
Grace Jones, his father being then dead and left her possessed of a very good
estate for her life, to the value of £100 per annum. And afterwards practising
for the space of two years in good reputation and credit in the place where
he lived did several times persuade his said mother Grace Jones to part with
her estate to him that he might enjoy the same. But his said mother, knowing that it was her right for her life and being then possessed of it, having no
other maintenance for her and the rest of her children, did refuse to grant his
request, but withal did not deny to assist and help him in his necessity and
occasion to the utmost of her ability.

Yet not being satisfied with the kindness of his mother in parting with
what she could afford, but coveting the possession in his own hands, [he] did,
on the eleventh day of October last past entice his said mother to walk with
him into the fields to a barn of hers about a quarter of a mile from Monmouth,
persuading her that she had lost corn out of it. And said, he had often told
her of it, yet she would never believe him, but now he could make it appear
plainly to her, if she would please to go with him to the barn to see, telling
his mother that she would do very well to look after it. At length, through
her son's much importuning of her, she went with him towards the evening in
her slippers, and coming to the barn, she found the corn scattered from thence
to a small wood about two furlongs[1] from it. Which corn Henry Jones and
his servant, George Briggis, had before scattered and carried into the wood,
the better to make his mother believe that to be true which he had before
affirmed to be so, and likewise to execute his bloody intent upon her, which
he had designed several times before. Which accordingly he brought to pass
in persuading his mother to go to the wood, and there she should find several
sheaves of her wheat.[2]

The mother, coming to the woodside, was very unwilling to have gone into
it and desired her son to bring the corn to the stile by the side of it. Yet at her
son's entreaty she went into it, where she found several sheaves as her son had
told her. And stooping down to feel whether it were wheat or straw, rubbing

it in her hands, her son shot her in the head with a pistol charged with a slug. Which done, he bade his boy George Briggis do his office, who thereupon cut her throat and told his master *That his mother's throat cut as tough as an old ewe's*. This done, the son took from her five pounds in money and several rings which was on her fingers. After all this, the son and his boy (who was a butcher's son near the town of Monmouth) endeavoured to draw the dead body to a river near the wood, but it proving too heavy for them, they were forced to leave it near to the place where they did the murder. The servant, for thus complying with his master's desire in the murder, had five pounds promised him by his said master and a new suit of clothes.

After which, the boy went to the farmhouse of his slain mistress near the wood and the son to his mother's house in Monmouth. Who had not above half a mile home at the most from the place where he committed the murder, yet he was four hours going thither, the Devil appearing to him in several shapes and leading him out of his way. At length he got to his mother's house, and coming to the door, giving a little rap with his fingers, his sister presently let him in (as was afterwards proved against her at the Assizes), who stayed up for him, and that night washed her brother's bloody clothes.

But early the next morning, a poor woman of Monmouth going to the wood to gather some sticks to make her a fire, chanced to see the dead body, and coming near to her found her to be Mrs. Grace Jones of Monmouth. Upon this, the woman returned back to the town and acquainted the magistrates that in such a wood there lay such a person murdered. Upon which they went to the house of Mrs. Grace Jones and found her son Henry Jones in bed, and told him, *They heard his mother was murdered.* He made very strange of it and seemed to be much troubled at it, but going with the townsmen to the place where his mother lay dead, by her was found several footsteps [footprints] and measuring the feet of them that were present they found those footsteps to fit the feet of Henry Jones. Suspecting him to be concerned, they charged him with the murder and had him and his man before two or three justices met for that purpose, who examined first the boy and then the master. The boy confessed that his master shot her in the head and the master said the boy cut her throat, and so the one impeached the other.

After this, the daughter, Mary Jones, was taken into examination, suspecting her to be guilty with her brother in this murder, not only for beating of the little children for crying and making inquiry after their mother, but for washing her brother's bloody clothes and endeavouring to conceal her mother's death. Yet some friends, thinking her to be innocent, became bail for her, and she went at liberty. But within five or six weeks after, she made her escape from Monmouth and was gone several miles towards London. But the bail [bondsman] hearing of it, she was pursued and apprehended and carried back again, where she was committed prisoner till the next Assizes.

For which bloody murder they were all three brought to trial at the Assizes held at Monmouth by the judges appointed for that circuit on Thursday the 7th of this instant March, 1671. Henry Jones, before the Assizes, confessed he shot his mother in the neck and the boy cut her throat after she lay gasping on the ground, but at the Assizes he stood mute and would not plead to his indictment. He had sentence to be pressed to death and was put under the press on Saturday the 9th of March, and was dead upon Monday the 11th of March about 12 o'clock.

George Briggis, the servant, was found guilty of the murder and was drawn upon a sledge to the gallows, and made this confession, *That he did cut his mistress's throat after she was shot*, for which he was hanged, according to his sentence, on Saturday the 16th of this instant March. Mary Jones, the sister, was also found guilty. She was drawn upon a sledge with the servant and was burned at a post near the gallows on the same day, being the 16th of March as abovesaid.

Notes

1 A furlong is approximately 200 metres.
2 In the early modern period, corn was a general term used to describe any cereal crop, such as wheat, rye, barley, and oats. In this case, the corn was wheat.

19 The widow's murder

One particularly interesting feature of this chapbook is that the first part appears to have been printed and distributed before the author had any knowledge of the murderer. Once John Randal was discovered and confessed his crime, the author or printer reissued the earlier tract, with the addition of the new information. (In fact, I have reversed the arrangement here to preserve the chronology; the original chapbook begins with the discovery of John Randal and then appends the first book.) Rather like modern newspaper reporting, the information was provided to the public as it became known, and guess-work was used to help complete the initial story. In the first book, the author predicts that the murderer was known to the victim because the robber did not have to force his way in, Widow Burton would not have let a stranger into the house, and, if it was a stranger, he would merely have bound and gagged her rather than kill her, as she would not know the robber's identity. The author is also certain that "time will produce and justice will reward" the murderer. As it turned out, the author's predictions came true in their entirety. John Randal was indeed known to Widow Burton, explaining both why he was allowed into the house and why he felt the need to murder her in order to rob Esquire Bluck's home, because she could easily have identified him to the authorities had she survived. Randal was captured because he returned to a nearby shop to collect razors he had previously brought in for sharpening, where a witness recalled that Randal had been the last person seen entering Bluck's home while Burton was house-sitting. Returning for his razors after murdering a woman and stealing more than forty pounds worth of silver plate led to Randal's undoing, and surely shows Randal to have been a greedy, arrogant, and over-confident man, in addition to an amateur murderer and thief.

***

The full discovery of the late horrid murder and robbery in Holborn, being the apprehension, examination, and commitment of John Randal, formerly butler to Esquire Bluck, where the same was done. With his confession of the fact and all particular circumstances before Sir William Turner. *London: Printed for John Millet, 1674*

The fifth of August, the squire being out of town with all his servants at his country house at Hunsdon in Hertfordshire, about twenty miles from London, having given charge and trust of his house to this ancient retainer to his family of known fidelity, whose care and diligence was manifested to the last, she having expressed both by the posture she was found in. The evening before this horrid murder, she charged the milk-woman that served the house that she should call the next morning, because she should have occasion for some milk, which accordingly she did, when coming to the door she found it open, not as it used to be. At which being amazed, she first knocked at the door for a considerable time, but neither seeing any person nor hearing any voice, she went in, where to her greater astonishment she found the body of the aforesaid Widow Burton lying in the parlor with her feet over the threshold, with a coverlet thrown over her. Which made the first discovery of this horrid murder and robbery, upon which coming forth strangely affrighted with this sad spectacle, the neighbours questioning the reason of her affrightment.

She relating the cause, immediately a constable was sent for, who came as speedily. At which time one of the esquire's servants from the country, accidentally coming to fetch some necessaries he was sent for, who meeting the constable and seeing such a tumult at the door, was much astonished. But hearing what was done, he, with the constable, was a spectator, not only of that sad spectacle of the murder of the housekeeper, but also went with the constable to observe what mischief was further acted, and upon search found all the doors and locks broke open. The loss is no way to be computed without the estimate of the esquire, who only knows that great loss he hath sustained; the jealousies concerning the actors as yet undiscovered. 'Tis hoped time will produce and justice will reward these two great and crying sins, rarely remaining without discovery and vengeance following at the heels.

'Tis strangely remarkable that this poor creature should thus horribly lie strangled, black in the face, and cold when she was first found, with her thread about her neck, wherewith she had been working. The bloody actor, not content with binding or gagging, which might have been security sufficient for his intended design of robbery, but 'tis feared the apprehension of his after discovery, prompted on that lamentable butchery, the expedition of which acts gives a further suspicion, it being so sudden, even the very day after the esquire went out of town, otherwise 'tis supposed his cruelty had not extended so far. 'Tis further observable that she never used to let in any into the house but such whose voice she well knew; and the street-door nor the lock were not broke, although after he had broke the other locks, both of room, trunks, etc.

were all broke, and all the said place miserably ransacked. The richest moveables no doubt taken away, all except one plate dressing-box which was left on a cupboard's head standing openly.

The coroner and jury found it murder.

Remember whatsoever hath been done in the most secret cell shall at last be discovered and proclaimed upon the house-top. Oh, that all these late sad examples, which several have so lately suffered the hand of divine and humane justice for, might take that good and everlasting rule given to Israel upon this account, might take effect, which was that Israel of old, was therefore spectators of the hand of justice, that so they might see justice executed and hear sentence passed, that they might hear and fear and do no more any such thing, which is the great design of the publication of these relations.

We gave you already as full an account as we could of that horrid murder committed at the house of Esquire Bluck, and though we were then in the dark altogether who it might be that should be guilty of that bloody fact, yet since the justice of Heaven, that rarely permits blood to go un-revenged even in this world, hath been pleased to make a full discovery thereof, which we think fit to publish, begins as follows.

One John Randal that was formerly butler to Esquire Bluck, and consequently was well acquainted with all the rooms and places in the house, and knew that when the family used to go out of town they left only this poor honest woman, the widow Burton, the party murdered, to look to the house, is found to be the bloody actor of this lamentable tragedy. He is a person of about thirty years of age and was turned away from the esquire's service about half a year since, which time he was married, and since that (as he pretends) has been in Holland or some part of the Low Countries, but he had not been near his master's house from the time of his going away till the day before the squire went forth of town.

So that 'tis probably thought, knowing what time he used to go forth with his family, he had before resolved on the wicked design. And then came when he might have an opportunity, for on Monday the third instant he came to a neighbour's house and, pointing to Esquire Bluck's house, asked who lived at that house? To which the shopkeeper, knowing of him and wondering he should ask, told him his master, to which he replied, he thought he had been gone. But, however, he went to the house and drank with this good old woman, whom he since murdered, who made him stay dinner and 'tis likely told him her master was to go out of town. The next day he came again and drank with her, and on Wednesday brought three razors to be set at the razor-shop next door, which he left and was seen to go into this house (where as since appears he did this horrid murder), and so went away with a considerable quantity of plate undiscovered. Nor was there any likelihood of finding him out.

But behold, on Friday the seventh instant, about eight or nine o'clock in the evening, he came to this shop for his razors, when a gentlewoman that has part of the shop, having some mistrust of him because he was the last she saw go into the house before the murder done, no sooner saw him again but she was violently persuaded he was the murderer. And therefore, running whilst he stood in the shop to Squire Bluck, who was then at home, they got a constable and apprehended him and carried him before a justice, where he first stoutly denied the fact, but being asked where his lodging was and answering such a place in Whitecross Street, the same was ordered to be searched whilst he was kept before the justice. Where in his trunk they found plate of the squire's to the value of forty pounds, which was brought and shewed him. And then he confessed the fact, declaring that he sat with the poor woman talking till night, and that then she telling him it was late and time for him to be gone, he struck her with his fist and killed her, but denied that he had any more plate or any money save four four-pence-half-pennies and one nine-pence, whereupon he was committed to Newgate.

And considering all the cruel circumstances of this most bloody fact and the clear evidence against this person, both by the place taken into his custody and his own confession, there is small grounds or reason left to hope that he can escape in this world without satisfying for her death with his own. Though it is to be wished that by sincere repentance he may wash his soul from the stains of blood and so escape the second death and punishment everlasting.

20 The drover's suicide

In early modern England, it was common for girls aged about twelve to twenty to be put into domestic service in the home of another family, which is possibly the situation of the young victim in this story. There, they learned the skills that would later be useful when they became wives and mothers, such as cooking and cleaning, washing and mending clothing, preparing fruit, vegetables, and meats for the cold months, and assisting in raising younger children. These girls often fell prey to the men of the household, whether – as in this case of William Stapeler – the master of the house, or one of his sons or male servants. The author of this tale emphasizes the girl's lack of consent for this licentious act, which was necessary, along with elements such as evidence of penetration, physical attempts to resist, and calling out for help, to prove rape in court. Perhaps surprisingly, but not unusually for a man with a family to support, Stapeler was given a chance to provide bail in exchange for his freedom until the case went to trial. He was thus allowed to return home, in the company of a constable, to secure the bail. After confessing to his wife and kissing her and his children goodbye, Stapeler promptly left the house and hanged himself in a stable, which is interpreted by the author as a clear admission of guilt and a warning to all other "loose livers." This was merely one of many similar cases that were, to the anonymous author, signs of the times.

***

Sad and lamentable news from Romford, being a true and dreadful relation of the sad and dreadful end of one William Stapeler, a drover, who committed a rape, or ravishment, upon the body of a young girl that lodged in his house. For which he was brought before a justice of the peace on Tuesday last, being the 15th of this instant September, who after his examination hanged himself. *London: Printed for B. W., 1674*

Strange and dreadful nowadays are the actions of poor sinful mortals. No sooner can the sinful and dreadful action of one be past but that another appears. No sooner can the dreadful action of theft be mentioned in the mouth of a man, but peradventure he shall presently hear of the like action of theft committed by another. If reports fly abroad of murder, committed upon the body of man or woman, no sooner can the fire of that be kindled but that another presently appears, springs forth, and is presently heard of. We can hardly sleep in our beds but that we shall quickly hear of one sad accident or other.

If you hear not of theft, it is a thousand to one if you don't hear of murder; if you don't hear of murder, peradventure but that you shall hear of dreadful matters committed by one wretch or other, either murder, theft, rape, or such like sad transactions. So that if a man had the wisdom of Solomon, who writ so many proverbs and cautions and admonitions, whereby the sons of men might be (if grace were, which they so much slight, given to them, to be) as a guide to their feet and a lantern to their paths, to prevent and shun those damnable courses of the Devil, who is the chief instrument and contriver of the lost and undone estate of poor mankind.

But alas, my poor genius is too weak as to speak one word in a proper sense of these things. Neither is this our age sufficient to blazen forth to public view the sad transactions of this our age, committed by the sons of men. How dreadful is it to hear that at one Sessions one and twenty should be justly condemned, most shamefully to suffer by the hand of justice for their sad and dreadful murders and thefts by them committed. God in mercy grant that those who were lately executed may be an example and a cause to make them yet remaining in Newgate, and all others, to be forewarned at the hearing of the cutting off of nine of those their companions, whose lives were then justly sacrificed by the hand of justice for their just deserts. That so they may fear and dread the just hand of God, who oversees the ways of all men, and rightly judges and takes an account of all that men shall do, whether it be good or evil.

As does appear even in this our days, for the dreadful news from the Sessions House, which ended but on Friday last, would affright one but would not in the least move the heart of this our sad object of whom we intend now to speak of. We say, could not in the least move him to repentance, but, like Judas, went and hanged himself. In the town of Romford in Essex, ten miles from London, lived a poor sinful wretch who regarded not the law of God in the least, neither gave he heed to his just hand of revenge upon those that obey not his commandments. Let all good Christian people beg of God for saving grace, that may deliver them in the day of evil and in the hour of temptation.

This sinful wretch, William Stapeler by name, was a man that by outward view and appearance was a sad sinful wretch, and a wicked and loose liver, so that by the report of his neighbours, he lived by little else but by pilfering and stealing. Some report that he got his living altogether that way. Some say it hath been his practice all his lifetime to rob and steal from his poor neighbours and others. Others say and report that if he had his just due he had been hanged a year ago for stealing. Others report him to be as sad a wretch for whoring, drinking, swearing, stealing, and such like as lived in those parts. And, although yet the mercy of God was such as that his sins went a long time unpunished and his notorious faults escaped without punishment.

Yet this poor wretch, who was a drover[1] so called, and usually brought cattle to Smithfield Market and elsewhere in London, would not forbear his sinful courses, but having a girl, about thirteen years of age, coming to his house to lodge and continuing in his house upon a time the Devil put it into his heart to commit uncleanness with this tender bud. Making his attempt, he was, by God's providence, and the good education of the young damsel, hindered of his hellish purpose. But he still going on in his unbridled lust, he takes an advantage upon a time when his wife and children were out of the way, and deluding the poor girl into a private room, where he most barbarously and most filthily and abominably committed rape, or ravishment, upon the body of this young girl, who endeavoured with loud shrieks and outcries to have made this unhuman wretch to be discovered. Although for a time it seemed to little purpose, but at length, before his departure, she was heard to cry out and immediately company came in, and understanding the matter and circumstance of the business of this beastly rape and ravishment, he was laid hold on and was carried before a justice. And evidence coming against him, he was found guilty of his accusation,[2] for which the justice was sending him to gaol, but he pleading to go under bail, it was at length granted him.

And going home with the constables to provide good security, he was admitted to go into his own house without the constable but was as thought severely watched by them. But he coming into his house, told his wife that he had been before a justice, and that he was to find bail or else to go to gaol. And moreover he told her that if that he was accused for should be proved against him at the Assizes, he should be hanged. Therefore he would get away from the constables and shift for himself. Whereupon he gave her five shillings in money and kissed her and his children, and went out at his back door, as though he had gone quite away from them all, but goes immediately into a stable, where he takes a line, and fastening it to the horse's rack, he most desperately hangs himself.

In the meantime the constable comes for him and his poor sorrowful wife tells them that she knows not of him, but great search was made but he could not be found. After it was over, a neighbouring woman came and told his wife that she see him go into such a barn, but the woman would not believe her for a long time, hoping that he had been further off than so. But at length, going to that stable where the woman told her, she found him hanging dead upon the horse's rack. And coming out, she shrieked and cried out in a most dreadful manner, tearing her hair and wringing of hands and begging that he may be a warning to all loose livers.

And that he so may, let every good Christian power out their prayers to God Almighty, that He may give wisdom to the foolish and grace to the graceless, that so they be prevented from those evil and dreadful ends as this poor wretch of whom we have spoken, which he committed upon his own body upon the 15th of this instant September.

Notes

1 A person hired to move or "drive" livestock from farm to market.
2 That is, there was sufficient evidence to produce an indictment.

21 The roasted apprentice

This brief tale is unusual in the crime chapbook genre because the criminals did not get their just reward. Instead, they made their escape while the victim was being removed from the spit on which he was being roasted alive. In many ways, this story is more about relationships – between husband and wife and master (or mistress) and servant – than it is about crime. While on an errand, the young apprentice in this case happened to discover that his mistress was visiting a house of ill repute and spoke honestly when questioned about this discovery by both his master and his mistress. His frankness was poorly rewarded. That the mistress chose such a brutal method for his murder, and then fled with her assistants, merely affirmed in the eyes of the author the woman's mean character. This was in sharp contrast to her upstanding husband, a tradesman and city councilor, and to his responsible apprentice. Like so many chapbooks, this was partly a cautionary tale that reminded husbands to keep closer watch over their households, wives to be more genteel and circumspect in their actions, and, perhaps, apprentices to know when to keep out of their employers' personal affairs.

***

Cruel and barbarous news from Cheapside in London, being a true and faithful relation of an horrid fact, acted by an unhuman mistress upon the body of her apprentice, who for want of the fear of God, hired two men to strip him naked and bind him to a spit, intending to roast him alive, but by the providence of Almighty God was prevented, for having stopped his mouth with a cloth, turning him about until he was very much scorched, with striving for life the cloth dropped out, and then crying out "murder" the neighbours by violence broke open the door, and delivered the poor wretch from the unmerciful flames, from which the Lord deliver us. *London: Printed for W. P., 1676*

How many wicked, cruel, and unhuman acts of murder do we almost daily hear of, so that we may justly cry out with the Prophet, "The people have sold themselves to do wickedness."[1] For want of the fear of God, they still run on in their wicked courses, until they destroy both body and soul to all eternity, not once thinking that they must one day give an account for all their wicked works which they do here commit. But who unto them that do harbor such thoughts in their breast, much more to commit such unheard of cruelties? Alas poor souls they think not what answer they must make before the great tribunal seat of God. Then they would wish they had never been born, or the mountains to fall upon them, or the hills to cover them from the presence of the most high God.

But now to leave this digression and come to the relation of this unhuman fact. I think that if it be considered in all the circumstances, there has not been heard of, in our age, a fact more barbarous than what this relation gives you, of a scale-maker's wife living near unto Cheapside. She was of light carriage and used to frequent taverns and playhouses, as many people do report; for she always took coach when she went out, but as she came back again she alighted in Cheapside and came home afoot, because she used to frequent a house thereabout, or not far from the place where she was set down.

Her husband being as I told you before a scale-maker and a common councilman of the city was many times from home about his occasions and did little think that his wife did follow such lewd courses and bad company. But one day coming home before he was expected, he asked the apprentice where his mistress was, to which he answered he knew not, and within a short time after, she came home and all was quiet.

About two or three days after her husband being home, she sent the apprentice into Cheapside to call a coach, which he did according to her command, and the coachman came to the door with him, and she being ready equipped for her (not long) journey, away she went.

This apprentice, that afternoon had been abroad in the city about his master's business, and as he was coming home, saw his mistress alight out of the coach, and went into this suspected house which I before told you of, and when he came home he went about his employment. Soon after his master came home and asked him where his mistress was and he told him that she was at one Mr. Drapyer's.

"Oh," said his master, "doth she lay up her time in a bawdy house? Sirrah,[2] go and call her."

And so he did, and when she came home her husband asked what her business was at that house, and told her it was accounted a bawdy house (she could have told him that) but she said she had been there to see a sick body, and so pacified her husband.

The next morning when her husband was gone out, she asked the apprentice how his master knew where she was. He told her that he saw her go thither.

"Sirrah," said she, "I will make you an example to all telltales."

From that time, and ever after, she told him that he should beware how he told any more tales. And he, poor wretch, little thinking what barbarous thoughts she harboured in her breast.

Upon a time when she knew her husband was from home, [she] sent for two men which she had the more love for than she had for her husband. She called in the boy and told him he should die the cruelest death that ever could be thought on, or devised. Immediately the two men that were there laid hold on him, and stripped him naked unto his skin, and bound him to a spit. Having kindled a fire and stopped his mouth with a cloth, they laid down this poor harmless creature to the fire and turned him round until he was sorely scorched. But with long striving for life he got the cloth out of his mouth, and cried out "Murder!" And with many doleful shrieks and cries that the neighbours made all possible speed to deliver this poor, innocent, and harmless wretch from this amazing and horrid death, which through God's infinite blessing they attained.

Whilst they were comforting this poor creature and hearing him give this present relation, his mistress and the two men her wicked assistants made their escape. This sad news being noised abroad in the city, the apprentices presently made a rising, intending to have pulled down the house, but the right worshipful the lord mayor, and his officers and constables of the city, and their assistants, desired them to forbear, promising them that if either the woman, or the two cruel men her companions, could possibly be apprehended, they should be proceeded against according to law.

Notes

1 II Kings 17:17.
2 "Sirrah" was a term used toward a man or boy who was of lower status than the speaker, and was commonly used for servants and apprentices.

22 The ordinary's work

This short chapbook describes two very different crimes, both of which were ultimately punished with death. Nathaniel Russell was a bailiff's follower who was assisting his master serve a warrant. Mistaking a curtain rod for a spit, which he interpreted as a threat to the life of himself and the bailiff, Russell ran the victim through with a sword, causing a mortal wound. Witnesses later testified that the victim did not offer any provocation that justified Russell's actions, which according to contemporary writers such as Matthew Hale technically constituted murder. Nonetheless, in the absence of clear evidence that Russell had acted with malice, he could have been charged with manslaughter and been allowed to claim benefit of clergy. The reason for the murder charge and conviction might have been because Russell was acting as an officer of the law, and thus was held to a higher standard, which seems to have been an aggravating factor in this case. Significantly, Russell suffered the same punishment as Stephen Arrowsmith, who was convicted of raping a child, a crime that was much more heinous than Russell's. The fact that Russell and Arrowsmith were both hanged for crimes of very different malignity shows that execution was sometimes too blunt an instrument for the punishment of felonies, something that later authors such as William Blackstone would sharply criticize.

Another significant factor in these cases is the involvement of the Newgate ordinary. It was the ordinary's responsibility to prepare the condemned for the gallows and for the afterlife. This usually involved securing a full and willing confession for their crimes, both the one for which they were ultimately sentenced to die, and any other sins they had committed, particularly those lesser crimes that had inexorably led to their ultimate punishment. In the cases of both Russell and Arrowsmith, the ordinary managed to get confessions, even though both men had previously been unwilling to accept responsibility for their actions. These private confessions and demonstrations of repentance and acceptance, and the public ones that followed at the site of execution, were important to convince the masses of the wages of sin, and that justice was a benevolent force designed to balance society and restore order, rather a malevolent force designed to upset it. It was precisely for these reasons that last-dying speeches and the ordinary's account of prisoners' behaviour and repentance while in Newgate awaiting execution – which began to be published in 1676 – were so important. These *Ordinary's Accounts* earned the chaplain a good income, but more than that, provided critical lessons on morality and penitence that were designed to deter criminal behaviour and emphasize the state's power to punish.

***

The confession and execution of the two prisoners, that suffered at Tyburn on Monday the 16th of December, 1678. Viz.[1] Nathaniel Russell, a bailiff's follower, for murdering a young man in White's Alley, and Steven Arrowsmith, for a rape committed on a girl between eight and nine years of age. Giving a true account of their behaviour after condemnation, the substance of the discourses that passed between them and Mr. Ordinary in Newgate that morning before they went into the cart, and their speeches at the place of execution. *London: Printed for R. G., 1678*

On Thursday the 12th of this instant December, six persons in all received sentence of death: one for murder, one for a rape, one for treason, one for clipping of money, one for stealing a mare, and a woman and a man (old offenders) for several felonies. Of these, four obtained His Majesty's gracious reprieve. The other two, viz. Nathaniel Russell, for murdering of a young man, and Steven Arrowsmith, for abusing and ravishing a girl between eight and nine years of age, were ordered for execution on Monday the 16th of this instant December.

Their crimes were thus: a bailiff and his follower in White's Alley, by virtue of a marshal's writ, went up into a chamber, having the door opened to them to arrest a young gentlewoman. Her brother, a lad about seventeen or eighteen years of age, being with her, stood before her with a piece of a curtain rod in his hand. The bailiff coming up to him, shoved him down in a chair, and presently the follower, having his sword drawn before he came into the room, run him into the body, so that he cried out he was killed, as indeed it proved. For on the Thursday night following he died, being run through the liver and midriff. It was proved by three witnesses that the young man neither struck nor thrust at the bailiffs, nor gave any provocation, and that the wound was given before any arrest made. Nor did they take away the young woman as prisoner, but returned a rescue upon the person dead. The bailiff alleged his warrant, justifying his coming there, but disowned that he any way contributed to the fact and was acquitted. The follower had little material to say for himself, only alleged that the young man made at him with a spit, which he took for a sword, and threatened to kill him (contrary to witnesses called even by themselves) and so was found guilty of wilful murder, as aforesaid.

The other, being apprentice to a victualler[2] in Barking parish, was indicted on the statute for having the carnal knowledge and abusing his master's daughter, a child between eight and nine [years] of age. It appeared he had seduced her with money and abused her several Sundays, as having then most opportunity, for many weeks together, till at last the child, being much hurt, was scarce able to go and then with much ado, she discovered [reported] it. The several circumstances, though they were necessary there to be proved, are too foul and unseemly here to be related. The child herself testified it fully, and another girl about ten years old gave evidence what posture she once saw them in. And four or five women proved the wrong done to the child upon their view of her body and what a sad disease was thereby contracted. So that the evidence seemed as home as could possibly be expected in a crime of this kind. Yet the jury at first appeared dissatisfied, but on better advice and more mature consideration, justly brought him in guilty, for which he now suffered.[3] A fit warning for all lascivious persons to deter them from the horrid practices of debauching and ruining poor children of such tender years. It being death by the law to have carnal knowledge of any female child under ten years of age, even although with her consent, which from those so young is reasonably presumed to proceed from an innocent indiscretion and ignorance of what they are tempted to.

During the short space between sentence and execution, Mr. Ordinary took great pains with them, both in private exhortations and in his sermons on the Lord's Day, and God was pleased to bless his good endeavours with such success that they both, at last, in the judgment of charity, appeared very penitent and fit to die. On Monday morning about nine o'clock, the said two prisoners, and another young man condemned for clipping, were brought into the hall of Newgate, where Mr. Ordinary applied himself to them in a very pertinent and pressing discourse, suitable to their condition. And in the process thereof, speaking particularly to Russell, he asked him what hopes he had of salvation, and upon what grounds? To which, lifting up his hands and eyes, he answered that though he were a vile sinner and his sins innumerable (repeating that word two or three times), yet he hoped and trusted to be saved by the infinite mercies of God in Christ Jesus, and that he had prayed earnestly for pardon and had hopes that God would grant it him, and then, of his own accord, fell into prayer with much affection and words as apt as could be expected from a person of his education.

After that, Mr. Ordinary instructed him more fully in the nature of the terms on which pardon from God was to be obtained, that he must pray not only for a pardon, but to have his heart changed and sanctified by regeneration, and then proceeded to inquire concerning the fact for which he died, laying open the heinousness of the sin. To which the prisoner replied that he did believe the man died by his sword, but affirmed he had no intention either to kill or wound him, and that he himself could not certainly tell how it happened, being in the evening and done suddenly in a hurry, but denied that the person deceased was pushed or held down by anybody in a chair. Mr. Ordinary told him, sure he formerly had been guilty of many grievous sins, that God should so give him up to such a fact without any provocation, providence oft-times punishing great sins with greater. To this he answered by confessing that all his life he had run on in a course of wickedness and rebellion against God, and particularly bewailed with tears his continual breach and neglect of the Sabbath and religious duties.

Then Mr. Ordinary spake particularly to Stephen Arrowsmith, who with many tears deplored his condition, yet blessed God that he had generally led a very civil life: never was guilty of theft, nor a frequenter of idle naughty houses, but used to hear very good ministers and rarely neglected his duty on the Sabbath, save only to visit his parents. Till Satan seduced him to this abominable wickedness, which he now very freely confessed himself guilty of, and that he deserved to suffer for the same, which was great satisfaction to some present, to whom he before refused to acknowledge it.

They both declared that they were willing to die, and died in the Protestant religion, and expected salvation not by any righteousness or works of their own, which were nothing but sin and vileness, but only and merely by the passion and merits of the Lord Jesus. Russell had before expressed something to one of the other persons condemned, as he informed against him, as if he did not believe or doubted whether there were any local Hell. But Mr. Ordinary inquired of him his belief in that point, whereupon he replied that he was well satisfied that there was a real place of Hell, and did trust God would deliver his soul from it and admit him into the Kingdom of Glory.

Then Mr. ordinary prayed with and for them a considerable time, very affectionately and with great enlargement towards their particular circumstances, they attending very reverently on their knees. After which another minister came in and gave them some exhortation and likewise prayed with them, then declaring to them that the only service they could now do Godward[4] would be to warn others at the place of execution to avoid passion, uncleanness, and all other sins themselves had possibly been guilty of and which hath brought them to this untimely end. And desiring them to compose themselves and keep their hearts close to God, the ministers for the present recommended them to God, and they were carried down to the cart, desiring most heartily, as they went, all people to pray for them. When they were putting on the halters in the lodge, he that did it, after it was on, asked Russell if it hurt him? "Tis," saith he, "somewhat straight, but," with a low voice, as to himself, "nothing can hurt me but sin."

At the place of execution, the ordinary exhorted and prayed for them, as likewise they for themselves. Then they did freely of themselves warn all spectators to take heed by their fatal example of all sin in general, and that they would get and maintain the fear of God in their hearts. Russell in particular desired them to beware of the great sin of Sabbath-profanation, as also of lewd company, wrath, passion, and drunkenness. Arrowsmith acknowledged his crime there again, and that he had often desired to resort to the public assemblies of God's people but was detained from them by a person who should rather have encouraged him to it. He also said that though he never took to any vicious course, yet as to his crime of brutish lust, for which he suffered the penalty of the law, he was surprised by the violent temptation of Satan, for which he could never sufficiently repent.

Upon consideration of the whole and more that might be said, it is charitably believed that they both died very penitent and with greater hope of their happy state than most that suffer death at that ignominious place.

Notes

1 Viz. is a common abbreviation of the Latin *videlicit*, roughly meaning "namely" or "that is to say."
2 A person who sells large quantities of food, often to travellers in an inn, or to outfit a ship.
3 The jury's dissatisfaction was likely because the girl had allegedly consented to the sexual acts. However, as the judge probably pointed out, the girl was legally too young to give consent, and thus Arrowsmith could be convicted based solely on evidence of penetration. This was proven when a jury of matrons discovered that Arrowsmith had given the girl a venereal disease, proof of emission and, therefore, penetration.
4 That is, regarding the worship of God, to help their salvation.

23 The beastly highwaymen

Highway robbery was considered to be the most serious form of theft. Not only were the king's subjects placed in great personal jeopardy because these robberies were always carried out with violence and force of arms, thus "putting the fear" into the victims, but infringing on the freedom of travel and stealing from wealthy merchants or, in this case, from a carriage that carried large sums of money, could damage the delicate English economy. Furthermore, because all roads and rivers were the "king's highways," committing robbery upon them was tantamount to stealing from the king himself, which stopped just short of treason. Some highway robbers were gentlemen riding on horseback, who were professionals in their trade and who, since the times of Robin Hood, had developed a celebrity status in English literature and society. As this chapbook makes clear, the reality was usually different: the crime was importuned by debt and necessity and was carried out by amateurs who did not have the common sense to mask their faces, a fact that quickly led to their arrests. The story of the boy and the lion that is appended to this tale provides an example of the author's belief that these highwaymen were to be counted among the beasts of prey. No matter how gentle they appeared to be, nor how well educated or refined they were, their "natural fierceness" will return at the least provocation. Like a number of other chapbooks in this collection, the criminals are treated as sub-human creatures. Thus, this story is a cautionary tale, warning readers to be always wary of the "natural estate" of their fellow man.

***

The great robbery in the west, or, the innkeeper turned highwayman. A perfect narrative how an innkeeper near Exeter, drawing in two others into his confederacy, lately robbed the Exeter Carrier of six hundred pounds of money, and for the same were executed at the said city the 13th of this instant August 1678. With the remarkable speech of the said innkeeper on the ladder. *London: Printed for L. C., 1678*

The Assizes for the County of Devon were held at Exeter, the 5th, 6th, etc. of this instant August, where among many malefactors tried, there happened this remarkable passage: one John Barnes, who lately kept the Black Horse Inn near Southgate in the said city, who had lived there in good repute for many years, increased by a formal hypocrisy, he being a great pretender of religion, and a constant frequenter of private meetings,[1] did about a year ago leave that place and took an Inn in Collumpton, a town about ten miles distant from Exeter.

In the same county, where being more out of the sight of his former acquaintance, he began to drop that religious mask before which he had worn, and now adventured to sin barefaced, by several extravagant courses, running himself behind hand as to his estate. He particularly became pretty considerably indebted to a Smith in Collumpton aforesaid, to whom having often promised payment, and as often failed him, at last, about three months since, being again importuned for money, this devout innkeeper having observed him to be a stout fellow of good natural courage, and at present mean and necessitous, took upon him the Devil's office to tempt him to be a partner with him in his wickedness. Telling him, *That if he would go with him such a day, and be secret, he would not only pay him all his money, but make him a man forever.*[2] In short, the Devil furnished him with such plausible arguments (as commonly a little rhetoric serves to persuade us to be wicked) that he not only prevailed with him, but also with a neighbouring worsted-comber[3] to join with him in his evil design.

Being all three confederated, he knowing by his old acquaintance and observation, when the Exeter Carrier had a great charge of money to convey up to London, they at a convenient place called Honiton Hill, set upon his men and took from them no less than six hundred pounds in ready money. This lusty booty encouraged our two freshmen in the mystery of padding,[4] and they began extremely well to like their new trade. But sweet meat must have sour sauce, the carrier's men knowing them by sight, though so discreet not to take notice during the robbery, which had been but to tempt them to add murder to theft, they were all three in short time after apprehended, and committed to gaol. Where, by the innkeeper's advice and his fellow prisoners' skill they got off their fetters [chains], or so much of them that they broke the prison by night and got abroad, nor has one of them been since heard of. The other two not being able absolutely to clear themselves of their irons were retaken the next morning. He that was retaken with the innkeeper was always very pensive, bewailing his condition, being the first time, as he protested, that he was ever concerned in such an unjust action, and blaming him, who cursed persuasions and insinuations had, contrary to his own inclinations, brought him to it.

The innkeeper carried it very confidently till his trial, where they were both found guilty, the evidence being clear and positive against them. There were many women of quality in Exeter, that made great intercession for the said innkeeper to get him a reprieve, not so much for his sake, as out of charity to his poor innocent wife and children, for she was generally reputed a very good, careful, industrious, and pious woman, and hath no less than nine very hopeful children. But the nature of his crime excluded him from mercy in this world, so that he and his comrade were on Tuesday the thirteenth of this instant August, conveyed to the usual place of execution, where there were two that presently suffered.

The innkeeper, desiring two hours' time, the better to prepare himself, had it granted, which he spent in prayer and Godly conference with several ministers. Then coming upon the ladder, he made a large speech, wherein first *He confessed not only the crime for which at present he suffered, but likewise diverse other sins, and particularly lamented of hypocrisy, earnestly begging the spectators' prayers, and exhorting them not to despair in any condition, but trust to the providence of God, rather than to take any indirect courses to supply their seeming necessities, acknowledging that his failing herein, had brought him to this untimely end.* And so with all the outward marks of a sincere penitent, submitted to his sentence, and was executed.

I think we may not improperly number highwaymen amongst the beasts of prey and therefore conceive it will be no great absurdity, if we add here the relation of a sad accident that happened in Gloucestershire. About the beginning of this instant August, there came to the borough of Winchcombe an itinerant family, consisting of a man and his wife, a boy about a dozen years old, a lion, and an ape. Which last two creatures they daily exposed to the view of such as had the curiosity to spend their pence. But whilst they remained there, the boy whose office it was to tend them, going one day to feed them, passed by the lion and went and gave the ape his commons first. Which so far affronted the royal animal, that in a rage he seized on the youth with his paws, who shrieked out in a lamentable manner. Before any could come to his rescue, the lion had got his head into his mouth and bit and crushed him to death and also had sucked all the blood out of his body. Nor had the ape, for all their old familiarity, fared much better, if he had not got up by the wall out of his reach. The coroner having viewed the lad's corpse, there was an order for the lion to be killed, which was accordingly executed with great solemnity, being shot to death in the presence of many hundreds of people.

In this instance we may see the rage and fury of these creatures and that though they seem never so tame and gentle, yet on the least disgust their natural fierceness returns. So it is with men in a natural estate. They may appear much civilized by education, but if grace have not made a through change in the heart, the smallest occasion or temptation shall revive and discover their lurking corruptions. And this let us remember, 'tis from the sin of man that the strongest beasts which before reverenced and obeyed him, do now presume to seize upon and destroy him. It being but just that he who proved a traitor to the King of Kings should forfeit his sovereignty over the creatures, and that they should rebel against him, as he had done against God.

Notes

1 Under the Conventicle Act (1664), it was illegal for five or more nonconformists (those who disavowed Anglicanism) to attend religious meetings together.
2 That is, Smith would become a "made man," or wealthy.
3 An artisan who prepared wool for spinning by combing its fibers to straighten them.
4 Sometimes called foot-padding, this term referred to common highwaymen who robbed on foot, instead of the higher-rank of highwaymen who travelled on horseback.

24 The fire in the garrett

Arson was among the most serious of crimes in early modern England, particularly in an old city such as London. Buildings were usually framed with wood, were often physically attached together for entire blocks, and typically housed multiple families on several floors. Thus, the act of setting fire to a dwelling place could result in catastrophic damage and death far beyond the intended victims if the fire was not immediately contained. The act of arson described in this chapbook was committed fourteen years after the Great Fire of London in 1666. A horrible event still in the living memory of many inhabitants of London, this conflagration destroyed much of the old City of London. It claimed more than 13,000 buildings, 80 parish churches, and the homes of nearly 100,000 people, and resulted in extensive restoration projects that are still visible today. The act of arson described here was at a minimum expected to destroy one house, which also housed several tenants, and could have had the unintended consequence of, once again, setting London ablaze.

This crime was made worse by the author's belief that the arsonist, Elizabeth Owen, was a Jesuit agent, possibly acting on the orders of her "cousin," and that many similar "firing-plots" had been ordered by the Jesuits. This event occurred in the midst of the Popish Plot (1678–81), a conspiracy concocted by Titus Oates, who alleged that the Jesuits – a secretive Catholic order that travelled incognito into Protestant countries – were conspiring to assassinate King Charles II so that his brother James, the Duke of York, a confirmed Catholic, could take the throne. Though later revealed to be a seditious libel for which Oates was subsequently imprisoned for perjury, the Popish Plot resulted in the execution of several suspected traitors, the unsuccessful parliamentary Exclusion Crisis that sought to remove James from the line of succession because of his religion, and an ongoing hysteria that was assuaged only by James's abdication in 1688, during the so-called Glorious Revolution. Shortly after, Oates was granted a royal pardon and a state pension for life for his services to the state. Whether or not Elizabeth Owen and her "cousin" were Jesuit agents, this anonymous author certainly knew how to tap into current national fears in order to sell his chapbook.

***

The Jesuit's firing-plot revived: or, a warning to housekeepers. Being the full and true relation how Elizabeth Owen, on the 8th of this instant November, set fire to the house of one Mr. Cooper, living in Fleet Street between St. Dunstan's Church and Fetter Lane End, she being a servant in the said house. With an account how she broke open and robbed several trunks, into which she put several lighted candles, which fired both the rafters and floors of the garrets. With the manner how it came to be discovered, and her clothes found ready bundled up among other things. As also her examination, confession, and commitment to Newgate in order to her trial. *London: Printed for L. Curtiss, 1680*[1]

Though Rome has been so often baffled in her weak and shallow contrivances, yet her agents think it not convenient to give over, although in every design and new contrivance their malice and folly is made to appear, to the abhorrence and detestation of all sober and civil persons. Nor can they prevail to work upon any but poor contemptible proselytes [strangers], whom they, by the powerful charms of gain, do bring into snares, that so their work may be perfected, though to their utter ruin, as may be observed in the many firing plots the cunning Jesuits have of late contrived. In which for the most part they employ silly servant-maids, promising them after the pernicious work is done that they shall receive much wealth, which makes them go boldly on to perpetrate the horrid deed. But then being taken by the hand of justice, they are left in great confusion and amazement, not knowing where to find the man that did enjoin them their destructive task.

An instance of which may be plainly seen in a late unlucky mischief which happened to the house of Mr. Cooper, commonly known by the name of the Sussex House, near to Fetter Lane End in Fleet Street, the manner of which was as followeth. About a month since, Mr. Cooper, having an occasion for a servant-maid by reason of the departure of his former, was by a friend of his wished [recommended] to one Elizabeth Owen who had of late dwelt in Gracechurch Street. And upon his friend's recommendation he accordingly entertained her in his house in nature of his servant, she behaving herself seemingly well and never was observed to have anyone follow her, unless one young man, whom she called cousin, pretending he was her uncle's son.

On Sunday last, being the seventh of this instant November, her mistress and she had a small falling out about the dressing of a dinner and some words passed, but in no likelihood of such force as to prompt her on to such a desperate revenge, the feud being reasonably pacified. She went about her work as at other times she was wont to do, continuing very cheerful all Sunday after and likewise Monday, which was the day wherein she acted the horrid deed. About nine o'clock in the evening, she was observed to go upstairs, at which time, as she since did not greatly deny and by circumstances does plainly appear, she went into the garret where the tapster of the house lay. And with a bunch of keys that were afterwards found about her, [she] opened several trunks, in which were clothes which she took out and bundled up, putting several of her own amongst them. After that, with several candles (the tallow of which being found melted on the floor) she set the trunks on fire, placing them where she thought they soonest would take hold of the timber.

This being done, and she seeing them to begin to blaze, went downstairs and placed herself in the bar, this being between ten and eleven o'clock. When immediately the smoke came downstairs, of which ere [before] any besides those of the house smelt it she began to complain of, saying that there was an intolerable smoke which almost put her eyes out. Whereupon her mistress answered she saw no such mighty smoke as she pretended, but if there was any, she believed that it proceeded from the burning of faggots [logs] in the chamber overhead, there having been some gentlemen of her acquaintance lately in the same. But the wench persisted that it could not come from thence, but that the house, she feared, was on fire, or words to that effect.

The smoke still increasing more and more, they were induced to believe there had some mischief indeed happened, or that some brand[2] rolling out of the chimney might have taken hold of the hangings. So that running upstairs, they went into the room where the fire had been made but found all things in good order. When looking farther, they observed a smoke to come down the other pair of stairs that were yet higher, so that when they went up them they found the garrets all on fire, being fired in several places, and that in one place it had burnt quite through the floor into the chamber underneath. Whereupon they immediately called for help, which was not long ere they had sufficient from their neighbours and through providence in a short time mastered that raging element which then began to blaze through the roof of the house. And Heaven knows, had it not been so stayed [solid], it being amongst old buildings, what harm it might have done or where have ended.

After the fire was beaten down and the hurry was over, they began to search into the cause of it or how it should happen, which they long had not done before they found, as we have already mentioned, several parcels of grease,[3] which come from the melted candles, and that the trunks being first opened were set on fire, which being light and dry had fired the rest. Both the garrets being fired in several places, the trunks burnt to ashes, but the ashes of no woollen apparel found amongst the rest, which made them enquire what might become of the woollen that was in them. And upon further search [they] found that it was thrown out at the window into a little paved yard and, as it is before-mentioned, many of Elizabeth Owen's own clothes packed up amongst them, which caused her master and mistress to suspect her as guilty of firing their house. And thereupon, by the advice of several neighbours, they caused her to be apprehended and for that night secured.

The next morning she was carried before the Right Worshipful Sir William Turner, alderman and justice of the peace for the City of London, who examined her strictly in all points but could not get nothing out of her, she being of a sullen dogged temper. Only she did declare to some persons of worth and credit that she did not design the fire should have begun so soon, but that it should have been much longer ere it had kindled so that it might have surprised her master and mistress, with all the rest of the family, herself only excepted, and have burnt them in their beds, so horrid and desperate was her hellish design. After a long examination she was committed to Newgate, where she now remains. Not long after she was committed, her pretended cousin came to look for her, who, perhaps had he been taken and narrowly sifted [examined], might have proved the Jesuit or the Jesuit's agent that employed her to act this desperate exploit and horrid villainy.

Notes

1 This case is the first in this collection that will also be found in the Old Bailey records, which began to be published in 1679 (oldbaileyonline.org, t-16801208-1).
2 A small piece of wood that escapes a fireplace and can cause a fire, commonly known as a firebrand.
3 At this time, candles of poor quality were made of tallow (fat and suet), as opposed to ones of higher quality made of beeswax.

25 The penitent apprentice

The story of Thomas Savage is one of the better-known seventeenth-century English crime tales. It was originally published in 1668, in a lengthier treatment of 48 pages, in which we also read about the execution of Savage's confederate, Hannah Blay, for her part in this murder. The version presented here is an abridgement, dated approximately 1680, of only eighteen pages, of which six comprise a ballad (not reproduced here) designed to be sung by the baser type of audience the abridgement was likely to attract. The popularity of this tale was due, in part, to the fact that it is a model of the crime chapbook genre, which balances rich description of a heinous and senseless crime with strong statements of morality, repentance, and deterrence. Savage was an impressionable young man of only sixteen years old, who was in service as an apprentice, precisely the type of training one might expect of any respectable youth. But he squandered away this opportunity for advancement through Sabbath-breaking, drinking, and whoring, a slippery slope that eventually led to murder and theft, and to his own death by being hanged, twice. After he committed the murder, Savage almost immediately lamented his act, and showed repentance during his time in Newgate and while standing on the ladder with the noose around his neck, awaiting his execution. This was, thus, a classic tale of sin and repentance, written, as the title page makes clear, "as an example for youth, to amend their lives, lest sin and Satan prove their overthrow."

***

The wicked life and penitent death of Thomas Savage, who was twice executed at Ratcliff, for murdering his fellow servant, with a full account of the manner of his fact, together with his flight, and how he was taken and committed close prisoner to Newgate, where he remained very penitent and truly sorrowful for his misspent life, and the many sins he had committed, especially the horrid sin of murder. Written as an example for youth, to amend their lives, lest sin and Satan prove their overthrow. *London: Printed for J. Back, at the black boy on London Bridge, near the drawbridge, {1680?}*

Thomas Savage, born of honest parents, in the parish of St. Giles in the Fields, was put apprentice to a vintner at Ratcliff, where he lived about one year and three quarters. In which time, he appeared to all that knew him to be a monster in sin, giving himself up to all sensual pleasures, and never so much as delighted to hear one sermon, but if he went into the Church at one door, but would soon go out at another, and accounted 'em fools that could spare so much time to hear the ministers of God's Word. He spent the Sabbath usually at an alehouse, or at least a base house, with that strumpet, H. Blay.[1] He came acquainted with her by a young man, who afterwards went to sea, and after that he often went by himself and used to bring her bottles of wine, which satisfied not her base desire, but told him, if he intended to be welcome, he must bring money with him. He said he had none, but what was his master's, and he had never wronged him of twopence in his life. But she enticed him to bring it privately. He replied he could not, for the maid was always at home with him.

"Hang her, jade,"[2] says this impudent slut, "knock her on the head, and I will receive the money." This she often repeated, and that day when he committed the murder, he having been with her, she made him drunk with burnt brandy, and wanting one groat to discharge his reckoning, tired him out of his life, and persuading him to murder the maid, and she would receive the money.

He going home about one o'clock, his master standing at the street door, did not dare to go in that way, but climbed over a backdoor, and comes into the room where his fellow servants were at dinner.

"Oh," says the maid, "you have now been at this lewd house, you will never leave till you are ruined."

He was much concerned at her words and while he sat at dinner the Devil and passion entered so strongly into him that he resolved to kill her. So when his master with his family was gone to Church, leaving none at home but him and the maid, he steps to the bar, and reaches a hammer, and goes to the fireside, and taking the bellows in his hand, sits down and knocks the bellows with the hammer.

The maid saying, "sure the boy is mad. Sirrah, what do you make this noise for?"

He said nothing, but went to the window, making the same noise there, and on a sudden he threw the hammer with great force at the maid's head, so that she fell down shrieking out. Then he took the hammer several times, but had not the power to strike her again. At last the Devil was so great with him, that he taketh the hammer and striketh her many blows with all the force he could, rejoicing that he had finished the murder. This done, he goes to his master's chamber, breaking open a cupboard, and taking a bag of money under his clothes, goes out at a backdoor to this base house again. The strumpet, seeing what he had done, would feign have had the money, but he refusing, gave her half a crown,[3] and so departed.

That night he wandered toward Greenwich, and coming over a stile,[4] he set down to rest himself, and considering what he had done, he began to lament, and would have given ten thousand worlds, if he could have recalled the blows again. After that he was in so much trouble of spirit that he imagined everyone he met come to seize him. That night, he got to Greenwich, where he lay, acquainting his landlord that he was bound for Gravesend. But in the night he arose and knew not what to do. Conscience so terrified him that he could take no rest.

In the morning he took his leave, but the landlady perceiving he had a sum of money, said to her husband, "I wish {hope} this youth came by this money honestly."

Upon which he was sent for back and he told them such a plausible tale, that he was an apprentice to a wine-cooper[5] in London Bridge and was carrying it to this master in Gravesend, and if they pleased he would leave the money with them and they might send to his mistress and be further satisfied.

Thus he parted and went forward for Woolwich, where he was soon taken in a victualing house sleeping and confessed the fact. So they took him back to the aforesaid house at Greenwich, where meeting with his master and some other acquaintances, he was immediately conveyed to a justice at Ratcliff, who committed him close prisoner in Newgate, where several eminent divines came to discourse him.

Whereof one said, "Are you the young man that committed the murder on your fellow servant at Ratcliff?"

Then he replied, "I did."

"Then what do you think of your dismal state and of your precious soul? You have not only brought yourself to public shame and punishment, but without God's infinite mercy, have brought your soul to eternal misery and torment. Were you not afflicted when you have considered what you had done and heartily sorry for committing so horrid a crime?"

Then he answered, smiting upon his breast, and tears trickling down his cheeks, "Yes, I was troubled to my very soul, that I had shed the blood of she who never thought me no ill. And so for aught I know, made her as miserable as myself, in that I gave her no warning, so much as once to call upon God, but sent her out of the world in the midst of her sins. Oh, how will I be able to appear before God, when she shall be present to accuse me of my crime, and say 'Lord, this villain bereaved me of my life, not affording me the least space of time to prepare for eternity.'"

Those ministers endeavoured still to lay the heinousness of the crime open to him, shewing him what a horrid sin he had committed in the breach of that commandment, "Thou shalt not kill," and God's threatening, "That whosoever sheddeth man's blood, by man his blood shall be shed."

Thus by their expressions, they wrought upon him so, that he burst forth into many tears, especially when he remembered that saying of one of the divines that said, "He would not be in his conditions for ten thousand worlds." This afflicted him more and more, adding sorrow to sorrow, being deeply tormented in his conscience, for what he had done.

Then they asked him his age. He told them sixteen years. "Then you are but youthful and blooming and yet indeed an old sinner. Oh turn, turn from thy sins, that the Lord may be gracious to thee." With this advice they left him for that time.

Soon after they visited him again, and asked him, how his soul stood affected towards God? And whether or no he had repented him of his sins?

He answered, "I daily endeavoured to do, but I find my heart so hardened that if there be a heart of iron, I have one, it is not fit to be called a heart. When I consider how many pray with me and are afflicted for my condition, and yet when they are done, I myself cannot be sufficiently troubled for my deplorable state."

The night before the Sessions, they asked, if they thought it not terrible to appear before this present bar of justice? Said he, "When I consider the bar of men, and comparing to the justice seat of God, it is not to be feared. Oh, when I think of appearing before the great tribunal, there instead of saying 'Take him to a gaoler', I may expect that dreadful sentence, 'Depart from me into everlasting torments.' Oh, this makes my very hair to stand on end, my heart to ache, and my soul to tremble."

Thus he continued lamenting his dismal condition, often in fervent prayer to God, that he would be graciously pleased to pardon him, so that before his death, he had a great deal of comfort in his soul, and could freely leave the world, not fearing the terrors of death, through the hope of having a being with God in glory, after these clouds of sorrow should be passed over. Thus, the nearer he grew to his end, the more comfortable hopes there appeared in him.

His speech at the place of execution

"Here am I come to suffer a shameful death, which I indeed most justly deserve. For I have shed the blood of an innocent creature, who never gave me the least provocation. I have not only murdered her body, but if God had no more mercy of her poor soul, than I had of her body, she is undone to all eternity. So that I deserve not only death from men, but damnation from God. I desire all that behold me, to take warning by me. The first sin I began with was Sabbath-breaking, whereby I got acquaintance with bad company, and so frequented alehouses at the time of divine service, and from the alehouse to the bawdy house, where I came acquainted with this vile strumpet, H. Blay, who enticed me to rob my master, and commit this murder.

"Young men, I would have you look steadfastly upon me and consider how one sin draws on another. First, Sabbath-breaking brought me to ill company, where I practiced not only drunkenness, but likewise whoredom, and was soon drawn away to wrong my master, for the accomplishment of which, murdered my fellow servant, and have brought myself to be a public shame to all that behold me.

"Oh, make me your example, and learn to amend you lives, before it be too late, for sin will not only bring your bodies to the grave, but your souls to Hell. Oh, walk in the ways of God, and He will be your guard and guide to support you from temptations. Now I am going to take my leave of the world, humbly entreat you all to pray with me to God, that he will have mercy upon my poor soul, and that I may be able to go through the bitter pangs of death, and not fall from him, and that my soul may find acceptance with him, through Jesus Christ our Lord. Amen."

His last prayer at the place of execution

"Oh most merciful and forever blessed Lord God, I beseech thee look down from Heaven upon my poor immortal soul, which now is ready to appear before thy bar. Lord, I humbly entreat thee to prepare me for it, and receive my soul into the arms of thy mercy, and though my body die a shameful death, yet let my soul live forever. Oh merciful Father, forgive all the horrid sins I have committed, as Sabbath-breaking, drunkenness, swearing, uncleanness, theft, together with that crying sin of murder, and all others that I have committed. Lord give me a new heart and grant me faith that I may lay hold on thee, and throw myself wholly and wholly upon thee. Enable me to go through the bitter pangs of death cheerfully. Let not my soul perish, though my body die. Lord, let me not be shut from thy presence, and let not all the prayers, tears, counsel, and instructions, that have been made and shed on my behalf, be in vain. Good God, I have repented for what I have done, from the bottom of my heart, yet am not worthy of the least of thy mercies. But for thy namesake, thy son's sake, and my soul's sake, lift up the light of thy countenance upon me. I am willing to leave this world in hopes of an interest with thee and thy son Jesus Christ. Oh pour down thy spirit upon my soul, and tell me my sins are forgiven. Here upon my bended knees, I present thee with a broken and contrite heart. Lord, receive my soul, one smile, one word of comfort, for my Lord and Saviour's sake. Oh, let me not go out of this world with my sins unpardoned, let not my soul perish though I killed a poor innocent creature. Lord, deal not with me as I dealt with her, but pity me, pity me, for Jesus Christ his sake. Amen."

After he rose from prayers, and his cap was over his eyes, he used these expressions: "Lord Jesus receive my spirit, Lord one smile, good Lord, one

Figure 25.1 Woodcut image from *The wicked life and penitent death of Tho{mas} Savage,*
1680. This image depicts a typical hanging at the gallows. The condemned
is surrounded by a large crowd and is blindfolded before being pushed from a
ladder, causing slow strangulation leading to death. The image is vague enough
in its details to have been used in several chapbooks.

Source: Reproduced by permission of the Bodleian Library, Oxford University.

word of comfort, for Christ's sake. Though death make a separation between
my soul and body, let nothing separate between thee and my soul. Good Lord
hear me; good Father of mercy hear me. Oh Lord Jesus receive my soul."

So he was turned off the ladder.

These melting expressions drew many tears from the beholders' eyes, to
see so much penitence from him, who was but sixteen years of age. After he
had hung the usual time, the sheriff commanded him to be cut down and his
body received by some of his friends, who carried it to a neighbouring house.
Where, being laid upon a table, he was discerned to stir and breath, so that
they immediately put him into a warm bed which recovered him so, that
he opened his eyes, and moved his body and hands, but could not attain his
speech. The news was soon abroad, so that officers came and conveyed him
to the former place of execution, and hung him up again until he was quite
dead, and never came to himself again. He was buried at Islington, where he

sleeps in the bed of his grave, until the morning of the resurrection, whence it is hoped he will rise to eternal glory.

Notes

1 We learn in another text that her first name is Hannah.
2 "Jade" was a term commonly used for loose women, the modern equivalent of "slut" or "hussy."
3 A half-crown coin was worth 1/8 of a pound, or 2 shillings and 6 pence.
4 A fixed passageway (as opposed to a moveable gate) through a fence or wall that is designed to allow people to pass through while preventing animals from doing so.
5 A tradesman who produced barrels and casks, in this case to hold wine.

26 The common witch, Goody Buts

Like the trials of the Suttons and the Faversham witches discussed earlier, the case of Joan Buts is typical. Goody Buts was believed to have consorted with the Devil and she admitted to having a passionate, outspoken nature. According to the author, she promptly appeared at her victim's home, contrary to her will and cursing freely, when the family followed a doctor's advice to bury the girl's urine in the earth and burn her clothing. Despite all of the evidence that suggested *maleficium* (evil doings)—including consorting with a familiar, hurling stones at windows, thrusting balls of clay with pins and thorns, and bringing about a languor that allegedly resulted in the death of Mary Farmer—Joan was acquitted for lack of evidence. This is a reminder that witchcraft trials were not mere formalities, and that they were less likely to result in conviction as the seventeenth century wore on. Paradoxically, the number of witnesses (nineteen or twenty) and the length of the trial (three hours) might have convinced the jury that the community was protesting rather too much and that they had other reasons to disapprove of Joan's behaviour. But, although Joan was acquitted, the trial likely served an important function in the community. The judge, no less than the lord chief justice of the King's Bench, the senior judge in England, took the opportunity to chastise Joan for her outspoken ways. This case was a roundabout way of returning Goody Buts to her proper gender and social role in her community.

***

An account of the trial and examination of Joan Buts, for being a common witch and enchantress, before the Right Honourable Sir Francis Pemberton, lord chief justice, at the Assizes held for the Borough of Southwark and County of Surrey, on Monday, March 27, 1682. *London: Printed for S. Gardener, 1682*

She was indicted by the name of Joan Buts, late of Yoel, in the County of Surrey, for that she being a common witch and inchantress, and not having the fear of God before her eyes,[1] but moved by the instigation of the Devil, she did by her wicked and devilish art, bewitch Mary Farmer, and brought her into a languishing condition, in which languishing condition she continued until she died.

She was indicted a second time, for that she being a common witch and inchantress, etc., she not having the fear of God before her eyes, but guided by the instigation of the Devil, she had by her wicked and devilish art, bewitched Elizabeth Burrige, and brought her into a languishing condition, etc.

To both which indictments she pleaded not guilty and for trial put herself upon God and her country.

The witnesses being sworn, the parents of Mary Farmer swore, that their child being taken ill in an extraordinary and violent manner, the neighbours told them it was bewitched and persuaded them to go to Dr. Borun, which they did. And Borun told them that their child was under an ill tongue and advised them to save the child's water [urine] and put it into a bottle, stopping it close, and bury it in the earth, and to burn the child's clothes, assuring them that then the witch which had done her the hurt would come in. And that according they did so, and when the child's clothes was burning, Joan Buts came in, and sat her down upon a stool, looking with a most frightful and ghastly countenance. And being asked by a woman that was there present, what she ailed, she answered she was not well, nor had been out in seven weeks before.

"Why would you come out now then?" said the woman.

"I could not forbear coming to see you," said she, and with that, she threw down her hat and tumbled down wallowing on the ground, making a fearful and dismal noise, and being got up she fell a-cursing in a most horrid manner. To this purpose swore diverse others, who were present at the same time.

Elizabeth Burrige, who was one of the persons bewitched, swore, that going out of her master's house in the evening, toward the barn door, she saw a goose, or some such creature, coming toward her. Whereat being much affrightened, she run indoors, telling them what she saw. Whereupon her mistress, with some others of the house, went out to see if they could see anything, and being out, there were stones thrown at them from every side, and they could not see from whence they came, so that they were forced to retire into the house. And having shut the door, the stones were thrown as fast in at the window, and yet not one quarrel[2] of glass broken.

Her master swore that she being in the middle of the room, she suddenly screamed out, saying, "Something is got into my back." When going to her, he pulled out a great piece of clay from about the middle of her back, stuck as full of pins as ever it could hold. The maid swore also, that going the next morning a-milking, she saw Joan Buts, bedaggling [soiling] herself among the bushes, whereat being affrightened, she came home and told them, that she had met such a woman that used to come a-begging to the house, she not then knowing her name. But they told her, it was Goody[3] Buts. Her master swore likewise, that sending her upstairs, to fetch him something out of a trunk, she called out, "Master, here is Goody Buts." But going upstairs with several others, they could not see her, but they saw several things in the chamber move out of their places, there being nobody near them, and that coming downstairs, an andiron[4] that stood in the chimney removed out of its place, and flying over their heads, fell down before them. And that the maid crying out again, that something was got into her back, he took out another great piece of clay, stuck as full of thorns as the other was of pins.

Others swore, that they had diverse times taken out pins from the arms and other parts of Mary Farmer, which was also proved by diverse others that had seen them taken out.

And one of the evidences swore that he heard her say that if she had not bewitched her, if all the devils in Hell could help her, she would bewitch her.

She pleaded she was innocent and that those things that were sworn against her were not true. My Lord asked her, if she did not speak those words? She acknowledged she did.

"But my Lord," said she, "I am a passionate woman, and they having urged me, I spake those words in passion, my Lord, but I intended no such thing."

She said of one of the witnesses, whose name is Hakeing, and reputed to be a very sober man, that he had given himself to the Devil, soul and body. My lord chief justice asked her how she knew he had done so, to which not being able to give any answer, my lord cheeked, and told her that she must not abuse the witnesses at that rate.

There was in all about nineteen or twenty witnesses against her and the trial was near three hours long. The jury having been some time out, returned and gave in their verdict that she was not guilty, to the great amazement of some who thought the evidence sufficient to have found her guilty. Yet others who considered the great difficulty in proving a witch, thought the jury could do no less than acquit her.

Notes

1 Although it does not appear often in this collection, the phrase "not having the fear of God before her [or his] eyes" was commonly used in felony indictments.

2 A diamond-shaped, coloured piece of glass forming part of a larger window.

3 Short for "Goodwife," "Goody" was a polite way to address common women; wealthier woman would have been addressed as "mistress."

4 An iron bracket used to hold wood in an open fire.

27 The madness of Mary Philmore

Infanticide was the most common type of homicide committed by women. A case of infanticide was normally proven in court through the presence of a number of elements, as determined by the 1624 Infanticide Act. These included the woman hiding her pregnancy, which was possible in a conservative society where women wore garments designed to hide their figures; failing to make preparation for the arrival of a child, such as acquiring linens and infant clothing; giving birth in seclusion and then hiding the body with a design to keep the birth and death a secret; and the presence of trauma upon the body of the deceased child, as determined by a coroner's inquest. Most "murdering mothers" were single, young, poor, servant women, whose pregnancy would be a source of shame to her family and might render her ineligible for marriage. When infanticide was committed by a married woman, this was usually because of abandonment, or a cruel, lazy husband who failed to provide for her and her other children. Many elements of Mary Philmore's crime were, therefore, quite unusual, in that Mary was married to a good husband and father, who provided financial and emotional support for his family. It is interesting that although Mary exhibited signs of mental distress, the author clearly has little sympathy for her moment of madness despite the common acceptance in court of a defence of *non compis mentis* (a person of unsound mind). In early modern England, a mother killing her own child was simply too heinous and unnatural an act to be forgiven, and regardless of Mary's mental condition, she had to be removed from society in order to restore balance and allow the community to heal.

***

A true and perfect relation, of a most horrid and bloody murder committed by one Philmore's wife, in Blue Boar Court in Field Lane, London, upon the body of her own child, together with the heads of her confession in prison. *London: Printed by T. M. for the author, 1686*[1]

Not to trouble the reader with a tedious prologue of the judgments of God upon murderers, etc., I shall presently fall into the relation of the following barbarous action committed by Mary Philmore, the sad subject of the ensuing narrative.

She is the wife of ———[2] Philmore in Blue Boar Court in Field Lane, where they lived in good honest repute for some years, she never having been observed to be addicted to ill courses, but living in very good order, being a kind wife to her husband, and a careful mother to her children. Her husband the said Philmore having had two by her, both boys, the eldest being about three years old and the youngest about nine weeks old. Neither were they poor so as to want necessaries, but lived very well, he being a shoemaker in the said place. Yet (see the deprivation of human nature!) on Sunday the 13th of this instant September, about two of the clock in the morning, having had some wrangling words with her husband, she took her youngest child from its father's arms, where it lay innocently sleeping (the father likewise being in a sound sleep, having watched with her the night before, because she had been ill, and taken a sweat) and lest he should wake and miss it, put her biggest boy in its stead.

And taking the harmless infant downstairs, put its head into a pail of water (which her husband had overnight brought in, to boil their Sunday's dinner), where she held it by the heels a considerable time, till she thought it was dead, and then taking it out, went and laid it on the bed. But some time after hearing the child cry, and the Devil still being busy with her to make it away, she brought it down again, and (O cruel and barbarous woman!) put its head into the same pail of water, where she continued it till it was quite dead, and then took it out again, and spreading her husband's leather apron upon the ground, laid it thereon.

After she had committed this inhuman deed and day began to approach, she forsook her house and came to the godmother of the child which she had murdered, who asking her what made her there so early?

"Mary," (said she) "I have killed your godchild."

"God forbid," answered the woman, "I hope not!"

"'Tis too true," replied the mother, "for I have done it."

The godmother still giving no credit to so amazing a story, desired her to stay till she had fetched some drink at a neighbouring alehouse, and she would go with her and see the child, which the other consented to. But no soon was she gone out of door, but this desperate creature went away, and being pursued by the terror of her guilty conscience, wandered up and down like a dissatisfied or rather distracted woman, into Southwark, etc., not knowing whither or upon what account she was going, till it growing late at night. She came again so far toward home as Puddle Dock, where she sat herself down upon a dunghill, and there continued till about two o'clock on Monday morning, when the watch coming by apprehended her, and examining her where she had been, whither she was going, etc., her only answer was, she was going she knew not whither, nor could she tell where she had been, for she had committed such a crime, that she knew not what she did.

And being asked what crime it was, she desperately answered, she had murdered her child. Upon which confession being secured by the watch, she was some hours after sent to the Poultry Compter (where she herself related the most material circumstances herein mentioned) from whence she was carried before a magistrate, who after examination committed her to Newgate, where she now remains to receive a reward due for so unnatural and barbarous a crime, and to be an example to all such bloody assassins.

On Tuesday, the coroner's inquest sat upon the dead body of the child, who found it to be willful murder. The child was wrapped in its blankets, with clean linen, and all things in as good order as an ordinary man's child could be desired.[3]

Notes

1 A close variant on this story will be found in the Old Bailey records (oldbaileyonline.org, t-16861013-25), in which the name of the woman is given as Anne Philmore of St. Andrews, Holborn. In most other respects, the stories are identical, suggesting that the author of this chapbook has either deliberately changed names and places or was a very poor reporter.
2 This device was often used to protect the name of an individual, or to prevent lawsuits if the content was later found to be libelous.
3 We learn the end of this case in the records of the Old Bailey and the *Ordinary's Account*. Mary (or Anne) was found guilty of murder and was condemned to death. The ordinary recorded as follows:

> I took some time and pains under her commitment to convince her of the unnatural barbarity of the fact, yet could not obtain from her any discovery of the motives, which Satan impressed on her mind, to prevail with her to commit the crime. I asked her whether it were fear of poverty, that she could not maintain the infant, she replied no, for she joined with her husband in getting a livelihood for four children.

She was executed at Tyburn on October 25, 1686.

28 The French midwife's miserable moan

This gruesome tale of murder, dismemberment, and deception is written as if this is the midwife's own confession and repentance. If this is true, it would have been unusual; not only is first-person narrative rare in this genre, but it is also uncommon for a woman to author such a tract. More likely, this chapbook was written by a man who had some knowledge of the case, possibly a minister who heard the midwife's last confession. It is instructive that even after the murderess pleaded guilty to her brutal and bloody crime, the judge in her trial allegedly recommended that she put the matter to a jury. Presumably, this was because he believed there to be circumstances that might have mitigated her guilt. Even though this case would have been heard before an all-male jury, there is some suggestion that its members would have understood and have been sympathetic to her situation. Years of neglect and abuse, coupled with the high degree of provocation that occurred at the time of the crime, might have resulted in a certain degree of judicial discretion and, perhaps, a partial verdict, reduced sentence, or a pardon, even for such a horrific crime. But the woman's conscience would not allow her to take the case to trial, and her guilty plea was upheld, resulting in her being sentenced to being burned at the stake. This sentence was required because the midwife admitted to committing petty treason, the crime of a social inferior rising up against a social superior, in this case, a humble and hard-working wife against her cruel and lazy husband.

***

A cabinet of grief, or the French midwife's miserable moan for the barbarous murder committed upon the body of her husband, with the manner of her conveying away his limbs, and of her execution, she being burned to ashes on the 2nd of March in Leicester Fields.[1] *London: Printed for J. Blare, at the Looking Glass on London Bridge, 1688*

Under a sense of that horrid and hellish sin of murder, which I lately committed, I desire to leave the world this following treatise. First, the cause of my provocation. Secondly, the manner in brief of the murder. And thirdly, my hearty and unfeigned sorrow for my offence, which I hope may stand as a monument to succeeding ages, of that unmerciful murder, which brings me to my miserable end.

First of the cause. Since the time I became the unhappy wife of that miserable man, his unnaturalness and cruelty has been such that no tongue is able to express the daily sorrows that I underwent. From my unhappy destiny let every man and wife be warned let not sin and Satan provoke your passions, but learn to live in love and unity with one another. For where it is otherwise, there is little hope of a happy life, or a blessing from God, as I by sad experience know full well.

Dennis, my husband, whom I murdered, through the bad company he kept, and the abuses he gave me, caused great confusion between us. Time after time would he ransack and rifle me of what I earned by my industrious care. Then would he ramble into foreign parts, till he had wasted and consumed the same. This being done, he would return to me home again, with promise of amendment of life. Yet in a few days he would run into the same extravagancy, to my discontent. Though I often endeavoured to persuade and reconcile him, yet it was all in vain. For the more I entreated the more he would revile me, vowing, that for the future it should be worse and worse. This aggravated my sorrows, and made them more than I was able to bear. So that groaning under the burthen of my afflictions, I knew not what course in the world to take, to ease myself of that miserable bondage I was in.

At these times the Devil was busy with me, so that I often before this time attempted to do the same, but was prevented by assisting grace of God. But he still running in this race of wickedness, it gave fresh occasion of the same temptations again. Yet the sorrows and sufferings that I underwent I own to be no argument that I should make myself guilty of his blood. Yet wanting the fear of God, I gave way to the temptation, which has proved the ruin of us both. My unhappy husband has fallen by my hand of cruelty, and now I for this bloody fact do wait for my just punishment, which is to end my days in flames, in view of thousands that will be there to see my end.

A brief account of the manner of committing this crime

January the 26th in the morning, when he had been all the foregoing night in such bad company as he kept, he returned to this home, the door being left for his coming in. He entered the room while I was in a sweet sleep, free from the thoughts of all manner of evil. He being disguised in drink, fell foul upon me, and bitterly abused me with blows, which did exasperate my spirits to that height of passion, that I resolved in my heart to be revenged of him, although it proved my overthrow.

In this manner did I contrive my desperate design: he going into his bed and falling into a sound sleep, I took my fair opportunity in this wise. A packthread[2] being near at hand, the which he has used for a garter, the same did I take, and putting it round his neck, made a noose and strangled him in his sleep. Though he struggled for his life, yet I hardened my heart against him, and resolved to go forward with my design. He being dead, continued in our lodging from Thursday till the Monday following, during which time the horror of conscience so tormented me that I could not be at rest until I revealed it to some of my friends, whom I thought I might trust with such a secret. But instead of their siding with me in this black and bloody crime which I had committed, they blamed me for my unnatural cruelty and was abhorred and held detestable in their sight.

Monday the 30th of January, I having contrived this following means to convey him away, I resolved then to put it into practice: For the more ease of conveying him out of our lodging, I first cut off his head from his shoulders. After that his arms and legs from his body. Then taking the trunk of his body, I wrapped it up in a cloth, and lugged it forth myself by night, throwing it upon a dunghill in Porker's Lane, and then his limbs I threw into a house of office [toilet] in the Savoy, over the side of the Thames; the head into a vault [archway], near the Strand.

This being done, I concluded all was safe and well. But the carcass was soon found, and the next day the limbs, which bloody tragedy put the whole town into a consternation, wondering who might be the actor of so bloody a deed. I remained unapprehended till the Thursday following at night, when being seized on by an officer, I trembled, for conscience began to afflict me. I was soon brought to examination, then hurried to prison, where I bitterly bewailed my unhappy state.

During the time of my imprisonment, I began to consider with myself what I had done, and likewise what I had brought myself unto. At which serious consideration, I was afflicted in my mind, wounded in my conscience, and

Figure 28.1 Woodcut image from *A cabinet of grief, or the French midwife's miserable moan*, 1688. This image depicts a woman being burned at the stake, the common punishment for heretics and women who committed petty treason against their husbands.

Source: Reproduced with permission of the Bodleian Library, Oxford University.

drowned in my tears. The guilt of my crime was the cause of my grief. Often did I earnestly desire of God that he would make me sensible of my sins, and likewise truly sorrowful for the same. Upon my bended knees often did I present him with a broken heart, truly humbled under a sense of unfeigned sorrow for that black crime that I had committed, earnestly begging of God to pardon my offences, and receive me into his favour. The short time I have in this world, I purpose with God's assistance to spend in holy meditations, and the company of such whose good instructions may help to prepare my soul for eternity. Having so few minutes in my glass, there's no time to dally and let them slip, but so to make a full improvement of the utmost of them, that I may find the comfort and benefit of the same to eternity.

Being brought to the court of justice, in order to trial, the fact I confessed and "Guilty" was all I could plead. But the court in tenderness bid me to put myself upon trial, notwithstanding all I had said. But conscience told me 'twas true, I pleaded only "Guilty," which was recorded, and so I received the due sentence: *To be burnt till I was dead*, which was the most terrible and astonishing sound in my ears, that I ever heard in my life.

Notes

1 Today this is Leicester Square.
2 A length of twine commonly used for packing parcels.

29 The wicked life of Captain Harrison

The story of Captain Harrison describes a familiar theme in crime chapbook literature. Like the story of "The penitent apprentice," it carefully outlines the slow and steady decline of a man of good upbringing and honest employment into a wicked life of debauchery, deceitfulness, and eventually murder. On several levels, this story serves as a warning to readers. First, it warns about the ease by which a good man could become corrupted. The author emphasizes Harrison's genteel upbringing, good education, and the strong examples and instruction of his parents, but asserts that "a good father may have a bad son," and challenges any notion that "virtue and vice" are created by "nature." That is, a man's behaviour is not dictated by his parentage or upbringing, but rather – in this case – by the company with whom he chooses to spend his time. Second, this story warns innocent readers about the "rooks" that surround and prey on them. This semi-organized criminal underworld used a wide variety of techniques – each distinct enough to deserve its own name – in order to swindle, deceive, and otherwise impoverish innocent people who came within their grasp. Finally, the story warns about the inexorable backsliding caused by seemingly innocent vice. Although gambling and whoring, in themselves, were not serious criminal activities, the author makes clear that the person who partakes in these activities starts down the path that leads to greater and greater deviance. Thus, Harrison's gambling eventually led to murder and his own death. This would also become a common urban theme in the eighteenth century, especially as described in the satirist William Hogarth's series of prints entitled "The idle apprentice," in which, like Harrison, a young man's loose living causes him to leave his apprenticeship, backslide into vice, and eventually be hanged at Tyburn Tree.

***

Murder will out[1]: an impartial narrative of the notorious wicked
life of Captain Harrison, who was arraigned, tried, and convicted
at the Sessions House in the Old Bailey on Wednesday last,
the sixth instant, for the late barbarous, cruel, and unheard-of
murder of Doctor Clench. Giving a particular account of his
birth, parentage, and education; of his first coming to London,
and his being clerk to Sir J. O. of Gray's Inn; of his cheating a
Royal Oak lottery man at Tonbridge of eight hundred pounds; of
his going a commission-officer against the Duke of Monmouth in
the West, and his rascally behaviour towards the said duke when
he suffered on Tower Hill; of his lately frequenting several ill
houses and bad company; and lastly, of the motives and reasons
that induced him to commit the said barbarous and unheard-of
murder on the body of the said doctor, with the manner of it
and the true causes of its discovery. Licensed according to order.
London: Printed for Ed. Golding by Temple Bar, 1692

*Chap. I. Containing admonitions against the crying sin of murder,
with respect to the fact of which Mr. Harrison is found guilty*

The sin of murder is not only an injury to our brother but even the highest
contempt and despite [outrage] towards God himself, for it is the defacing of
his image which he hath stamped upon man, "For in the image of God made he
man" (Gen[esis] 9:6). Nay, yet further, it is the usurping of God's proper right
and authority, for it is God alone that hath right to dispose of the life of man;
'twas he alone that gave it and it is he alone that hath power to take it away.
But he that murders a man does, as it were, wrest this power out of God's hand,
which is the highest pitch of rebellious presumption, and as the sin is great, so
likewise is the punishment; we see it frequently very great and remarkable even
in this world (besides those most fearful effects of it in the next). Blood not
only cries, but it cries for vengeance, and the great God of recompenses, as he
styles himself, will not fail to hear it. Very many examples the scripture gives
us of this: Ahab and Jezebel, that murdered innocent Naboth for greediness of
his vineyard, were themselves slain, and the dogs licked their blood in the place
where they had shed his, as you may read in that story.[2] So Absalom, that slew
his brother Amnon after he had committed that sin, fell into another, that of
rebellion against his king and father, and in it miserably perished.[3]

And it is worth our notice what strange and even miraculous means it hath
often pleased God to use for the discovery of this sin. The very brute creatures
have often been made instruments of it; nay, often the extreme horror of a
man's own conscience hath made him betray himself. So that it is not any close-
ness a man uses in the acting of this sin that can secure him from the vengeance
of it, for he can never shut out his own conscience, that will, in spite of him, be
privy to the fact and that very often proves the means of discovering it to the
world. Or, if it should not do that, yet it will sure act revenge on him; it will be
such a Hell within him as will be worse than death. This we have seen in many

who, after the commission of this sin, have never been able to enjoy a minute's rest, but have had that intolerable anguish of mind that they have chosen to be their own murderers rather than live in it. These are the usual effects of this sin even in this world, but those in another are yet more dreadful, where surely the highest degree of torment belong to this high pitch of wickedness. For if, as our Saviour tells us (Matth[ew] 5.22), "Hellfire be the portion of him that shall but call his brother fool," what degree of those burnings can we think proportionable to this so much greater an injury?

Chap. II. Containing reasons for publishing these memoirs. Also, brief remarks on Mr. Harrison's birth, parentage, and education, with his being a clerk to Sir John O—— of Gray's Inn, etc

The occasion of writing these memoirs was not with a design to add affliction to the afflicted, or to load the memory of him who is ready to pay the dear price of his blood for the crimes and immoralities he has been guilty of, and of which herein the reader shall meet some account; but that in the description thereof, I may set up the same as a buoy or sea-mark for others to avoid those courses wherein he was wrecked.

Mr. Harrison was descended of an honourable family near Newcastle, his parents being well reputed and honest, who was likewise possessed of a considerable estate. Nor is it any wonder that persons so qualified should have the misfortune of such a child, since every day's experience demonstrates this as truth. A good father may have a bad son, virtue and vice rarely running in the channels of nature, though certainly their crimes are greater who are the offspring of such parents, and run counter not only to their examples and instructions, but also the benefits of that education they generally bring them up under. And which was not wanting to the person of whom we now treat, who was liberally educated (with all the care and caution that good parents could bestow upon him) at two grammar schools, where he made a considerable progress as to his learning. And in the spring of his youth [he] promised a better harvest than the summer of his life produced. For he was a pretty hopeful young gentleman till he had lived for some time with Sir John O—— of Gray's Inn as his clerk, when it's probable the great deceiver of mankind, taking notice of his early ripeness, was resolved to corrupt the root and blast the fruit that might be expected thence. For about this time it was he began to shew his future carriage in lewdness and debauchery.

Chap. III. Mr. Harrison leaves Sir John, and living at large, spends his whole time in gaming-ordinaries and bawdy-houses, where he soon spends his fortune, after which he sets up for a bully or hector. A brief character of those places and persons

Mr. Harrison, during his being with Sir John O——, was too much addicted to the unhappy and lewd conversations of the town bravos [coarse men], though not so public till after his leaving of Gray's Inn, when he pulled off his mask, seldom frequenting any other places but gaming ordinaries and bawdy houses, his companions being those of the first rate in rudeness and debauchery. As for the first of these vices, namely gaming, it is an enchanting witchery begot betwixt idleness and avarice, which has this ill property above all other vices: that it renders a man incapable of prosecuting any serious action. One propounded this question: whither men in ships at sea were to be accounted among the living or the dead, because there were but few inches between them and drowning? The same query may be made of great gamesters, though their estates be never so considerable, whether they are to be esteemed poor or rich, since there are but a few casts at dice betwixt a person of fortune (in that circumstance) and a beggar?

Blaspheming, drunkenness, and swearing are here so familiar that civility is by the rule of contraries, accounted a vice. As to whoring (besides that of ruining the soul), Solomon tells us that by the means of a whorish woman, a man is brought to a morsel of bread, which saying was verified in Mr. Harrison. For he had not pursued these extravagant courses long before his fortune became bankrupt, and our blind bubble or cully [innocent friend] was at last forced to turn bully or hector himself, coming into the list of hectors, trappaners, silts, biters, crossbiters, etc., under the general appellation of rooks.[4] And now he was got into the high road to ruin, these being a nursery for Tyburn, for there's scarcely a Sessions passes without someone of this gang marching thither.

When a young gentleman or apprentice comes into this school of virtue, unskilled in the quibbles and devices there practised, they call him a lamb, then a rook (who is properly the wolf) follows him close and engages him in advantageous bets and at length worries him; that is, gets all his money. And then they smile and say, "The lamb is bitten." Of these rooks, some will be very importunate to borrow money without any intention of repaying. Others will watch, if when you are serious at your game, your sword hang loose behind, and lift that away. Others will not scruple, if they spy an opportunity, directly to pick your pocket. Yet if all fail, some will nim [take] off the gold or silver buttons off your coat or steal your cloak if it be loose. Others will throw at a sum of money with a dry fist (as they call it); that is, if they nick you, 'tis theirs; if they lose, they owe you so much, with many other quillets [subtleties or rules]; or if you chance to nick them, 'tis much if they do not wait your coming out at night and beat you. Towards night, when ravenous beasts usually seek their prey, there comes into this ordinary shoals of these rooks. And when it grows late and the company thin, and your eyes dim with watching, false dice are often put on the ignorant, or they are other ways cozened [cheated] with topping or slurring, with diverse other ways too many here to enumerate.

Chap. IV. How Mr. Harrison gets the name of a famous bully or sharper.
How he cheated the Royal Oak Men at Tonbridge of £800 by palming a
false ball on them. How he gets a commission to go against the Duke of
Monmouth; his behaviour towards the said duke at the guard on Tower
Hill. His becoming a gallant to a merchant's widow

Mr. Harrison, continuing this loose and extravagant way of living, acquired
in time so great a proficiency in the art and mystery of rooking that he was
accounted one of the greatest sharpers or bullies about the town. For it was
this Mr. Harrison that about [?]⁵ years past, being at the Royal Oak Lottery at
Tonbridge, palmed a false ball on the Oak Men, and that so dexterously that they
had not the least jealousy of it, till by his continually setting very high upon one
figure (for several days together) he had gotten of the bank about £800 sterling.

When the late Duke of Monmouth landed in the west of England,⁶
Mr. Harrison got a commission in the Regiment of Fusiliers, commanded
by the late Lord Dartmouth, and commanded on the guard at Tower Hill
when the said duke was executed, vilifying his person at a strange rate. Not
long after this, he was broken for some misdemeanor, as some say for cowardice, after which he was forced to have recourse to his old employment.
And though oftentimes he was wretchedly poor, bare of money, and exposed
to many wants, yet by one means or other he would have good clothes and
a footman always attending him, though neither man nor master for several
days had 12d [pence] to bless themselves. He seldom kept one footman any
longer than till his livery⁷ was worn out and then seeks after another. For his
way was, whenever he saw a footman with a pretty whole livery (be it of what
colour it will) that was out of place, he would be for getting of him into his
service. About two years since, he got acquaintance with one Madam O——,
a merchant's widow, who then lived in Bridewell precinct, with whom he kept
company as her gallant, which he had not long done before they removed into
a house in Buckingham Court near Charing Cross.

Chap. V. Harrison, having spent his mistress' fortune, removes with her to
Salisbury Court. A difference between her and Doctor Clench, supposed to be the
main reason or motive that induced Harrison to commit the late horrid and most
barbarous murder on the body of the doctor, with a relation of the manner of it.
His being seized and sent to Newgate, tried and found guilty at the Old Bailey

Mr. Harrison and our madam lived so long together in Buckingham Court,
in riotousness and extravagancy, that thinking it not safe to be there any
longer, about 15 months since, they removed from thence into Salisbury
Court, not far from their former lodgings. Not long before this, one Doctor
Clench (a very worthy and honest physician living in Brownlow Street) had
lent Mr. Harrison's mistress a sum of money on a mortgage. Which afterwards, 'tis said, finding the thing mortgaged to another⁸ or diverse other
reasons, calling in his money, which the widow was so far from paying that
she desired more on the same account. In short, a great difference arising,
the doctor pursued the gentlewoman at law, which Harrison resented so

heinously, on the behalf of his mistress, that some time before the doctor was murdered, at Joe's Coffee House at Holborn he was heard to say that *Dr. Clench was a rascal and a villain, and that he would be the death of him,* or words to that effect.

And he was not long after as good on his word. For, on the fourth of January, about the hour of ten at night, Mr. Harrison and another person, not yet known, called a coach at the Temple Gate and ordered the man to drive to Brownlow Street End. Where being come, they sent the coachman to Dr. Clench's house to desire the doctor to come to them, in order to visit a considerable [wealthy] patient that was dangerously ill, by the Magpie-without-Aldgate. Upon which he went with the coachman to the coach, where they persuaded him to take coach with them to the said place. But in the way, or coming back, these two persons (after the Turk's manner[9]) most barbarously murdered the doctor by strangling him with a handkerchief. They made a very short stay at Aldgate, but as they came back, passing near Leadenhall Market, they made the coachman stop and gave him money to buy the best capon he could get. The coachman was no sooner gone but the two ruffians made their escape. The coachman, returning with the poulterer, found the coach door open, the two gentlemen gone, and, to their great surprise, the doctor alone lying dead in the coach. The body, by order of the constables, etc., was, for that night, carried to the Bull Inn and sometime after removed to his own house.

The Wednesday following the murder, Harrison was taken in Whitefriars by warrant from the Lord Chief Justice [John] Holt. And when brought before His Lordship, being examined to give an account where he was from 9 to 12 on Monday night, which he could not do but by very scandalous persons and that in a very lame manner. And being able to give but a very slender account of himself, and there being, at that time, very corroborating circumstances fixed on him, the lord chief justice committed him to Newgate that night, where he continued till the 6th instant, on which said day, being brought to the Old Bailey, he was there arraigned and tried for the willful murder of Doctor Clench. Where upon hearing the full evidence, he was found guilty. The trial lasted above four hours, and certainly never man had a fairer trial; never man of his character had a more substantial and intelligent jury; and never man had the happiness to come before more patient and merciful, more learned and impartial judges.[10]

A true copy of a letter written by Mr. Harrison, in Newgate, to a near relation, after his condemnation for the murder of Doctor Clench (London: Printed for Randal Tayler near Stationers' Hall)[11]

Dear Cousin,

Now accept of my hearty thanks for all your services and loving kindnesses; and God Almighty reward you. I am now preparing myself for another world and do heartily forgive all my enemies. There was four of my witnesses that did not appear: one Mr. White and his wife, Mrs. Fair-elesse,[12] and the maid where I was that night.[13] Let not God lay my blood to their charge and God forgive all those that swore falsely against me. And whither before my execution, or after, God is pleased to do it (but I am sure he will reveal it) and when it is brought to light, the world then will know my meanings. In the meantime, I resign my soul and body to him, who is a just God, and by this means will bring me to himself. This affliction is a great one, and more than human nature can bear. But I trust in him, that he will not lay more on me, than he will give me the grace of his Holy Spirit to undergo. And indeed I look upon it as a fatherly chastisement, *for whom he loves he doth chastise.* And if I had my deserts, he would have taken me off in the midst of all my sins, and have rewarded me with the punishment of the everlasting prison (*Hell*) prepared for all impenitent sinners. But I hope he will give me the grace of His Holy Spirit to repent myself of all my sins; which I have, and do, and shall, with a humble, lowly, and obedient heart, and not in the least cloak, or dissemble them before my heavenly Father, who gave up his only begotten son to die for sinners (and me the greatest.) And I hope he will give me the grace to follow his example, who was falsely accused, condemned, and suffered a shameful death upon the cross; I being now falsely to suffer a shameful death. At which time I sincerely and heartily beg of him to support me, which I trust in God he will, humbly begging pardon and confessing the sins I have been guilty of.

Now I have two things to beg of you, for Christ his sake: the first is that you will take it from me, a dying man, without the least hopes of pardon here from any mortal man, *That I am innocent, clear, and free, in thought, word, and deed* of this bloody, barbarous, unheard of, and inhumane murder, for which I do suffer, surely knowing and certainly believing no salvation can be had from the Almighty God, the searcher of hearts, that at the hour of death dies with a lie in his mouth. Therefore I desire your prayers (for me being innocent) and all other good Christians' prayers, that God Almighty will be pleased to bring to light this bloody deed, not when he would have him, but at his own appointed time (not our will, but his own be done.) The other is that you would be pleased to speak to your minister or any other divine you know, to visit me, and get him to come as soon as you can, and let me see you, for I have desired that nobody may come at me but yourself and cousin William and some divines. I will not now discourse any persons relating to worldly affairs, but what may tend for the salvation of my pour soul.

So recommending you to God, I rest *The most wronged man, the most unhappy man, as to this world; yet one of the most happy men through Christ my savior, in whom I trust for my eternal salvation.*

HENRY HARRISON

Notes

1 This common phrase was first used by Geoffrey Chaucer in the story "The Nun's Priest's Tale" from *Canterbury Tales* (circa 1390s). It meant that murder will always be discovered, or more generally, that bad deeds will eventually become public.

2 1 Kings 21.

3 2 Samuel 13.

4 These various terms were used to describe swindlers, deceivers, and confidence men, although each had its own distinctive methods.

5 The number appears against the right margin in the original and has been obliterated in the British Library's edition (shelfmark 10826.i.15).

6 Monmouth's Rebellion (1685) was the failed effort of a bastard son of Charles II to claim the throne from his uncle, now James II.

7 The uniform worn by servants. Usually, a master would have all his servants wear the same livery to distinguish them as members of his staff.

8 That is, they had borrowed money from others, using the same property as collateral.

9 This refers to the practice of strangling a person to death with a handkerchief or bowstring, as was then believed to be a common method of assassination for members of the royal line in the Ottoman Empire.

10 Some details of Harrison's crime and trial will be found in the Old Bailey records (oldbaileyonline.org, o16920115-1; f16920406-1; t16920406-1; OA16920415). The *Ordinary's Account* records that Harrison was hanged on April 15, 1692.

11 The following letter did not appear in the original chapbook, but is a separate publication appended to the British Library's copy (shelfmark 10826.i.15).

12 Part of this name has been obliterated from the British Library copy; the name "Fairelesse" appears in the Old Bailey trial record.

13 Throughout this letter, Harrison repeatedly claims that he did not murder Dr. Clench. Here, he is lamenting that fact that witnesses did not appear to support his alibi.

30 The soldier and the magpie

The trial of John Foster – by far the least serious case in this collection – shows that the English criminal justice system had its share of incompetence. All forms of theft in England were felonies, including the theft of goods valued at less than 1 shilling, or 12 pence, which was known as petty larceny. Petty larceny was the only non-capital felony, and as such was typically handled by JPs, although in this unusual case it was heard at the Old Bailey, an Assizes jurisdiction that commonly handled much more serious cases. There is evidence to suggest that the trial judge actually believed Foster to have committed the crime for which he was charged: he suggested that Foster, a soldier, should have been turned over to his captain for punishment, and warned him to "have a care how you meet a magpie again," a hint that the judge remained at least a bit suspicious of Foster's actions. But the choice of a JP to commit Foster to gaol for three weeks (in itself a longer punishment than Foster would likely have suffered had he been convicted), and then send him up to the Assizes as a result of such a "silly business," clearly engendered a great deal of sympathy for Foster's cause. This sympathy came from the trial judge who called Foster a "poor fellow!", from the victim Mr. Connisbey, who did not even want to bring the case to trial, and from the jury, which swiftly acquitted the accused. It was cases of incompetence such as this that occasionally resulted in JPs being removed from the annual Commission of the Peace because of their inability to perform their duties. One of the more interesting aspects of this case is the fact that the usual trial procedure – from the reading of the indictment to the final disposition – even in such a trifling business as this, was followed to the letter.

***

The trial of John Foster, a private sentinel, at Justice Hall in the Old Bailey in London, on Thursday the fifth day of June, anno dom. 1693, and in the fifth year of Their Majesties' reign, etc, for felony, in stealing a certain live bird called or known by the name of a magpie, and a cage, at the parish of New Brentford in the County of Middlesex. *London: Printed for Richard Baldwin, near the Oxford Arms in Warwick Lane, 1693*

The court being set, and proclamation made for silence, as is usual, the court proceeded as followeth:

Clerk of the Crown: Keeper of Newgate, bring the body of John Foster to the Bar (which was done). John Foster, hold up thy hand (which he did) thou standest indicted for felony by the name of John Foster of the parish of Hanwell in the county of Middlesex, labourer, as in the indictment is set forth, etc. What sayest thou John Foster? Art thou guilty of this felony where of thous standest indicted, or not guilty?

Foster: Not guilty, my Lord.

Clerk of the Crown: Culprit, how will you be tried?

Foster: By God and my country.

Clerk of the Crown: God send you a good deliverance.

After which the prisoner was taken from the bar, and within a little time after that, he was set to the bar again by order of the Court, etc.

Clerk of the Crown: Cryer make proclamation.

Cryer: O yez, if any one can inform Their Majesties the king and queen's[1] justices, their sergeant, their attorney, before this inquest be taken, between our sovereign lord and lady the king and queen, and the prisoner at the bar, of any felonies, treasons, or misprision of treason, let them come forth and they shall be heard. God save King William and Queen Mary.

Court: Amen.

Clerk of the Crown: You the prisoner at the bar, these men that you shall hear called, and personally do appear, are to pass between our sovereign lord and lady the king and queen, and you, upon trial of your life and death; if you will challenge them, or any of them, your time is to speak to them as they come to the book to be sworn, and before they be sworn.

The prisoner made no exceptions, and the jurors sworn to try the issue are these gentleman, whose names follow, who were called over, and appeared every one at the first call.

JURORS

Matthias Cupper	Henry Cripps
Crisp Grange	Charles Longland
John Hynde	John Holding
Robert Hynde	Robert Longland
Paul Winkle	Francis Barry
William Webb	Emanuel Davis

Clerk of the Crown: Cryer count these.

Cryer: One, two, three, etc. Twelve good men and true, stand together and hear your evidence.

Clerk of the Crown: John Foster hold up thy hand (which he did). Gentlemen of the jury, and you that are sworn, look upon the prisoner, and hearken to his cause. He stands indicted by the name of John Foster of the parish of Hanwell in the county of Middlesex, labourer, for that he the 14th day of May in the fifth year of the reign of our sovereign lord and lady the king and queen, with force and arms, at the parish aforesaid, in the county aforesaid, one bird called a magpie value two pence, and one birdcage value four pence, the goods and chattels of one Robert Connisbey, gent., then and there being found feloniously, he did steal, take, and bear away, against the peace of our sovereign lord and lady the king and queen, their crown and dignity, etc. To this indictment he hath pleaded not guilty, and for his trial he hath put himself upon God and his country, which country you are. Your business is to enquire whether he be guilty or not guilty. If you find him guilty, you are to enquire of his goods and chattels, and whether he fled for it. If you find him not guilty, nor that he did not fly for it, say so, and no more, and hear your evidence.

Cryer: Call Robert Connisbey and [Constable] Richard Searing.

Who appeared in court and were sworn, and Mr. Connisbey stood up.

Court: Come sir, what have you to say against the prisoner at the bar about a magpie that you lost?

Mr. Connisbey: My lord, I lost a magpie and a cage the 14th of May last, it was taken from my door off the hook that it hung upon; but truly, my lord, I can't say the prisoner at the bar stole it from me.

Court: What made you bring him here then? It is a very small inconsiderable business to put a man into Newgate for.

Mr. Connisbey: My lord, it was none of my doings, it was the justice of peace his fault that committed him. I was unwilling he should go to prison. I am sorry it happened so, my lord.

Court:	What is the justice of peace his name?
Mr. Connisbey:	His name is Hawley, my lord.
Court:	Pray, where does he live?
Mr. Connisbey:	At New Brentford.
Court:	He was but a foolish man for his pains to commit a poor fellow to gaol for such a silly trifling business as this is. He had better have sent him to his captain and let him run the gauntlet.[2] Have you any other witness sir?
Mr. Connisbey:	I have no more, but the constable that took the prisoner.
Court:	Took him, d'ye call it? Why surely you had no great difficulty about the taking of him, he was not in such fear as to run away for a magpie. However we will hear the constable.
Clerk of the Crown:	Stand up, Mr. Constable (which he did).
Court:	Is the constable sworn?
Mr. Constable:	Yes, my lord, I am sworn.
Court:	Come Mr. Constable, what say you to the matter? Do you know the prisoner at the Bar?
Mr. Constable:	Yes, my lord, this gentleman brought me a warrant from Mr. Justice Hawley against the prisoner at the bar, and I served it upon him at his quarters at Old Brentford, where I found the cage and a magpie, and I took them and the prisoner, and carried them before Mr. Justice Hawley, and his worship was pleased to commit the fellow to prison.
Court:	Poor fellow! Friend, how long hast thou been in prison?
Foster:	Almost three weeks, my lord, and I have endured a great deal of hardship, and many a hungry belly I am sure. God help me; I am very poor, my lord.
Court:	Hark you, Mr. Connisbey, pray what did the worthy justice of peace bid you do with the magpie after he had committed the prisoner?
Mr. Connisbey:	My lord, he order'd me to keep the magpie and the cage safe till the Bishop of London's bailiff came for it, it being a waif,[3] he said it was forfeited to the lord of the manor.

At which the court laughed heartily.

Court:	Pray, Mr. Connisbey, what was your magpie worth, and your cage? Was it a wire cage?
Mr. Connisbey:	Worth, my lord, I do not know well what it was worth, about a groat [four pence] or six pence, as the indictment sets forth. The case was a twiggen cage.
Court:	Fie, fie! A silly business, a wise justice indeed! He deserves to be committed himself, till he learns more wit. Have you done for the king and queen, Mr. Connisbey?

Mr. Connisbey:	I have no more to say, my lord, I would not have come here to say this, if I could have helped it.
Court:	Come, Mr. Foster, you have heard what hath been sworn against you. Now make your defence.
Mr. Foster:	My lord, indeed my lord, I did not steal the magpie. There was a man overtook me (a stranger to me) in the way between the two Brentfords, and desired me to carry the bird and the cage for him, which I did. And when he came to Old Brentford, he desired me to keep it, till he call'd for it. He went away, my lord, but never came any more. So, my lord, I was loath to kill the bird, and I did not know whose it was, if I had, I should have restor'd it to the owner.
Court:	A good defence. Look you, gentleman of the jury, the prisoner at the bar, John Foster, stands indicted of felony for stealing and magpie and a cage, of the value of 6 pence, which is a very inconsiderable value. And you have heard the evidence for the king, who told you that the magpie was lost, and that it was found upon the prisoner. But Mr. Connisbey does not take upon him to swear that the prisoner stole it from him, and the prisoner he denies it, and tells you, that truly he did not take it away, but that he had it of a stranger that he accidentally met withal upon the road between the two Brentfords. Therefore I don't see any colour of evidence against the prisoner. And I must needs say it was a very simple weak thing done of the justice of peace to commit the poor fellow for such a trifle. I shall leave it to you to consider the evidence, and if you find him guilty, you are to say so. But if you think in your conscience that he did not steal the magpie, then you are to acquit the prisoner. You had best go over to each other, and consider. You need not give yourselves the trouble to go out of the court, about such a small indifferent matter as this.

Then the jury having considered of their verdict, and being return'd to their seats, the Court spake as followeth:

Clerk of the Crown:	Gentlemen of the jury, are you agreed of a verdict?
Jury:	Yes.
Clerk of the Crown:	Keeper, set John Foster to the bar (which was done). John Foster hold up thy hand (which he did). Gentlemen of the jury, look upon the prisoner. How say you, is he guilty of the felony whereof he stands indicted, or not guilty?
Foreman:	Not guilty.

Court:	Keeper, bring the prisoner about the middle of the court (which was done). Look you, Foster, because you are a poor man the court has considered of your condition, and acquitted you of the fees. Get you home about your business, but have a care how you meet a magpie again.
Foster:	Indeed, my lord, I will. Pray God bless King William and Queen Mary, and all the honourable bench. God be with you, my lord.

Notes

1 Uniquely in English history, at this time the monarchs were jointly William III and Mary II, thus "Their Majesties."

2 Running the gauntlet was a form of military punishment in which a malefactor ran between two ranks of soldiers while they struck him with sticks and switches. Though embarrassing and painful, it was usually considered to be a minor punishment.

3 A waif, or stray, was a domestic animal that had gained its freedom and, if unclaimed by its owner in a reasonable time, was forfeited to the landlord on whose land it was found.

Glossary

acquit: the act of a trial jury finding the accused not guilty.

actus reus: a "guilty act," the physical component of committing a crime.

allocutus: a plea for mercy made between conviction and sentencing.

arson: the malicious burning of a house or outbuilding.

assault: a broad category of crime involving physical violence against another person.

Assizes: twice-annual meetings held by travelling crown justices and sergeants-at-law to judge capital felonies and clear the gaols of prisoners (gaol delivery).

bail: a sum of money paid to a court to ensure the accused returns for trial.

bailiff: an appointee of a sheriff who served writs (warrants) and carried out arrests.

bar: the railing or wall separating the litigants in a case from the judges and court officers; more generally, the courtroom.

bawdy house: a brothel run by a bawd, or madam; commonly referred to as a "house of ill repute."

benefit of belly: a plea for mercy made by a pregnant woman to avoid execution; usually followed by a pardon after the birth of the child.

benefit of clergy: a plea for mercy made by a man to avoid execution; successful pleading involved being branded on the thumb.

bond: a sum of money pledged to a court, usually by a bondsman, and paid to the court if a defendant fails to appear.

buggery: the act of engaging in anal intercourse, usually between two men.

burglary: the act of breaking into a house at night.

burned at the stake: the punishment commonly used for women convicted of high or petty treason, or of men and woman guilty of religious heresy.

capital punishment: any form of state punishment involving loss of life.

chance medley: a verdict exculpating the accused from an accidental killing.

clipping: the act of removing small amounts of gold and silver from coins.

coining: the act of counterfeiting coins or possessing moulds for counterfeiting.

Common Pleas: a royal common law court that also provided justices for the Assizes.

commission of the peace: an annual list produced under the authority under the lord chancellor empowering JPs to hear cases as magistrates.

compter: a local gaol used to hold prisoners awaiting trial.

condemned: term used to describe a convicted felon who has been sentenced to death.

constable: a local volunteer appointed annually by a council of elders (aldermen).

convict: a term used for a criminal defendant after being convicted of a crime.

coroner: a royal official responsible to determine the cause of suspicious deaths.

coroner's inquest: a pretrial proceeding used to determine culpability for suspicious deaths.

culprit: a legal term used for a person against whom an indictment has been found true (*billa vera*), roughly meaning "we are ready to prove guilt."

cutpurse: the act of using a knife to remove a purse from a man's waist.

Exchequer: a royal common law court, comprised of judges known as barons, that also provided justices for the Assizes.

executioner: a member of the community who is responsible to carry out punishments, especially executions.

felonious killing: the act of killing another person without malice; more commonly known as manslaughter.

felony: a serious crime theoretically punishable by death, with the single exception of the felony of petty larceny.

gallows: the physical structure on which prisoners were hanged by the neck until dead.

gaol: a place where those accused of serious criminal offences awaited trial; also known as a compter.

gaol delivery: a commission given to Assizes judges to hear cases against any prisoner currently in gaol, even if the crime was not a felony or an indictment had not been prepared.

gaoler: an individual who contracted with the local sheriff for the right to run the gaol.

gibbeting: a punishment involving a corpse (and occasionally a live person) being placed in chains or a cage, suspended from the ground, and left to rot, a process sometimes known as "hanging in chains"; more generally, the gallows.

grand jury: a body of men who determined whether a presentment was true (vera) or should be dismissed (ignoramus); if true, it became an indictment.

hanged by the neck: the punishment of being hanged by strangulation at the gallows.

hanged, drawn, and quartered: the common punishment for traitors, involving the body being drawn to the place of execution, the traitor being hanged until nearly dead, taken down, eviscerated, emasculated, and beheaded, after which the body was quartered and displayed in a prominent place.

housebreaking: the act of breaking into a house during the day and therefore less serious than burglary.

house of correction: a workhouse intended to rehabilitate convicts by training them for an apprenticeship; also known as Bridewells.

hue and cry: a process by which able-bodied men are summoned (by "shouting and crying out," *huer et crier*) to assist in the apprehension of a criminal.

ignoramus: the decision of a grand jury to reject a bill of indictment; literally "we do not know."

indictment: a document reciting the details of a crime usually prepared by a JP or coroner and presented to the grand jury or inquest.

infanticide: the act of killing a newborn child, usually by its mother.

jury: see **grand jury** and **petty jury.**

jury of matrons: a body of woman selected to determine whether a woman was pregnant or had been sexually active or raped.

justice of the peace (JP): a gentleman of the local community appointed to serve as a magistrate, particularly in Quarter Sessions courts.

justices: the judges appointed to the royal common law courts, who travelled on the criminal Assizes; sometimes refers to JPs.

keeper: the title given to the guards at Newgate and other prisons.

King's/Queen's Bench: a royal common law court that served primarily as a civil court, but also as a criminal court for Middlesex County, oversaw and heard appeals from the Assizes, and also provided justices for the Assizes; the name depended on the gender of the current monarch.

larceny: the felonious act of stealing, usually unaccompanied by violence; petty larceny involved theft of goods valued at under 1 shilling and was non-capital; grand larceny involved theft of goods valued at more than 1 shilling and was theoretically capital.

magistrate: title often used by JPs and mayors when sitting as judges.

mainprise: an order allowing a private person to take an accused person into his custody, usually on friendly terms, upon security given for his appearance at trial.

maleficium: the act of a witch using supernatural forces to inflict evil or violence against another person.

mayor: the elected head of a town council, and as chief magistrate automatically enrolled annually as a JP.

mens rea: a "guilty mind," the mental component of committing a crime.

misdemeanor: a minor crime typically judged summarily or in Quarter Sessions by JPs.

mitigation: the act of reducing the severity of punishment for a specific crime.

mittimus: a document issued by a JP to a gaoler ordering him to keep a person or persons in custody until trial.

murder: premeditated killing committed with malice aforethought.

Newgate: a prison used to hold prisoners awaiting trial at the adjacent Old Bailey, and awaiting punishment after conviction.

non compis mentis: the legal term for a person of unsound mind who was not responsible for his or her actions.

Old Bailey: a standing felony court in London, located adjacent to Newgate.

ordinary: the chaplain of Newgate Prison, formally known as the minister-in-ordinary, who was responsible to help the condemned prepare for their deaths.

oyer et terminer: a commission given to JPs and Assizes judges authorizing them "to hear and determine" cases within their jurisdiction (e.g. felonies for Assizes judges) on the king's behalf; often given with a commission of gaol delivery.

pardon: a royal release from punishment following a criminal conviction; could be free (complete release) or conditional (lesser punishment).

partial verdict: finding the accused guilty of a lesser offence.

pederasty: the act of an adult, usually a man, engaging in sexual acts with a child, usually a boy.

peine forte et dure: an ordeal involving the use of iron weights or stones to force a defendant to plead guilty or not guilty, or die in the process.

perjury: willfully giving false testimony under oath.

petty jury: a body of twelve men chosen to hear evidence of a crime and determine the guilt of the accused; also known as a trial jury.

petty treason: the act of an inferior killing a superior, resulting in the punishment of drawing and quartering for men and burning for women.

Quarter Sessions (Sessions of the Peace): courts held by a panel of justices of the peace to hear misdemeanours and regulatory offences, typically four times per year in the counties.

quorum: a select body of JPs who had legal training and heard most criminal misdemeanours in their counties.

rape: the act of a man sexually assaulting a girl or woman through violence and intercourse.

recognizance: an order issued by a magistrate requiring an individual to be of good behaviour or to keep the peace toward the person who made a complaint, until further action was taken.

reprieve (respite): a stay of punishment pending royal review, usually leading to a pardon.

riot: an unlawful assembly by three or more people resulting in a violent breach of the peace.

robbery: the act of forcibly stealing something from the body of a person, thus placing their life in jeopardy; highway robbery was a particularly serious form.

rook: a general term used for swindlers and deceitful people.

scolding: the misdemeanor crime of a woman rebuking her husband in public, which upset the social order.

Sessions: the regular meetings of the Assizes throughout England and at the Old Bailey courthouse in London (the "Sessions House"); sometimes a general term for Quarter Sessions.

sheriff: a royal appointee responsible for administering the court system, ensuring punishment was carried out, and overseeing bailiffs and constables.

sodomy: any sexual act, normally anal or oral, between a man and another man, woman, or beast, that could not result in procreation; commonly used to prosecute homosexuals.

summary justice: trial by judge alone for minor crimes, particularly lesser misdemeanours.

treason: the act of conspiring against the state, monarch, or his immediate family; certain crimes, such as coining and counterfeiting, were also deemed treason.

trial by water: a method of determining the guilt of accused witches based on whether the accused floated (a sign of guilt) or sank (innocence) when placed into water.

true bill: the decision of a grand jury or coroner's inquest that there is sufficient evidence to indict; also known as *billa vera*.

Tyburn Tree: the permanent triple gallows located in London near Hyde Park until 1783.

vi et armis: literally "by force and arms," but more accurately "putting in fear," the act of making a victim fear for their life; usually an exacerbating factor in criminal trials.

witchcraft: the act of conspiring with the Devil to cause violence against another person through supernatural means (*maleficium*).

Bibliography

The subjects of crime, criminal biography, popular print, and oral culture in early modern England have seen a remarkable amount of scholarship since the 1980s. Although this bibliography is representative of this literature, it is not comprehensive. Rather, it includes the sources that were used to prepare the introduction and the discussions preceding each text.

Amussen, Susan Dwyer. "Punishment, Discipline, and Power: The Social Meanings of Violence in Early Modern England." *Journal of British Studies* 34 (1995): 1–34.

Beattie, J. M. *Crime and the Courts in England, 1660–1800*. Princeton: Princeton University Press, 1986.

Beattie, J. M. "Scales of Justice: Defense Counsel and the English Criminal Trial in the Eighteenth and Nineteenth Centuries." *Law and History Review* 9 (1991): 221–67.

Briggs, John, Christopher Harrison, Angus McInnes, and David Vincent. *Crime and Punishment in England: An Introductory History*. London: UCL Press, 1996.

Clegg, Susan Cyndia. *Press Censorship in Elizabethan England*. Cambridge: Cambridge University Press, 1997.

Cockburn, James S. *A History of English Assizes, 1558–1714*. Cambridge: Cambridge University Press, 1972.

Devereaux, Simon. "Recasting the Theatre of Execution: The Abolition of the Tyburn Ritual." *Past and Present* 202 (2009): 127–74.

Devereaux, Simon, and Paul Griffiths, eds. *Penal Practice and Culture, 1500–1900: Punishing the English*. New York: Palgrave Macmillan, 2004.

Dolan, Frances E. *Dangerous Familiars: Representations of Domestic Crime in England, 1500–1700*. Ithaca, NY: Cornell University Press, 1994.

Dolan, Frances E. *True Relations: Reading, Literature, and Evidence in Seventeenth-Century England*. Philadelphia: University of Pennsylvania Press, 2013.

Durston, Gregory. *Crime and Justice in Early Modern England 1500–1750*. Chichester: Barry Rose, 2004.

Edelstein, Laurie. "An Accusation Easily to be Made? Rape and Malicious Prosecution in Eighteenth-Century England." *American Journal of Legal History* 42 (1998): 351–90.

Faller, Lincoln B. *Turned to Account: The Forms and Functions of Criminal Biography in Late Seventeenth- and Early Eighteenth-Century England*. Cambridge: Cambridge University Press, 1987.

Faller, Lincoln B. *Crime and Defoe: A New Kind of Writing*. Cambridge: Cambridge University Press, 2008.

Fletcher, Anthony, and John Stevenson, eds. *Order and Disorder in Early Modern England.* Cambridge: Cambridge University Press, 1985.

Fox, Adam. *Oral and Literate Culture in England, 1500–1700.* Oxford: Oxford University Press, 2000.

Fumerton, Patricia, Anita Fuerrini, and Kris McAbee, eds. *Ballads and Broadsides, 1500–1800.* Burlington, VT: Ashgate, 2010.

Gaskill, Malcolm. *Crime and Mentalities in Early Modern England.* Cambridge: Cambridge University Press, 2000.

Gaskill, Malcolm. *Witchfinders: A Seventeenth-Century English Tragedy.* London: John Murray, 2005.

Gladfelder, Hal. *Criminality and Narrative in Eighteenth-Century England: Beyond the Law.* Baltimore: Johns Hopkins University Press, 2001.

Griffiths, Paul. *Lost Londons: Change, Crime and Control in the Capital City, 1550–1660.* Cambridge: Cambridge University Press, 2008.

Hackel, Heidi Brayman. *Reading Material in Early Modern England: Print, Gender, and Literacy.* Cambridge: Cambridge University Press, 2005.

Herrup, Cynthia. "Law and Morality in Seventeenth-Century England." *Past and Present* 106 (1985): 102–23.

Herrup, Cynthia. *The Common Peace: Participation and the Criminal Law in Seventeenth-Century England.* Cambridge: Cambridge University Press, 1987.

Herrup, Cynthia. *A House in Gross Disorder: Sex, Law, and the 2nd Earl of Castlehaven.* Oxford: Oxford University Press, 1999.

Hoffer, Peter C., and N. E. H. Hull. *Murdering Mothers: Infanticide in England and New England, 1558–1803.* New York: New York University Press, 1984.

Johns, Adrian. *The Nature of the Book: Print and Knowledge in the Making.* Chicago: University of Chicago Press, 1998.

Kermode, Jenny, and Garthine Walker. *Women, Crime and the Courts in Early Modern England.* Chapel Hill, NC: University of North Carolina Press, 1994.

Kesselring, K. J. *Mercy and Authority in the Tudor State.* Cambridge: Cambridge University Press, 2003.

Kesselring, K. J. "Felony Forfeiture and the Profits of Crime in Early Modern England." *Historical Journal* 53 (2010): 271–88.

Kesselring, K. J. "Rebellion and Disorder" in *The Elizabethan World.* Eds. Susan Doran and Norman Jones. London: Routledge, 2011.

Lake, Peter. *The Trials of Margaret Clitherow: Persecution, Martyrdom and the Politics of Sanctity in Elizabeth England.* London: Continuum, 2011.

Langbein, John H. *The Origins of Adversary Criminal Trial.* Oxford: Oxford University Press, 2003.

Lockwood, Matthew. "From Treason to Homicide: Changing Conceptions of the Law of Petty Treason in Early Modern England." *Journal of Legal History* 34 (2013): 31–49.

Marshburn, Joseph H., and Alan R. Velie. *Blood and Knavery: A Collection of English Renaissance Pamphlets and Ballads of Crime and Sin.* Rutherford, NJ: Fairleigh Dickinson University Press, 1973.

McGowen, Randall. "The Body and Punishment in Eighteenth-Century England." *Journal of Modern History* 59 (1987): 651–79.

McKenzie, Andrea. "'This Death Some Strong and Stout Hearted Man Doth Choose': The Practice of Peine Forte et Dure in Seventeenth- and Eighteenth-Century England." *Law and History Review* 23 (2005): 279–313.

McKenzie, Andrea. *Tyburn's Martyrs: Execution in England, 1675–1775.* London: Hambledon Continuum, 2007.

Pettegree, Andrew. *The Book in the Renaissance*. New Haven: Yale University Press, 2010.

Porter, Roy. *Madness: A Brief History*. Oxford: Oxford University Press, 2002.

Raymond, Joad. *The Invention of the Newspaper: English Newsbooks, 1641–1649*. Oxford: Oxford University Press, 1996.

Raymond, Joad. *Pamphlets and Pamphleteering in Early Modern Britain*. Cambridge: Cambridge University Press, 2003.

Raymond, Joad. *News Networks in Seventeenth Century Britain and Europe*. London: Routledge, 2006.

Raymond, Joad. "News" in *The Elizabethan World*. Eds. Susan Doran and Norman Jones. London: Routledge, 2011.

Robison, William B. "Murder at Crowhurst: A Case Study in Early Tudor Law Enforcement." *Criminal Justice History* 9 (1988): 31–62.

Shapiro, Barbara J. "Oaths, Credibility and the Legal Process in Early Modern England: Part One." *Law and Humanities* 6 (2012): 145–78.

Sharpe, J. A. *Crime in Seventeenth-Century England: A County Study*. Cambridge: Cambridge University Press, 1983.

Sharpe, J. A. *Crime and the Law in English Satirical Prints, 1600–1832*. Cambridge: Chadwyck-Healey, 1986.

Sharpe, J. A. *Crime in Early Modern England, 1550–1750*, 2d. ed. London: Longman, 1999.

Sharpe, J. A. *The Bewitching of Anne Gunter: A Horrible and True Story of Deception, Witchcraft, Murder, and the King of England*. New York: Routledge, 2001.

Sharpe, Kevin. *Reading Revolutions: The Politics of Reading in Early Modern England*. New Haven: Yale University Press, 2000.

Shepherd, Simon, ed. *The Woman's Sharp Revenge: Five Women's Pamphlets from the Renaissance*. London: Fourth Estate, 1985.

Sherman, William. *John Dee: The Politics of Reading and Writing in the English Renaissance*. Amherst: University of Massachusetts Press, 1995.

Spufford, Margaret. *Small Books and Pleasant Histories: Popular Fiction and Its Readership in Seventeenth-Century England*. London: Methuen, 1981.

Thomas, Courtney. "'Not Having God Before His Eyes': Bestiality in Early Modern England." *The Seventeenth Century* 26 (2011): 149–73.

Thomas, Keith. *The Ends of Life: Roads to Fulfilment in Early Modern England*. Oxford: Oxford University Press, 2009.

Wall, Alison. "'The Greatest Disgrace': The Making and Unmaking of JPs in Elizabethan and Jacobean England." *English Historical Review* 119 (2004): 312–32.

Walsham, Alexandra. *Providence in Early Modern England*. Oxford: Oxford University Press, 1999.

Watt, Tessa. *Cheap Print and Popular Piety, 1550–1640*. Cambridge: Cambridge University Press, 1991.

Weatherford, John W. *Crime and Punishment in the England of Shakespeare and Milton*. Jefferson, NC: McFarland & Company, 2001.

Webb, Simon. *Execution: A History of Capital Punishment in Britain*. Stroud: The History Press, 2011.

Wrightson, Keith. "Two Concepts of Order: Justices, Constables and Jurymen in Seventeenth-Century England" in *An Ungovernable People: The English and Their Law in the Seventeenth and Eighteenth Centuries*. Eds. J. Brewer and J. Styles. London: Hutchinson, 1980.

Index